In a Shade of Blue

Pragmatism and the Politics of Black America

Eddie S. Glaude Jr.

16pt

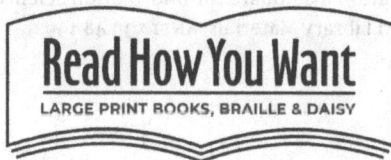

Copyright Page from the Original Book

EDDIE S. GLAUDE JR. teaches religion and African American studies
at Princeton University. He is the author of *Exodus! Religion, Race, and Nation
in Early Nineteenth-Century Black America* and the editor of *Is It Nation Time?
Contemporary Essays on Black Power and Black Nationalism*, both published by
the University of Chicago Press, and coeditor, with Cornel West, of *African
American Religious Thought: An Anthology.*

The University of Chicago Press, Chicago 60637
The University of Chicago Press, Ltd., London
©2007 by The University of Chicago
All rights reserved. Published 2007
Printed in the United States of America

16 15 14 13 12 11 10 09 08 07   1 2 3 4 5

ISBN-13: 978-0-226-29824-5 (cloth)
ISBN-10: 0-226-29824-8 (cloth)

Library of Congress Cataloging-in-Publication Data

Glaude, Eddie S., 1968–
  In a shade of blue : pragmatism and the politics of Black America /
Eddie S. Glaude, Jr.
      p.   cm.
  Includes bibliographical references and index.
  ISBN-13: 978-0-226-29824-5 (cloth : alk. paper)
  ISBN-10: 0-226-29824-8 (cloth : alk. paper)
    1. Pragmatism. 2. Dewey, John, 1859–1952. 3. African Americans—
Religion. 4. African Americans—Politics and government. I. Title.
B832.G53 2007
973'.0496073—dc22

                                                  2006033988

⊗ The paper used in this publication meets the minimum requirements
of the American National Standard for Information Sciences—Permanence
of Paper for Printed Library Materials, ANSI Z39.48-1992.

TABLE OF CONTENTS

TABLE OF CONTENTS

In loving memory of Pattie Pride Jones

DECEMBER 28, 1963–APRIL 14, 2006

Preface

"Knowledge is power," declared a young African American man attending the Tavis Smiley Foundation Leadership Institute. The institute was founded to train young people between the ages of thirteen and eighteen to become leaders in their communities. They learn how to take stock of their strengths and weaknesses, to lay plans and set goals, to communicate effectively and build networks. They also learn how to apply these skills to make successful lives for themselves and, ideally, to bring about change in their communities. I was able to spend some time with these remarkable young people in the summer of 2006 at Texas Southern University. Cornel West, Tavis Smiley, and I held a town-hall meeting to discuss with them *The Covenant with Black America,* Smiley's best-selling book on the current conditions of African Americans, and its relevance to their ambitions as future leaders. The young man who spoke was obviously excited about the occasion, and so were we. He went on to say with profound conviction, "I will do everything in my power to continue to get knowledge."

Another young man stood up and offered a slight correction to his colleague's impassioned remarks. He said, "I agree with what has just been said, but we should know that knowledge without action is useless. We must *do* something with that knowledge." The conversation that followed was instructive. Students weighed in on the matter. West and Smiley offered their views. I asked, "What if we understand knowledge not as separate from doing, but rather as a *consequence* of it? What if knowledge is simply the fruit of our undertakings?" To use one of Tavis Smiley's favorite words, we proceeded to "marinate" for a while on the implications of the relation between how we think and how we act. At one level, my questions had been aimed simply at countering an implicit anti-intellectualism. But what I had also done was to invoke, verbatim, John Dewey's definition of knowledge as the "fruit of our undertakings." In a room full of young people with varied backgrounds and challenges in their lives, we found ourselves thinking with distinctly *pragmatic* tools about epistemology and how our thoughts about the subject could affect how we seek to change the world.

Why John Dewey in this context? Because I believe that the tradition of American pragmatism exemplified by Dewey offers powerful resources for redefining African American leadership and politics. This book seeks to make that case. I argue that pragmatism, when attentive to the darker dimensions of human living (what we often speak of as the blues), can address many of the conceptual problems that plague contemporary African American political life. How we think about black identity, how we imagine black history, and how we conceive of black agency can be rendered in ways that escape bad racial reasoning—reasoning that assumes a tendentious unity among African Americans simply because they are black, or that shortcircuits imaginative responses to problems confronting *actual* black people.

The relationship I propose between pragmatism and African American politics is mutually beneficial. Pragmatism must reckon with the blues or remain a stale academic exercise. The blues, of course, are much more than a musical idiom. They constitute, as Albert Murray notes in his classic book on the subject, "a statement about confronting the complexities inherent in the human situation and about improvising or experimenting or riffing or otherwise playing with (or even gambling with) such possibilities as are inherent in the obstacles, the disjunctures, and the jeopardy." Murray goes on to say, in words that I hope will resonate through the pages that follow, that the blues are "a statement about perseverance and about resilience and thus also about the maintenance of equilibrium despite precarious circumstances and about achieving elegance in the very process of coping with the rudiments of subsistence."[1] In one sense, to take up the subject of African American politics is inevitably to take up the blues. That is to say, the subject cannot but account for the incredible efforts of ordinary black folk to *persevere* with elegance and a smile as they confront a world fraught with danger and tragedy. To embrace pragmatism is to hold close a fundamental faith in the capacities of ordinary people to transform their circumstances while rejecting hidden and not-so-hidden assumptions that would deny them that capacity. To bind pragmatism and African American politics together, I hope to show, is to open up new avenues for thinking about both.

My book does not offer a political blueprint nor is it concerned with putting forward concrete solutions to specific political problems. It seeks instead to open up deliberative space within African American communities and throughout the country for reflection on *how we think* about the pressing matters confronting black communities and our nation. Reflection is not opposed to action. I hope to make clear how the theoretical and the practical are intimately connected.

To be sure, the bleak realities of our country constitute the backdrop of my efforts. Our democratic way of life is in jeopardy. Fear and our clamoring need for security have revealed the more unsavory features of American culture. The foundational elements of a free and open society are being eroded, and our political leaders lie to justify their destruction. The corrosive effects of corporate greed on the form and content of our democracy are also apparent: the top 1 percent of the population is getting richer while the vast majority of Americans, of whatever color, struggle to make ends meet. In many African American communities in particular, we see the signs of crisis: deteriorating health, alarming rates of incarceration, the devastating effects of drug economies, and the hyperconcentration of poverty because work has simply disappeared. Political factions stay the course, exploiting faith communities, stoking the fires of homophobia (while denying the epidemic of HIV/AIDS in black communities), and appealing to uncritical views of black solidarity that often blind our fellow citizens to the destructive policies that, ultimately, undermine the values of democratic life. All the while, established African American leaders seem caught in a time warp in which the black revolution of the 1960s is the only frame of reference, obscuring their ability to see clearly the distinctive challenges of our current moment.

In dark and trying times, particularly in democracies, it is incumbent upon citizens to engage one another in order to imagine possibilities and to see beyond the recalcitrance of their condition. Participatory democracies are always fragile, and moments of crisis serve as easy excuses to discard the values that sustain them. When we stop talking with and provoking our fellows we in effect cede our democratic form of life to those forces that would destroy it. *In a Shade of Blue* seeks, among other things, to make explicit the values and commitments that inform my own thinking about African American politics and democratic life. The book continuously asserts the primacy of participatory democracy, the necessity for responsibility and accountability, and the pressing need for more imaginative thinking about African American conditions of living.

For me, these are not abstract concerns. I have been blessed over the last couple of years to be able to speak all around the country and talk with fellow citizens about the challenges confronting African American communities specifically and our democratic form of life generally. On college campuses from New Haven to Denver to Urbana, and in town-hall meetings from Oakland to Houston, I have invoked my pragmatic commitments as a basis for reimagining African American politics—to reject specious conceptions of black identity, facile formulations of black history, and easy appeals to black agency. I have insisted that we hold one another accountable and responsible in light of an understanding that democracy is a way of life and not merely a set of procedures—that it involves a certain moral and ethical stance and requires a particular kind of disposition committed to the cognitive virtues of free and open debate. I have urged young African Americans to take up the challenge to forge a politics that speaks to the particular problems of this moment and not simply to mimic the strategies and approaches of the black freedom struggle of the 1960s. I have done so because of my philosophical commitment to the idea that publics come into and out of existence all the time and that our challenge is to find the requisite tools to respond to the shifts and transformations that call new publics into being.

This book emerged out of these encounters. It carries the burden of making the case that pragmatism, rightly understood, offers resources for thinking about African American politics in the twenty-first century. As such, *In a Shade of Blue* isn't for the philosophically faint of heart. Chapter 1 is perhaps the most challenging, as it seeks to make clear the significance of John Dewey's moral and political philosophy. I hope that the general reader will find it worthwhile to persevere through the book's more difficult passages. My argument ends with the call for a "post-soul politics"—a form of political engagement that steps out of the shadows of the black freedom struggles of the sixties and rises to the challenges of our current moment with new voices, innovative thinking, and an unshakable commitment to the values of participatory democracy.

The challenges are indeed many. At the same meeting of the Leadership Institute where the young man spoke so eloquently about the power of knowledge, he and many others acknowledged the profound challenges confronting our communities and the conditions that often discourage them from engaging or believing in matters of democracy. Many of these talented young people spoke of imprisoned fathers whom they barely knew and of dysfunction as part of their daily lives. One young woman spoke passionately about her mother, a single parent who has given everything to make a better life possible for her daughter. Another young man talked about the failures of the adults in his life. He wondered how he was supposed to learn the ethics of work and the importance of virtuous character when so many around him didn't seem to care about either. But these young people do not simply place the blame on the older generation. They are their own harshest critics *and* most passionate advocates. They struggle for a language to describe their moment and for a politics to address it effectively. *In a Shade of Blue* is my small contribution to that enormous and critical task.

Acknowledgments

This book came to life in the context of the Covenant Tour, a coast-to-coast series of town-hall meetings related to Tavis Smiley's book *The Covenant with Black America.* Participating in these extraordinary discussions gave me an opportunity to test my thinking about African American political matters in real time. I owe a special debt of gratitude to Tavis for making them possible and for enabling me to experience a historic moment in the life of this nation. But all of my work is indebted to Cornel West. Cornel's first book, *Prophesy Deliverance!,* sparked my interest in John Dewey and provided a blueprint for thinking about pragmatism and African American life together. More important, Cornel has modeled for me how to be an intellectual, how to be committed to principles of justice and get my work done, how to avoid letting my anger consume me, and how to enact love in a world shot through with so much hatred. I will forever be his student.

I have had the good fortune to teach in the best religion department in the country. My colleagues at Princeton are simply wonderful. In particular, I'd like to thank Jeffrey Stout and Marie Griffith. Marie offered helpful comments on a draft of chapter 4. Jeff has been a precious conversation partner since my graduate school days, and his work in moral philosophy fundamentally informs my thinking. Special thanks are also owed to Albert Raboteau. He was the inspiration for chapter 4 and serves as an inspiration in my life generally.

The constant support of friends has helped me survive the demands of writing this book. I am grateful to my best friend, Paul Taylor. We have been thinking together about pragmatism, John Dewey, and race for close to fifteen years. He read and commented on drafts of chapters and provided much-needed support when my faith in the project wavered. Melvin Rogers—to my mind, the most sophisticated reader of Dewey's political philosophy writing today—also read a draft of the manuscript. William Hart also read a draft of the manuscript in less than two weeks and helped me avoid an egregious error. He disagrees with my reading of Sethe's choice in *Beloved;* I would expect nothing less.

Countless others have contributed directly or helped me indirectly to finish this book. I owe much to Jonathan Walton, Tommie Shelby, Bill Lawson, Donald Koch, Eduardo Mendieta, Ira Berlin, Raymond Ross, Lucius Outlaw, Howard Winant, Terri Harris-Reed, Valerie Smith, Noliwe Rooks, Robert Gooding-Williams, Victor Anderson, Jeffrey Ferguson, David Wills, Farah Jasmine Griffin, Nikhil Singh, and Robin D.G. Kelley. Brittani Kirkpatrick and Joshua Anderson wrote excellent senior theses under my direction, which greatly helped my efforts. The anonymous reviewers of the manuscript offered constructive criticism and helpful suggestions that greatly improved the manuscript. A special debt of gratitude goes to Alan Thomas, my editor at Chicago, for his continued support and encouragement (I believe he is one of the best editors in the country); to all of those folks, especially Randy Petilos, who under severe time constraints assisted the production; and to Joel Score, my remarkable copyeditor.

I also owe much to Ronald Sullivan and Stephanie Robinson (and their wonderful son, Tre), to Keith and Terri Jones (along with their beautiful children, Tyler and Aaron), and to Vince and Traci Hall (along with their beautiful kids, Vandy and Jade). They have been wonderful friends to keep a brother sane in the midst of the work.

My family is my foundation and makes everything I do possible: my mother and father, Juanita Glaude and Eddie S. Glaude Sr.; my two sisters, Bonita Glaude and Angela Glaude-Hosch; and my brother, Alvin Jones, who has always been my hero. I love them with all of my heart and soul!

I am indeed so loved. Finally, I want to thank Marie and Langston, the loves of my life. Nothing I do is ever complete until I say how much I love you both.

Chapter 1 was first published as "Tragedy and Moral Experience: John Dewey and Toni Morrison's *Beloved*" in *Pragmatism and the Problems of Race,* edited by William Lawson and Donald Koch (Bloomington: Indiana University Press, 2004).

An earlier version of chapter 2 was published as "Pragmatism and Black Identity: An Alternative Approach" in *Nepantla: Views from the South* (vol. 2, issue 2, 2001) and was reprinted in *Pragmatism, Nation, and Race: Community in the Age of Empire,* edited by Eduardo Mendieta (Bloomington: Indiana University Press, forthcoming).

An earlier version of chapter 3 was published as "Pragmatic Historicism and the Problem of History in Black Theology" in the *American Journal of Theology and Philosophy* (vol. 19, no. 2, May 1998), a brief section of which was reprinted in "Myth and African American Self-Identity" in *Religion, Myth, and the Creation of Race and Ethnicity: An Introduction,* edited by Craig Prentiss (New York: New York University Press, 1999).

And finally, chapter 5 contains a brief excerpt from an encyclopedia entry entitled "Nationalism in the United States in the 19th Century" in *Encyclopedia of African American Culture and History: The Black Experience in the Americas,* edited by Colin A. Palmer (Detroit: Macmillan Reference USA, 2006).

In a Shade of Blue: An Introduction

Now, as then, we find ourselves bound, first without, then within, by the nature of our categorization. And escape is not effected through a bitter railing against this trap; it is as though this very striving were the only motion needed to spring the trap upon us. We take our shape, it is true, within and against that cage of reality bequeathed us at our birth; and yet it is precisely through our dependence on this reality that we are most endlessly betrayed.

JAMES BALDWIN, *Notes of a Native Son*

This is ... a first rate test of the value of any philosophy which is offered us: Does it end in conclusions which, when they are referred back to ordinary life-experience and their predicaments, render them more significant, more luminous to us, and make our dealings more fruitful?

JOHN DEWEY, *Experience and Nature*

The blues is an impulse to keep the painful details and episodes of a brutal experience alive, in one's aching consciousness, to finger its jagged grain, and to transcend it, not by the consolation of philosophy but by squeezing from it a near-tragic, near-comic lyricism.

RALPH ELLISON, *Shadow and Act*

Pragmatism is as native to American soil as sagebrush and buffalo grass. So is white supremacy. But classical pragmatists like Charles S. Peirce, William James, and John Dewey rarely took up the question of white supremacy in their philosophical writings. For them, race and racism remained marginal intellectual categories despite the long, looming shadow of slavery that framed their extraordinary lives. I am not convinced, however, that their failure to address white supremacy philosophically constitutes an unforgivable moral failing. Professional philosophy, after all, isn't the first place one looks for courageous social advocacy. And James and Dewey did in fact demonstrate in their daily lives a commitment, however limited, to antiracist politics (Peirce is a different story). We need to recognize that American pragmatism emerged in the context of a nation committed to democracy *and* slavery, to ideas of equality *and* to the insidious ideology of Anglo-Saxonism. American pragmatism indeed reflects the haunting duality at the heart of this country: a simultaneous commitment to democratic ideals and undemocratic practices. To say then that pragmatism is native to American soil is to acknowledge that it carries with it all the possibilities and limitations that have defined our fragile experiment in democracy.

One would hope that matters had changed among scholars who call themselves pragmatists today. But even now, most pragmatists fail to take seriously the issues of race in their philosophical work. Cornel West's account of pragmatism in *The American Evasion of Philosophy* inserted W.E.B. DuBois into the pantheon of pragmatist thinkers, and we have seen, due in large part to the indefatigable work of Leonard Harris, a resurgence of interest in Alain Locke. But too often DuBois and Locke remain mere personalities. Their insertion into the pantheon of American pragmatism is much like the use of gender-specific pronouns to draw attention to feminist concerns in philosophical writing: the impression it creates—that patriarchy, or in this instance white supremacy, has been seriously considered—is too often an illusion.

When, for example, Richard Rorty invokes the work of James Baldwin in his book *Achieving Our Country,* one expects more than a passing mention of the problem that so exercised Baldwin throughout his career. Instead, Baldwin stands simply as an exemplar of moderation—someone willing, unlike the leftists Rorty so vehemently chastises, to criticize America without rejecting it outright. This is interesting as far as it goes; Rorty's nostalgia for the old white left and his eloquent commitment to the ideals that animate the life of the country are hard to dislike. But Rorty evades the more fundamental challenge that Baldwin's writings present to anyone willing to engage them: that America must confront the fraudulent nature of its life, that its avowals of virtue shield it from honestly confronting the darkness within its own soul.

Rorty might claim that his liberal commitments offer adequate resources for addressing these concerns; that is to say, if good liberals are to be consistent they must condemn racism insofar as it denies the maximization of opportunity for individual variation. Rorty, like most good pragmatists, believes that the liberal goal of maximal room for individual variation requires "no source of authority other than the free agreement of human beings,"[1] that we must work to diminish human suffering and make possible the conditions for human excellence, and that we must commit ourselves to the goal that every child should have an equal chance of happiness. Nothing further needs to be said. But Rorty knows, as we do, that liberals have failed miserably in these areas, primarily because of their equivocation in the face of white supremacy's insidious claims. Pragmatists need to offer something more than assertions that "good liberals don't behave in this way." Sustained attention needs to be given to the kinds of claims and practices that frustrate the liberal vision Rorty commends. The same can be said about John Dewey, the consummate philosopher of American democracy: shouldn't he have engaged philosophically the ways in which white supremacy frustrated his philosophical claims about democracy? We know he did not, and Rorty, one of his most famous contemporary disciples, also has not. That kind of work is left principally to those of us who bear the brunt of such practices.

A Tradition of African American Pragmatism

We know African Americans have taken up the task. Not so much by participating in professional philosophical debates about truth and meaning as by tackling the complex problems of American racism. To be sure, the political philosophy of W.E.B. DuBois carries the imprint of pragmatism, and Alain Locke's theory of value and critical theory of race reflect pragmatic commitments. Both take up the pressing issues of American democracy in light of the history and political economy of white supremacy, which gives their pragmatism a timbre and tone different from that of Dewey and Rorty. But DuBois and Locke do not stand alone. One encounters in Anna Julia Cooper's magisterial work, *A Voice from the South* (1892), a pragmatic defense of religious belief in the face of a debilitating skepticism in which "all hope in the grand possibilities of life [is] blasted."[2]

Several years before William James's classic 1896 essay, "The Will to Believe," Cooper argued for the necessity of belief as a source of what James called the strenuous mood. She recounted the story of a slave who attempted to escape to the North. "He believed that somewhere under the beckoning light, lay a far away country where a man's a man. He sets out with his heavenly guide before his face—would you tell him he is pursuing a wandering light? Is he the poorer for his ignorant hope? Are you the richer for your enlightened suspicion?"[3] In Cooper's view, much depends on our belief in "the infinite possibilities of devoted self-sacrifice and in the eternal grandeur of a human idea heroically espoused." Such faith—that is, "treating truth as true"—compels us to work to transform our world and is essential, she argued, if African Americans are to rise to the challenges confronting them. Cooper closed her marvelous work with words much like those of William James but with the gravitas of someone struggling against white supremacy: "The world is to be moved one generation forward—whether by us, by blind force, by fate, or by God! If thou believest, all things are possible; and as thou believest, so be it unto thee."[4]

We also find African American cultural workers during the Harlem Renaissance, alongside DuBois and Locke, drawing on the insights of pragmatism to formulate their claims about the beauty of black life. These formulations aided in their attempts "to explain America to itself" in light of the doings and sufferings, as well as the expressive traditions, of African Americans. Charles Johnson, the Chicago-trained sociologist and editor of *Opportunity,* thought of himself as a Deweyan of sorts, and his reading of pragmatism informed his conception of African American politics. In his "Notes on a Personal Philosophy of Life," for example, Johnson rejected a formulation of black community predicated on an abstract notion of racial essence, an idea of blackness antecedent to the actual experiences of black individuals. For him, meaning and the values that we come to cherish emerge out of transactions with our environment—out of experience: "Adherence to any body of doctrines and dogmas, based upon a specific authority, as adherence to any set of beliefs, signifies distrust in the power of experience to provide, in its on-going movement, the needed principles of belief and action. [Dewey] challenges to a new faith in experience itself as the sole ultimate authority."[5] This view of experience led Johnson to emphasize the centrality of African Americans to the actual meaning of democratic community and social justice in the United States. Neither could be known, in his view, except by confronting candidly those who have been denied just treatment and access to democratic life.

Ralph Ellison makes a similar claim. He recognized that the grand democratic vision of Ralph Waldo Emerson was limited by his racial myopia, in the sense that Emerson failed fundamentally to recognize African-descended people as autonomous agents. In *Invisible Man,* for example, Ellison puts forward a profound reconstruction of Emerson's vision by drawing a circle, to invoke the title of one of Emerson's important essays, around his powerful but limited vision of American democratic life. Emersonian ideas of self-reliance and representativeness, both of which presuppose a white American subject, are recalibrated to provide those consistently marginalized in Emerson's "imaginative economy" a central and canonical place in the very construction of American identity. Indeed Ellison claimed to be an inheritor of Emerson's language. But in claiming that inheritance, he also makes an argument about the direction and meaning of American pragmatism. As Michael Magee writes, "In returning to Emerson, Ellison recalls the uncanny truth about pragmatism, that it is 'the partial creation of black people.'"[6] This provocative formulation signals the extent to which American pragmatism is the direct reflection of the unique character of America itself, which is inextricably connected to the presence of its darker citizens—America's blues people.

There has indeed been a longstanding tradition of African Americans explicitly taking up the philosophical tools of pragmatism to respond to African American conditions of living. Cornel West stands in this tradition even though he has, over the years, distanced himself from the label. West's prophetic pragmatism, as expressed in *The American Evasion of Philosophy,* ushered in a formal articulation of the sensibility that I have generally outlined here. In his hands, pragmatism encounters the underside of American life, it grapples with the tragic dimensions of our living, it gives attention to individual assertion and structural limitations, and it asserts the need for a fuller grasp of the realities of white supremacy (and other forms of oppression) that inform our self-understanding. He rightly notes that American pragmatism "tries to deploy thought as a weapon to enable more effective action" and that "its basic impulse is a plebian radicalism that fuels an antipatrician rebelliousness for the moral aim of enriching individuals and expanding democracy."[7] But West knows of pragmatism's blind spots—that its commitment to expanding and enriching democratic life has been continuously "restricted by an ethnocentrism and a patriotism cognizant of the exclusion of peoples of color, certain immigrants, and women yet fearful of the subversive demands these excluded peoples might make and enact."[8] Like those before him he takes up the task of attempting to explain America to itself, and we find that, when assessed in light of the history and political economy of white supremacy, pragmatism—whether Emersonian, Jamesian, or Deweyan—looks and sounds different. It has been colored a deep shade of blue.

Coloring Pragmatism

In a Shade of Blue is my contribution to the tradition I have just sketched. My aim is to think through some of the more pressing conceptual problems confronting African American political life, and I do so as a Deweyan pragmatist. I should say a bit about what I mean by this self-description. John Dewey thought of philosophy as a form of cultural and social criticism. He held the view that philosophy, properly understood as a mode of wisdom, ought to aid us in our efforts to overcome problematic situations and worrisome circumstances. The principal charge of the philosopher, then, is to deal with the problems of human beings, not simply with the problems of philosophers. For Dewey, over the course of his long career, this involved bridging the divide between science, broadly understood, and morals—a divide he traced to a conception of experience that has led philosophers over the centuries to tilt after windmills. Dewey declared, "The problem of restoring integration and co-operation between man's beliefs about the world in which he lives and his beliefs about values and purposes that should direct his conduct is the deepest problem of any philosophy that is not isolated from life."[9]

Dewey bases this conclusion on several features of his philosophy: (1) antifoundationalism, (2) experimentalism, (3) contextualism, and (4) solidarity.[10] Antifoundationalism, of course, is the rejection of foundations of knowledge that are beyond question. Dewey, by contrast, understands knowledge to be the fruit of our undertakings as we seek "the enrichment of our immediate experience through the control over action it exercises."[11] He insists that we turn our attention from supposed givens to actual consequences, pursuing a future fundamentally grounded in values shaped by experience and realized in our actions. This view makes clear the experimental function of knowledge. Dewey emphasized that knowledge entails efforts to control and select future experience and that we are always confronted with the possibility of error when we act. We experiment or tinker, with the understanding that all facts are fallible and, as such, occasionally afford us the opportunity for revision.[12]

Contextualism refers to an understanding of beliefs, choices, and actions as historically conditioned. Dewey held the view that inquiry, or the pursuit of knowledge, is value-laden, in the sense that we come to problems with interests and habits that orient us one way or another, and that such pursuits are also situational, in the sense that "knowledge is pursued and produced somewhere, somewhen, and by someone."[13] Finally, solidarity captures the associational and cooperative dimensions of Dewey's thinking. Dewey conceives of his pragmatism as "an instrument of social improvement" aimed principally at expanding democratic life and broadening the ground of individual self-development.[14] Democracy, for him, constitutes more than a body of formal procedures; it is a form of life that requires constant attention if we are to secure the ideals that purportedly animate it. Individuality is understood as developing one's unique capacities within the context of one's social relations and one's community. The formation of the democratic character so important to our form of associated living involves, then, a caring disposition toward the plight of our fellows and a watchful concern for the well-being of our democratic life.

With these four general features in mind, Dewey's view is consistent, as one would expect, with the characterization of pragmatism provided by Williams James. In *Pragmatism*, James powerfully describes the pragmatist as one who

> turns away from abstraction and insufficiency, from verbal solutions, from bad *a priori* reasons, from fixed principles, closed systems, and pretended absolutes and origins. He turns towards concreteness and

adequacy, towards facts, towards action, and towards power.... It means the open air and possibilities of nature, as against ... dogma, artificiality, and the pretence of finality.[15]

The good pragmatist, then, encourages a view of philosophy as social and cultural criticism, where the neat conundrums of the scholar's professional practice give way to a certain kind of responsibility in our intellectual lives, where we take the tools of our training and work to offer some insight into specific conditions of value and into specific consequences of ideas. In this view, philosophy becomes, as Dewey argued, "a method of locating and interpreting the more serious of the conflicts that occur in life and a method of projecting ways for dealing with them: a method of moral and political diagnosis and prognosis."[16]

A sensibility or general temperament, to use James's language, informs this philosophical orientation: it places an accent on an open, malleable, and pluralistic universe, a view in which change is a central feature of our living, demanding of us variety, ingenuity or imagination, and experimentation in practical matters. It places a fundamental accent on human agency or powers. This can be thought of as a reflection of its Emersonian lineage. Pragmatists express a profound faith in the capacity of everyday, ordinary people to transform their world. There are certainly constraints, but it is through our various practical transactions that we work to make a substantive difference in our conditions of living.

Pragma is Greek for things, facts, deeds, affairs. Pragmatists hold the view that our practice is primary. Knowledge, for example, does not require, in the pragmatist view, philosophical foundations in direct personal awareness. Instead, it is bound up in culture, society, and history. It results, in part, from our doings and sufferings, our ability or inability to secure desired aims in a somewhat hostile environment. The good pragmatist, in the end, seeks to avoid dogmas that settle matters prior to experience and calls us to see the ethical import of our actions—that what we believe about the world has ethical significance and that what we do has ethical implications for how we will live our lives. C. I. Lewis best captures this view of pragmatism: "At bottom, all problems are problems of conduct; all judgments are implicitly judgments of value; that as there can be ultimately no valid distinction between the theoretical or practical, so there can be no final separation of questions of truth of any kind from questions of the justifiable ends of actions."[17]

This book attempts to show that pragmatism can help address some of the more challenging dimensions of contemporary African American politics. But I maintain that it first ought to undergo a reconstruction of sorts. Pragmatism must be made to sing the blues. In chapter 1, I argue that, contrary to standard accounts, John Dewey's reconstruction of moral experience insists on the tragic dimension of our moral lives: that we are consistently confronted with competing values that often require that some good or value is butchered. I then put Dewey in conversation with one of America's greatest writers, Toni Morrison. Dewey indeed has resources capable of addressing what Stanley Cavell describes as the work of mourning,[18] but my reading of Morrison aims to reconstruct those resources in light of the *racialized* experiences that haunt American life. What might it mean to think of the tragic in the context of those black persons forced to forge a self amid the absurdities of a society still fundamentally committed to racist practices? I suggest that Morrison's novel exemplifies what it means to hold a pragmatic view of the tragic that takes seriously the often brutal realities of white supremacy. Morrison, then, teaches Dewey a lesson about race, American democracy, and the often tragic choices imposed on this country's darker citizens. The chapter thus opens the way for a more sustained encounter between pragmatism as I understand it and African American political life.

Chapters 2, 3, and 4 examine how pragmatism might aid us in rethinking the various ways appeals to black identity, history, and agency impact the form and content of African American political activity. Too often such appeals settle political matters beforehand. Black history, for some, constitutes a reservoir of meaning that predetermines our orientation to problems, irrespective of their particulars, and black agency is imagined from the start as bound up with an emancipatory politics. When identity is determined by way of reference to a fixed racial self, the complexity of African American life is denied. Moreover, the actual moral dilemmas African Americans face are reduced to a crude racial calculus in which the answers are somehow genetically or culturally encoded.

My aim in these chapters is not to deny the viability of black identity talk, appeals to black history, or something like black agency. Instead, I bring my pragmatic commitments to bear on these notions in order to open up ways in which we might reimagine African American politics for the twenty-first century. In chapter 2, for example, I maintain that we have approached the issue of black identity in the wrong way: that it is not some fixed and unchanging point of reference that determines, in advance of our actions, who we are. Rather, our identities turn out to be the products of efforts to dispose of problematic situations. This pragmatic approach gets us past some of the more troublesome dimensions of identity politics precisely because it locates identity formation in the messiness of our living and the problems we confront.

African American Christianity has been central to constructions of black identity. In chapters 3 and 4 African American Christianity and those who study it provide my point of entry for reflections about how we might conceive of black history and agency in pragmatic terms. In chapter 3 I seek to recast how appeals to African American history ground black theological claims. My interest here is not to recoup the project of black liberation theologians but to consider African American history as predicated on experience, as informed by John Dewey's account of the term.

I then turn to the concept of black agency in chapter 4. Accounts of African American Christianity and slavery have been plagued by old debates about agency, such as whether African American conversion to Christianity amounted to an act of assertion or fortified the regime of slavery. Using the concept of experience put forward in chapter 3, I argue for a more nuanced view of black agency free of the preordained constraints of emancipatory politics.[19] I take particular issue with the tendency in black theology to subordinate complex religious meanings to concerns about liberatory practice.

Throughout these chapters I hope to dislodge what I take to be simplistic descriptions of African American conditions of living. In each instance, I insist that we turn our attention from antecedent matters to consequent phenomena—that is to say, from fixed and unchanging points of reference to the complexity of actual doings and sufferings.[20] My aim, like that of any good pragmatist, is to call our attention to the ethical significance of our beliefs and actions in the context of a society still beset by racism and of our efforts to forge a better world for our progeny.

Reconstructing some of the central categories of African American politics is one of my primary ambitions. In chapter 5, I take up the difficulty surrounding discussions of black power and its attendant politics. I do so because much of the politics of the 1960s and 1970s presuppose conceptions of black identity, history, and agency that I reject in the preceding chapters. My intention, however, is not to debunk black nationalism as such but to look more closely at what we mean by the term. We need thicker descriptions of the politics of this historical moment, which continues to inform contemporary African American political life.

In my final chapter, I argue that one of the consequences of our failure to offer thicker descriptions of the black power era has been a fundamental mischaracterization of our contemporary moment, a moment marked by profound transformations, both national and global, in the lives of African Americans.

Here again I take my cue from John Dewey, who in *The Public and Its Problems* maintained that certain events can transform the very nature of a public and the ways members of that public deliberate. I show how the lingering prestige of the black freedom struggle of the sixties and seventies today blocks the path to the formation of what I call a post-soul politics. This politics would recognize the diversity of African American political interests and foreground the importance of participatory democracy. I argue that our continual reference to the strategies and descriptions of the era points to our failure to ask some fundamental questions: What is the African American public under present conditions? What are the reasons for its eclipse? And how are we to help it effect the political changes called for by current social realities?

I end with a brief epilogue in which I discuss the implications of Tavis Smiley's February 2006 symposium and the resulting book, *The Covenant with Black America*. Together they constitute, in my view, an extraordinary moment in African American history. They have galvanized a deliberative public space in which African Americans, at the local and national level, have applied what Dewey called critical intelligence to real social problems, exemplifying the ideal of democratic participation and exhibiting faith in the capacities of ordinary people to transform their circumstances. In short, this moment serves as an example of the kind of work needed to reimagine African American politics for the twenty-first century. Explicit in this effort is a profound trust in everyday black people and an insistence that we take seriously in our analysis of American democracy what James Baldwin described as the beauty of black life (in all of its complexity). *In a Shade of Blue* attempts to do just that with the philosophical resources of pragmatism.

A Return to James Baldwin

In *The Fire Next Time* Baldwin invokes the beauty of black life and struggle, not out of blind deference to the authority of those experiences, but as a means of exposing the adolescence of this fragile experiment in democracy and proposing an approach to what he describes as the difficult task of "raising our babies." For Baldwin, the traumas of African American life have given "the American Negro ... the great advantage of having never believed that collection of myths to which white Americans cling."[21] Invocations of the beauty of black life and struggle, then, disrupt a certain utopian imagining of America as "the shining city on the hill"—disclosing for all to see the lie of American innocence.

Beyond this, such invocations reveal a deep insight about American democratic living. Black life and struggle force the nation to encounter the grim realities of suffering and thus undermine the belief that America is an example of democracy realized. They serve as a corrective to the myth of American innocence, the false comforts of moral righteousness, which would insulate us from what Cornel West calls the funk of life[22]—the fact, as Baldwin put it, that life is inescapably tragic:

Life is tragic simply because the earth turns and the sun inexorably rises and sets, and one day, for each of us, the sun will go down for the last, last time. Perhaps the whole root of our trouble, the human trouble, is that we will sacrifice all the beauty of our lives, will imprison ourselves in totems, taboos, crosses, blood sacrifices, steeples, mosques, races, armies, flags, nations, in order to deny the fact of death, which is the only fact we have.[23]

The fact of death, for Baldwin, ought not tempt us into a quest for certainties that secure us from the evils of living. Instead we should earn our death "by confronting with passion the conundrum of life," and we should do so nobly, in part *"for the sake of those who are coming after us."* [24]

In Baldwin's view, such an understanding of life remains elusive for Americans precisely because of our refusal to look the facts of our country's racialized experiences squarely in the face. To do so would shatter the illusion that ours is a white nation and would force our fellow white citizens to see and finally know these blues people who may "reveal more about America to Americans than Americans wish to know." In this sense, Baldwin's invocation of the beauty of black life and struggle constitutes a profoundly democratic act aimed at rescuing democratic ideals from the ghastly implications of the idolatry of color. This insight, I believe, cuts in a number of directions.

Baldwin recognized, perhaps in ways we have yet to grasp, the extent to which appeals to blackness were warranted in a country so fundamentally committed to white supremacy. But he also understood those appeals instrumentally and as inherently limited. Color, in his view, was a political reality, which revealed little about our moral capacities. The challenge was somehow to transcend color, narrowly understood, and to do so in the name of the complex experiences of African American life. Baldwin powerfully pleads in *The Fire Next Time:*

At the center of this dreadful storm, this vast confusion, stand the black people of this nation, who must now share the fate of a nation that has never accepted them, to which they were brought in chains. Well, if this is so, one has no choice but to do all in one's power to change that fate, and at no matter what risk—eviction, imprisonment, torture, death. For the sake of one's children, in order to minimize the bill that they must pay, one must be careful not to take refuge in any delusion—and the value placed on the color of the skin is always and everywhere and forever a delusion.[25]

Baldwin offers here a serious cautionary note. Invocations of the reality of black pain and suffering ought not lead us to embrace conceptions of black identity and history that would further deny how deeply implicated we are in this country's past, present, and future. To be sure, one of the lessons we are to learn from his discussion of the Nation of Islam in *The Fire Next Time* is the organization's failure to understand how profoundly American black folk in this country actually are.

Baldwin's was not an invocation of the idols of the past: the past does not constitute a refuge from the horrors of life. Baldwin invoked the beauty of black life in order to orient us to the future, to the task of creating a better world for our children. His was a profound act of piety and an extraordinary expression of love.

But Baldwin's discussion of the Nation of Islam also reveals something else: the radical rage that results from the conditions of black living in the United States. One would expect individuals who experience systemic degradation to be angry. This is not to suggest that rage should completely define their lives. For some this may be the case. But for the majority of African Americans rage stands alongside the joys of living, and it is precisely in this intense juxtaposition that the edginess of some facets of black life can be found. Indeed, Baldwin renders intelligible the strangeness of the Nation of Islam's theodicy by translating it into the idiom of everyday black life, where rage is a constant companion: we all have our private Bigger Thomas living within our skulls. Baldwin's prose, even when he writes of our desperate need to work together, in love, to better our country, drips with rage—not a consuming, destructive anger but a rage that incites us to act to transform our circumstances and to *memorialize* loss.

Some argue that Baldwin's later writings suffered from an all-consuming rage—that politics and its consequences overwhelmed his aesthetic choices.[26] I disagree. *No Name in the Street,* for example, far from marking a decline, elaborates in interesting ways the insights of *The Fire Next Time.* Take the theme of translation. Here Baldwin, through a retelling of the history of the civil rights movement and his autobiography, renders the Black Panthers in particular and the black power movement in general intelligible to those who might view it as simply the rantings of crazed African American youth. The theme of love recurs as well. He writes of his finding love in Paris, and how "it began to pry open ... the trap of color, for people do not fall in love according to their color."[27] This conception of love extends to the great paradox of African Americans working passionately for American democracy. As Baldwin writes at the end of *No Name in the Street:*

> To be an Afro-American, or an American black, is to be in the situation, intolerably exaggerated, of all those who have ever found themselves part of a civilization which they could in no wise honorably defend—which they were compelled, indeed, endlessly to attack and condemn—and who yet spoke out of the most passionate love, hoping to make the kingdom new, to make it honorable and worthy of life.[28]

To my mind, such formulations are hardly less acute than the powerful views of *The Fire Next Time.*

Even Baldwin's view of color, as evidenced briefly in his remarks about love, remains consistent. He still sees color instrumentally and as inherently limited. But he understands the significance of appeals to color for those who have suffered because they are black. As African Americans struggle with the difficult tasks of self-creation and identity formation—both of which, he suggests, are "arrived at by the way in which the person faces and uses his experience"[29]—the reconstruction of blackness becomes a key tool in finding one's place in a civilization committed to white supremacy. The slogan "black is beautiful," Baldwin argues, is not an expression of reverse racial chauvinism; rather, it registers the fact that "black is a tremendous spiritual condition, one of the greatest challenges anyone alive can face." He goes on to say that "to be liberated from the stigma of blackness by embracing it is to cease, forever, one's interior agreement and collaboration with the authors of one's degradation."[30]

Color has no intrinsic value here. Even as Baldwin asserts its importance he insists that such ideas must inevitably be transcended.

> If it is difficult to be released from the stigma of blackness, it is clearly at least equally difficult to surmount the delusion of whiteness. And as the black glories in his newfound color, which is his at last, and asserts, not always with the

very greatest politeness, the unanswerable validity and power of his being—even in the shadow of death—the white is very often affronted and very often made afraid. He has his reasons, after all, not only for being weary of the concept of color, but fearful as to what may be made of this concept once it has fallen, as it were, into the wrong hands. And one may indeed be wary, but the point is that it was inevitable that black and white should arrive at this dizzying height of tension. *Only when we have passed this moment will we know what our history has made of us.* [31]

Again, this does not constitute a great departure from Baldwin's early work.

Yet there remains an importance difference between *No Name in the Street* and *The Fire Next Time*. The tone is decidedly different. A history of loss—loss of life and loved ones—is central to the story of the African American sojourn in the United States. In *No Name in the Street* Baldwin places this history in the foreground, and rightly so, for here he witnesses death and tells the tale of the mighty dead who struggled to change America. Indeed, the deaths of Martin Luther King Jr., Malcolm X, and Medgar Evers reveal for Baldwin the depths of the sickness that infects the soul of America—and perhaps also a more general, unseemly truth: that "most people are not, in action, worth very much; and yet, every human being is an unprecedented miracle. One tries to treat them as the miracles they are, while trying to protect oneself against the disasters they've become."[32] Baldwin's invocation of "all that beauty," then, entails, among other things, a memorializing of this loss. What is ironic about the criticism of Baldwin during this period is the refusal to take seriously what the dead might mean for him and for America.

The term *invocation* has a special resonance here. The political theorist Sheldon Wolin distinguishes usefully between vocation and invocation. Vocation, in his view, involves a commitment to an ideal evidenced in a particular practice: a calling of sorts that shapes one's choices and guides one's actions. Invocation, however, is a response to a certain kind of loss, a "recalling" that entails the recognition that "something irreplaceable has gone" and that we and our world are irreparably diminished by that fact. Typically, and this is especially true for a society like ours, so committed to notions of progress and the like, loss is banished to history; it is something to "get over." But Wolin rightly notes that loss "is related to power and powerlessness and hence has a claim upon theory." The question, and a powerful one it is, then becomes how to memorialize loss theoretically.[33]

Baldwin answers not with an account of the role of theory in our lives but with an insistence that the memory of loss must inform our current practice. Memory constitutes a constraint on hubris and enables passionately intelligent action. To ignore the past is to fall victim to its undertow. It dooms us, as Santayana famously noted, to repeat the past, and for those who have suffered irreparable loss such repetition is unacceptable. Baldwin wrote of history in "White Man's Guilt":

> History, as nearly no one seems to know, is not merely something to be read. And it does not refer merely, or even principally, to the past. On the contrary, the great force of history comes from the fact that we carry it within us, are unconsciously controlled by it in many ways, and history is literally *present* in all that we do. It could scarcely be otherwise, since it is to history that we owe our frames of reference, our identities, and our aspirations.[34]

The memory of loss then reminds us—and this is especially important to the marginalized and subjugated in our society—of the bodies and broken souls that lie hidden beneath our cherished form of life. This "rememory," as Toni Morrison describes it, holds at arms length America's beliefs about its commitment to the inherent rights of all human beings without distinction; it also tempers any conviction that we are the progenitors and perennial defenders of such ideals.

For Baldwin, then, invocations of the past orient us appropriately to the tasks of self-creation and reconstructing American society.

> In great pain and terror one begins to assess the history which has placed one where one is and formed one's point of view. In great pain and terror because, therefore, one enters into battle with that historical creation, Oneself, and attempts to recreate oneself according to a principle more humane and more liberating; one begins the attempt to achieve a level of personal maturity and freedom which robs history of its tyrannical power, and also changes history.... But, obviously, I am speaking as an historical creation which has had bitterly to contest its history, to wrestle with it, and finally accept it in order to bring myself out of it.[35]

No Name in the Street enacts this Emersonian formulation with relentless courage, foregrounding loss at every turn in order to disclose, amid the extraordinary transformations wrought by black struggle, the daunting challenge of how we, as Americans, must work through the reality of our dead.

Wolin makes another important point about loss and invocation that bears mentioning. In moments of rapid transformation, loss appears to be as much a prerequisite as a side effect of change. And, for Wolin, when losses (or what he refers to as casualties) far exceed the capacities of those who endure them, resulting in little time "to mourn, to absorb the loss and make sense of it, then there is the political equivalent of *blocked grief.*" [36] Blocked grief can take many political forms. Wolin mentions religious and patriotic fundamentalism. In the case of African Americans, we may memorialize in various ways the deaths of Martin, Malcolm, Medgar, and all of the loved ones we know little about, but the resentments and questions associated with their loss remain unresolved. I want to suggest that blocked grief has resulted, among African Americans, in the persistence of black quests for certainty—forms of racial politics that secure us from American hypocrisies.

Baldwin recognized this. However, he remained concerned about America precisely because he understood African Americans as intimately connected to this fragile experiment. He saw that it was *necessary* to embrace this flawed country even as he grasped, perhaps more clearly than most, how blocked grief altered these peculiar blues people's orientation to this place. Baldwin's insight frames my own embrace of pragmatism and informs this modest act of piety and love.

1

Tragedy and Moral Experience: John Dewey and Toni Morrison's Beloved

This time, although he couldn't cipher but one word, he believed he knew who spoke them. The people of the broken necks, of fire-cooked blood and black girls who had lost their ribbons.

What a roaring.

TONI MORRISON, *Beloved*

To be loved, baby, hard at once, and forever, to strengthen you against this loveless world.... We have not stopped trembling yet, but if we had not loved each other none of us would have survived. And now you must survive because we love you, and for the sake of your children and your children's children.

JAMES BALDWIN, *The Fire Next Time*

When the future arrives with its inevitable disappointments as well as fulfillments, and with new sources of trouble, failure loses something of its fatality, and suffering yields fruit of instruction not of bitterness. Humility is more demanded at our moments of triumph than at those of failure. For humility is not caddish self-depreciation. It is the sense of our slight inability even with our best intelligence and effort to command events; a sense of our dependence upon forces that go their way without our wish and plan.

JOHN DEWEY, *Human Nature and Conduct*

No one really questions John Dewey's commitment to democracy. His philosophical works and his political life stand as grand examples of his struggle for the formation of a genuinely cooperative society. But what do we make of his relative silence about the problem of race in the United States? To be sure, Dewey's political choices reflected a desire to end racism. His participation in the formation of the NAACP and his 1922 essay "Racial Prejudice and Friction" demonstrate his interest in the challenge race and racism posed to his conception of democracy. But Dewey was never truly attentive *in his philosophical work* to the problem of racism in America; in none of his major books on democracy did he grapple with the challenge that race presents to his ideas. How are we to think about Dewey's philosophical insights about democracy in light of this? Does he offer us any tools for thinking about contemporary problems of race in the United States?

I want to argue that that Dewey's pragmatic philosophy offers unique insights that can help us address, creatively and intelligently, some of the more intractable problems posed by racism in the United States, from the difficulties of identity politics to the persistence of structural racism. But first

Dewey's philosophy of democracy must be reconstructed in light of the realities of race that have defined this nation. That is to say, a sustained encounter must take place between Deweyan commitments to participatory democracy and the perennial problems of race that frustrate those commitments—what Cornel West describes as the "night side" of American democracy. If American pragmatism is to be understood, in part, as a specific historical and cultural product of American civilization, and as a particular set of social practices that articulate certain American desires, values, and responses, then it must address explicitly the tragedy of race in America.

Many scholars hold the view that Dewey's version of pragmatism is marred by a naïvely optimistic faith in science or a grievous lack of attention to the operations of power. His views, they maintain, are inattentive to the "night side" of life generally. These accounts of Dewey trade on a misconception: that his undying faith in our capacity to work on our world means that he believed there are no limits to what we can do. It is certainly true that in reflecting on the meaning and value of American democracy Dewey emphasized, like Ralph Waldo Emerson, the heroic capacities of ordinary people in a world of radical contingency. But how we understand the place of contingency in Dewey's overall philosophical outlook frames how we ought to understand the scope of human agency in his thinking, as well as its tragic dimensions.

The chapter is divided into two parts. In the first, I argue that behind Dewey's notion of contingency lies what can be called a tragic sensibility. Dewey held the view that uncertainty pervades our lives and involves us in the peril of evils, that there are dimensions of life that are far beyond our control (which deepen "our sense of dependence upon forces that go their way without our wish or plan"[1]), and that this uncertainty defines our moral life in the sense that we can have no recourse to fixed, universal rules that resolve our moral dilemmas. Our moral lives instead require us constantly to choose between competing values and to live with the consequences of those choices without yielding to despair. Dewey holds on to a Sophoclean insight about practical reason and refuses to streamline the complexity of our moral lives. I suggest, then, that the underlying orientation of Dewey's work is predisposed to an effort to reconstruct it in light of the tragedy of race in the United States.

After setting out this view in general terms, I defend it against Hilary Putnam's and Cornel West's influential critiques of Dewey. Readers less interested in these philosophical debates may wish to skip to the second part of the chapter, although the debates should intrigue even nonspecialists. In *Renewing Philosophy,* Putnam claims, among other things, that Dewey's view of intelligence fails to capture what is really at stake in tragic moral situations: what kind of persons we take ourselves to be. For him, Dewey's invocation of intelligence is simply about the maximization of goods and betrays a naïve faith in science, broadly understood. West, for his part, argues in "Pragmatism and the Sense of the Tragic" that Dewey simply fails to grapple seriously with tragedy and the problem of evil. In his view, Dewey's pragmatism does not address the realities of dread, disease, and death, which threaten our democratic ways of thought and life. For West, Deweyan faith in critical intelligence simply fails to meet the challenge posed by the debilitating pessimism that can overtake us in the face of these realities. I maintain that both Putnam and West fail to grasp the importance of contingency and conflict in Dewey's philosophy of action. Nor, I think, do they appreciate how his view of such matters limits the scope of critical intelligence and offers resources for a much more developed pragmatic view of tragedy.

In the second part of this chapter, I deepen my reading of the tragic dimensions of Dewey's thought through a brief examination of Toni Morrison's novel *Beloved.* [2] I suggest that the decision of Morrison's character Sethe to have her children escape slavery by death is best characterized by the pragmatic sense of the tragic I develop in my interpretation of Dewey. I also discuss the way in which the character Baby Suggs, in her exhortation to "Know it, but go on out the yard," gives voice to an understanding of tragedy and evil as part of the moral exigencies of life. Both are ineluctable features of the world of action: always we must know it, but act anyway. I read this as a particularly powerful reconstruction of what Dewey called intelligently guided experimentation. My reading of *Beloved*, then, offers an outline of a pragmatic view of the tragic that takes seriously the realities of race that have shaped this country—realities that in turn make explicit the tragic implications of Dewey's moral and political philosophy. The lesson Morrison's novel holds for Deweyan pragmatism is that the problems of race in the United States are best dealt with by confronting our past and the tragedy therein precisely in order to invade intelligently the future. Creative intelligence and an experimental approach enriched by the knowledge of our *racial* experiences allow us to locate the serious conflicts that plague America and offer up ways to deal with them. Tragedy remains. We must know it and act anyway.

Dewey, Tragedy, and Moral Experience

Sidney Hook argues in *Pragmatism and the Tragic Sense of Life* (1974) that William James and John Dewey held a view of tragedy that framed the central themes of their pragmatism—an open-ended universe, an accent on human agency and the importance of critical intelligence—with the vital options, inescapable limitations, and piecemeal losses we all confront as we act in the world. Drawing on the work of James, Hook suggests that "no matter how intelligent and humane our choices, there are real losses and losers."[3] Tragedy, then, is a part of the moral exigencies of life. It involves principally the moral choices we make between competing and irreconcilable goods, and it entails the consequences we must endure, if we live, and the responsibility we must embrace without yielding to despair.[4] Tragedy, in this view, is a moral phenomenon, "rooted in the very nature of the moral experience and the phenomenon of moral choice. Every genuine experience of moral doubt and perplexity in which we ask 'What should I do?' takes place in a situation where good conflicts with good."[5]

Hook doesn't go very far toward demonstrating how this notion of tragedy informs the work of James and Dewey. He simply assumes it and moves on. But one can easily see this view of tragedy in the work of William James. James's talk about the sick-soul and his tortured attempt to hold off the view that the world is a sea of disappointment testify to his intense grappling with tragedy. In "The Moral Philosopher and Moral Life" James argues that the conflict of goods is an essential feature of our moral lives. He writes, "The actually possible in this world is vastly narrower than all that is demanded; and there is always the *pinch* between the ideal and the actual which can only be got through by leaving part of the ideal behind. There is hardly a good which we can imagine except as competing for the possession of the same bit of space and time with some other imagined good." And when we make our choices between them, some ideal is always butchered. "It is a tragic situation," he notes, "and no mere speculative conundrum with which [we have] to deal."[6] For James, the *pinch* is a constitutive feature of the world of action. Victories abound. But so do defeats. Everywhere we look we see what he describes as "the struggle and the squeeze," and our task is somehow to lessen them. In this effort, we do not have recourse to fixed principles or rules. In James's words, "Every real dilemma is in literal strictness a unique situation; and the exact combination of ideals realized and ideals disappointed which each decision creates is always a universe without a precedent, and for which no adequate previous rule exist."[7] At the moment of decision, we can only act on what we hold dear.

Making the case that John Dewey holds a tragic vision is a bit more difficult. Dewey's talk about scientific method and critical intelligence suggests, for some, that he was excessively optimistic about our capacities to resolve conflicts (particularly of the sort that concerned James). Interestingly though, Dewey begins in the same place as James. In *The Quest for Certainty* he writes of genuine moral dilemmas

All the serious perplexities of life come back to the genuine difficulty of forming a judgment as to the values of the situation; they come back to a conflict of goods. Only dogmatism can suppose that serious moral conflict is between something clearly bad and something known to be good, and that uncertainty lies wholly in the will of the one choosing. Most conflicts of importance are conflicts between things which are or have been satisfying, not between good and evil.[8]

This view presupposes formulations laid out in his *Ethics* (1932), and I will turn to this text later in the chapter. But for my purposes here it signals that Dewey recognizes, like James, that our moral lives are characterized by conflicts of values.

In "Three Independent Factors in Morals," for example, Dewey writes that uncertainty and conflict are inherent in morals—that conflict is internal and intrinsic to every moral situation. Dewey's talk about critical intelligence and method, then, ought to be understood in light of this recognition of the centrality of conflict. As he writes in *Human Nature and Conduct:*

> It is not pretended that a moral theory based upon realities of human nature and a study of the specific connections of these realities with those of physical science would do away with moral struggle and defeat. It would not make the moral life as simple a matter as wending one's way along a well-lighted boulevard. All action is an invasion of the future, of the unknown. Conflict and uncertainty are ultimate traits.[9]

The conflict runs deep for Dewey, whose *faith,* unlike James's, resides in our capacity to engage in intelligent action: he is reluctant to fix belief even in the face of conflict of goods. Thus it becomes all the more urgent to develop habits and virtues with which we can intelligently seek to ameliorate problematic situations.[10] For Dewey, *preoccupation* with the pinch—the struggle and squeeze of the world of action—can become debilitating. We should instead take the world for what it is: uncertain, in process, and always acting on us, for weal or woe. This understanding of the precariousness of the world of action is absolutely crucial for understanding the tragic vision implicit in Dewey's pragmatic philosophy of action.

In Dewey's view, we have responded to the hazards of this world of uncertainty in, at least, two ways. First, we have constructed rituals of supplication and sacrifice in the hope of appeasing the uncontrollable forces that impinge upon us. The aim here is to ally ourselves with powers that dispense fortune in order to escape defeat and, perhaps, to experience triumph in the face of destruction.[11] Second, we have invented arts: Housing, clothing, irrigation—all are examples of attempts to "construct a fortress out of the very conditions and forces" that threaten us.

The first response entails, in Dewey's terms, changing the self in emotion and idea, a method that informs traditional philosophical reflection. The second is the method of changing the world through action.[12] Both reflect our efforts to respond to a world of hazards. Yet we have often viewed the arts as an inadequate response.

Why? The world of action, of doing and making, involves us in activities that in no way remove uncertainty. As Dewey writes: "The distinctive characteristic of practical activity, one which is so inherent that it cannot be eliminated, is the uncertainty that attends it. Of it we are compelled to say: Act, but act at your peril."[13] Practical activity involves change, and it has been our desire to escape the frightening consequences of change that has led to misguided quests for certainty. In Dewey's view, modern philosophy has conceived of knowledge, for example, as a private affair in which the disclosure of the invariant—the Real in itself—is the object of inquiry. Here philosophers strip away the imaginative formulations of a religious outlook, in which a sharp division between the ordinary and the extraordinary animates how we see ourselves in relation to our world and the universe, only to replace them with their own doctrine of what Dewey termed "the antecedently real," which when grasped by thought, discloses fixed and immutable Truth. For Dewey, this search translates efforts to escape the exigencies of life into rational form. Deliverance from the vicissitudes of existence by means of rites and sacrifice gives way to a form of deliverance through reason, a theoretical affair that stands apart from our actual conditions of living.[14]

The world of action, by contrast, is fraught with uncertainty. In it, events for which we have neither wished nor planned happen to us and transform our lives. Circumstances may force us to choose wrongly or to betray those whom we love. People we cherish die. We die. Indeed, the contingency of our lives and the apparent indifference of nature to our efforts jeopardize human aspirations to live good lives.[15] Deliverance from the exigencies of life is, in some ways, deliverance from what some take to be the tragedy of brute chance. For in the end, Dewey writes, "the quest for certainty is a quest for peace which is assured, an object which is unqualified by risk and the shadow of fear which action casts. For it is not uncertainty per se which men dislike, but the fact that uncertainty involves us in peril of evils."[16]

This understanding of contingency forms the background for Dewey's philosophical formulations; it extends the Darwinian outlook, which presupposes that the world is processive. Dewey believes that Darwinian evolution dislodged an Aristolelian conception of the world in which all changes reflected an overarching order and were cumulative, in the sense that they tended in a predetermined direction.[17] Darwin's influence on philosophy resided in his rejection of this particular view and its replacement by the principle of transition: that the environment exerts pressures on its inhabitants and that random variations among these living creatures affect how they will get on in the environment as it acts upon them.

Our activity in the world, then, is one of constant adaptation and adjustment in light of the limit conditions of existence.

Three crucial points for Dewey's philosophy follow from this principle: (1) that philosophy must give up inquiry after absolute origins and fixed Truth and turn its attention to the actual conditions of experience that generate specific values, (2) that philosophy must abandon efforts to prove that life *must* have certain qualities and values, over and beyond experience, because of some predetermined end, and (3) that such an outlook introduces responsibility into intellectual life. We must, in Dewey's view, look the facts of experience in the face, acknowledging both the evils they present and the goods they *may* promise. As Dewey writes:

> As long as mankind suffered from this impotency, it naturally shifted a burden of responsibility that it could not carry over to the more competent shoulders of the transcendent cause. But if insight into specific conditions of value and into

specific consequences of idea is possible, philosophy must in time become a method of locating and interpreting the more serious conflicts that occur in life, and a method of projecting ways for dealing with them: a method of moral and political diagnosis and prognosis.[18]

The quest for certainty, then, is seen for what it is: an effort on the part of fragile, finite creatures to secure themselves and their world in the face of unrelenting change.

Such efforts have led us to turn our backs on the world of action and, to some extent, to absolve ourselves of the strenuous work of "making and remaking" our world. Fixed reality, complete in itself, provides us with a sense of assurance that order stands behind what we experience as contingent. It is similar to the relief from grief we feel when we know that our loved ones are resting peacefully in heaven. But Darwin's insights, Dewey maintains, force us to reject this view. Disclosure of the antecedently real does nothing to arrest the changes in our world (just as knowing that our loved ones are in heaven does not change the fact that they are dead and no longer with us). Change still happens—for better or for worse.

If we turn instead to experience, we give up efforts to secure our world by means of transcending it. The search for security remains. Our efforts, however, are located in practical activity, not in quests for absolute certainty. In this view, knowledge is the fruit of our attempts to resolve problematic situations and is understood in the context of communal inquiry, not in terms of private mental activity. The turn to the actual conditions of our living, then, tilts our understanding of knowledge in a different direction. It is no longer about absolute certainty and fixed Truth. Instead, knowledge can be properly understood only as a functional activity in the context of our experience, that is to say, in the context of interactions with our environment. The qualities and values of these experiences are not predetermined and set. Nor are they reducible to an inner event or to a backward-looking affair in which the past counts exclusively. Experience, for Dewey, "is a matter of *simultaneous* doings and sufferings,"[19] a process of undergoing in which agent-patients seek experimentally to find the best tools to cope with the obstacles their environment presents and to anticipate future problems.

This connection to the future forms the primary basis for responsibility. For in the effort to secure our world for our children and ourselves, we employ methods that generate foresight. We make moral and political prognoses with an eye toward securing and expanding for future generations the values we cherish. As Dewey writes in "The Development of American Pragmatism":

Pragmatism ... does not insist upon antecedent phenomena but upon consequent phenomena; not upon precedents but upon the possibilities of action.... The doctrine of the value of consequences leads us to take the future into consideration. And this taking into consideration of the future takes us to the conception of a universe whose evolution is not finished, of a universe which is still, in James's terms "in the making, in the process of becoming," of a universe up to a certain point still plastic.[20]

Dewey's accent on human agency presupposes a world that is always evolving. No guarantees. No fixed truths. Just the fragile attempts of finite creatures to flourish in an environment that impinges upon them daily. Here the mystery and awe we have felt in the face of a universe that is extraordinary (and which requires that we approach it with ceremonial scruples) is transferred to the human future.[21] Our primary responsibility, then, is to act intelligently in order to ensure, as much as humanly possible, that this future is better than our present.

MORAL EXPERIENCE AND HILARY PUTNAM'S CRITIQUE

Contingency forms the backdrop for Dewey's philosophical reflection. Once we grasp its place in his overall outlook we get a sense of his view of human agency and the task of philosophy. That is to say, once we realize that there is never a metaphysical guarantee to be had for our beliefs, we can give up efforts to discover the antecedently real and realize that what human beings do in the face of problems and how they go about doing it *is* the primary topic of philosophical reflection. Questions like Is the universe friendly to democratic possibility? can be abandoned. Instead we will ask how the consequences of our choices serve or defeat our efforts for genuine democratic living. The shift, as Dewey puts it, is "from an intelligence that shaped things once for all to the particular intelligences which things are even now shaping."[22]

It is essential that we recognize that, even with all Dewey's talk about intelligent action, uncertainty remains. Action involves risks and by no means guarantees satisfactory outcomes. Dewey makes this point powerfully near the end of his Gifford Lectures:

At best, all our endeavors look to the future and never attain certainty. The lesson of probability holds for all forms of activity as truly as for the experimental operations of science and even more poignantly and tragically. The control and regulation of which so much has been said never signifies certainty of outcome, although the greater need of security it may afford will not be known until we try the experimental policy in all walks of life. The unknown surrounds us in other forms of practical activity even more than in knowing, for they reach further in the future, in more significant and less controllable ways. *A sense of dependence is quickened by that Copernican revolution which looks to security amid change instead of to certainty in attachment to the fixed.* [23]

Dewey suggests here that our immodest pains to uncover the fixed and immutable principles of the universe provide a level of comfort (assurance) that is not available once we turn to the world of action. *This* world forces us to humble our efforts to the work of hypotheses for the amelioration of individual and social problems. We stand unprotected by the armor of traditional metaphysics only to encounter the full brunt of change and its potential misery and joy. Our best recourse in the face of these moments is not to seek refuge from the troubles of existence[24] but rather to act as intelligently as possible to secure for ourselves what we deem, at a given moment, desirable. The problems of evil then are understood, for Dewey, within the stream of experiences, and we need only turn to his conception of *moral* experience to see their tragic dimensions and implications.

Our moral experiences are characterized by conflicting moral demands.[25] We confront situations that demand of us a choice between competing values, and the conflict produces a genuine moral dilemma. Moral experiences and deliberation, then, are always situated in the context of some particular problem—some perceived moral perplexity. For Dewey, there are at least two kinds of moral struggle. One, which is most often emphasized in traditional moral writings, is the case when an individual is tempted to do something she knows is wrong. Dewey uses the example of the bank employee who is tempted to embezzle money. She knows that she shouldn't, though she may try to convince herself otherwise, to permit her desires to govern her beliefs. No real thinking, however, takes place, even if she seeks to justify embezzlement, for there is no sincere doubt as to what should be done.[26]

The other kind of moral struggle is the case when two values conflict. Dewey's example is worth quoting at length:

> Take ... the case of the citizen of a nation which has just declared war on another country. He is deeply attached to his own State. He has formed habits of loyalty and of abiding by its law, and now one of its decrees is that he shall support war. He feels in addition gratitude and affection for the country which has sheltered and nurtured him. But he believes that this war is unjust, or perhaps he

has a conviction that all war is a form of murder and hence wrong. One side of his nature, one set of convictions and habits, leads him to acquiesce to war; another deep part of his being protests. He is torn between two duties: he experiences a conflict between incompatible values.... The struggle is not between a good which is clear to him and something else which attracts him but which he knows to be wrong. It is between values each of which is an undoubted good in its place but which now get in each other's way.[27]

For Dewey, moral theory represents an extension of the kind of reflection that goes on in such moments. It does not emerge in the situation where we already know, by way of custom and habit, why one course of action is right and the other wrong. Moral theory takes place when we are confronted with situations in which opposing goods and incompatible courses of action seem to be morally justified.[28]

This approach evades some of the pitfalls of traditional moral theory. Dewey notes that traditional moral philosophy tends to isolate and reify specific features of our moral life in an effort to uncover one single principle of morality. These efforts, in whatever form, fail to acknowledge the centrality of uncertainty and conflict to our moral experiences. Instead, a litany of dualities—good and evil, justice and injustice, duty and caprice, virtue and vice—render moral conflict as only specious and apparent, not as an inherent part of the good, the obligatory, and the virtuous.[29] In such a view, with its ready-made distinctions and dualities, "the only force which can oppose the moral is the immoral."[30]

Dewey argues that uncertainty and conflict in moral experience ought not to be understood in this way. Instead, moral experience and the attendant notions of moral progress and character development involve the activity of making "delicate distinctions, to perceive aspects of good and evil not previously noted, to take into account the fact that doubt and the need for choice impinge at every turn," and the mark of moral decline is the loss of an ability to make such distinctions.[31] He goes on to suggest that there are at least three independent variables—good, right, and virtue—in moral action. Each has its own origin and mode of operation, and because of this, each can get in the others' way.[32] From this point of view, Dewey argues:

> Uncertainty and conflict are inherent in morals; it is characteristic of any situation properly called moral that one is ignorant of the end and of the good consequences, of the right and just approach, of the direction of the virtuous conduct, and that one must search for them. The essence of the moral situation is an internal and intrinsic conflict; the necessity for judgment and choice comes from the fact that one has to manage forces with no common denominator.[33]

In such situations the correct choice is rarely apparent. We stand somewhat ignorant of the end and the consequences that may follow from whatever choice we make. Nevertheless, we must choose, knowing not that our choice is based in some fixed, universal principle but that our choice is the best, most intelligent choice we can make in a particular problematic situation.

Hilary Putnam has found this dimension of Dewey's philosophy less than satisfactory. He argues that Dewey's emphasis on intelligence and the maximization of goods does not take us far enough in resolving the moral dilemmas we often face, particularly when what's at stake is what kind of individual we take ourselves to be. Putnam writes:

> Consider the famous case of an existential choice that Sartre employed in his *Existentialism and Humanism.* It is World War II, and Pierre has to make an agonizing choice between joining the Resistance, which means leaving his aging mother alone on the farm, or staying and taking care of his mother, but not helping to fight the enemy. One of the reasons that Dewey's recommendation to use intelligently guided experimentation

in solving ethical problems does not really help in such a case is Dewey's consequentialism. Pierre is not out to "maximize" the good, however conceived, in some global sense, he is out to do what is right. Like all consequentialist views, Dewey has trouble doing justice to considerations of the right. I am not saying that Dewey's philosophy never applies to individual existential choices. Some choices are just dumb. But Pierre is not dumb. Neither of the alternatives he is considering is any way stupid. Yet he cannot just flip a coin.[34]

For Putnam, when individuality is at stake—like the need for Pierre to decide who Pierre is—intelligently guided experimentation doesn't really help matters. And so Putnam turns instead to William James.

For Putnam, we need not restrict ourselves to "consummatory experiences which are brought about and appraised." Often we have to act on our belief that a course of action is right even though relatively little in our experience suggests that it is, or even though we lack the time to assess the consequences. Sometimes we have to run ahead of the evidence. To make this point, Putnam evokes James against what he considers Dewey's more "scientistic" position:

James thought that every single human being has to make decisions ahead of the evidence of the kind that Pierre had to make, even if they are not as dramatic.... James argued again and again that our best energies cannot be set free unless we are willing to make the sort of existential commitment that this example illustrates. Someone who acts only when the "estimated utilities" are favorable does not live a meaningful life. Even if I choose to do something of whose ethical and social value there is absolutely no doubt, say to devote my life to comforting the dying, or helping the mentally ill, or curing the sick, or relieving poverty, I still have to decide not whether it is good that someone should do that thing, but whether it is good that I, Hilary Putnam, do that thing. The answer to that question cannot be a matter of well-established scientific fact, in however generous a sense of "scientific."[35]

Many readers come away from Dewey's appeals to science thinking that he believes in inevitable progress and a human capacity to transform any circumstance, and that these positions blind him to the existential dilemmas that we fragile and finite creatures confront. But to read Dewey in this way, as does Putnam, obscures the tragic dimensions of his thinking.

Dewey understood that conflict and uncertainty arise because of the complexity of the problem of discovering what is good, what is right, and what is virtuous. For Dewey, the more thoughtful the individual moral agent is about the quality of her moral acts, the more aware she will be of the complexity of the problem of discovering what is good. He goes on to say, sounding a lot like Putnam, that the moral agent "hesitates among ends, all of which are good in some measure, among duties which obligate him for some reason. *Only after the event and then by chance, does one of the alternatives seem simply good morally or bad morally."* [36] Dewey maintains that dilemmas of this sort are not recognized by moral theory because, whatever the differences that separate different moral accounts, they all offer a single principle as an explanation of our moral lives. Pierre's sort of dilemma—in this case, the conflict between good and right—is exactly Dewey's point of entry into reconstructing moral philosophy.

But Putnam's worry goes beyond this. He would have to concede that, like James, Dewey recognizes the experience of a conflict between incompatible values as the starting point of his ethics. The problem, however, lies with Dewey's talk of intelligence in the context of such dilemmas. In Putnam's view, Dewey simply fails to capture what is really at stake when we are confronted with conflicting goods. What is at stake, Putnam suggests, is who we take ourselves to be. And yet on this point Dewey would emphatically agree. Putnam's worry points to a problem in his description of Dewey's moral philosophy. He fails to account for the importance Dewey places on habit and custom in the formation and continued development of our *individual* characters. What's at stake for Dewey in situations like Pierre's, among other things, is precisely what kind of person Pierre takes himself to be and will become. Dewey makes this point quite explicit in *Human Nature and Conduct.*

> The poignancy of situations that involve reflection lies in the fact that we really do not know the meaning of the tendencies that are pressing for action. We have to search, to experiment. Deliberation is a work of discovery. Conflict is acute; one impulse carries us one way into one situation, and another impulse takes us another way to a radically different objective result. Deliberation is not an attempt to do away with this opposition of quality by reducing it to one amount. It is an attempt to uncover the conflict in its full scope and bearing. What we want to find out is what difference each impulse and

habit imports, to reveal qualitative incompatibilities by detecting the different courses to which they commit us, the different dispositions they form and foster, the different situations into which they plunge us. *In short, the thing actually at stake in any serious deliberation is not a difference of quantity, but what kind of person one is to become, what sort of self is in the making, what kind of world is in the making.* [37]

In light of this, Putnam's criticism is puzzling. Dewey, like James, begins with the conflict between values. He also, like James, understands that our deliberations in the face of moral dilemmas are, in some ways, deliberations about what kind of person one is to become. In both views, individuality is at stake. Putnam, however, makes no mention of Dewey's talk about character and its relation to conduct. He fails to see that, for Dewey, what we do—even if that entails running ahead of the evidence—depends on the history of the organism engaged in the action. Dewey's invocation of intelligence, then, goes beyond the maximization of goods and reveals an existential commitment. To use his language, intelligence is, in some ways, about discovery: our attempt to figure out, as best we can, given the circumstances, why one impulse carries us this way and the other that way.

Unlike James, Dewey is not willing in these critical moments—moments that are as much about who we will become as they are about who we are—to allow us to rest solely on established habits. There may be cases where this is necessary. But we must not render the notion of "running ahead of the evidence" in such a way that it amounts only to a blind jab in the darkness. To run ahead of the evidence can very well be, and in some cases is, an intelligent act. Beyond this Dewey would agree with James when James writes,

> We stand on a mountain pass in the midst of whirling snow and blinding mist, through which we get glimpses now and then of paths which may be deceptive. If we stand still, we shall be frozen to death. If we take the wrong road,

we shall be dashed to pieces. We do not certainly know if there is any right one. What must we do? "Be strong and of good courage". Act for the best, hope for the best, and take what comes.... If death ends all, we cannot meet death better.[38]

THE PROBLEM OF EVIL AND CORNEL WEST'S CRITIQUE

We could easily throw up our hands about any possibility of flourishing in such a world. Experiencing the dark side of nature is all too much a part of what it means to be an agent. Evil, absurdity, and (to paraphrase Josiah Royce) the hideously petty dimensions of our failures and losses, could easily lead us to conclude, with Schopenhauer, that "earthly happiness is destined to be frustrated, or recognized as an illusion," and that "the grounds for this lie deep in the very nature of things."[39] For Schopenhauer, suffering is an ineliminable feature of this worst of all possible worlds. Here the nastiness of experience makes it such that, for each of us, it would have been better not to have been born. Indeed for Schopenhauer, our world can be described quite accurately as hell, and we "are on the one hand the tormented souls and on the other the devils in it."[40]

Classical pragmatists like Dewey reject the pessimistic conclusions drawn from the recognition of our precarious position in the world.[41] Dewey, for example, would readily agree with Schopenhauer that suffering is a constitutive feature of the world of action, but would insist that it points to only one side of the "double connection" of experience. Of course experience involves suffering. It is "primarily a process of undergoing: a process of standing something; of suffering and passion, of affection, in the literal sense of these terms."[42] But the process of undergoing is never merely passive: experience is not simply a matter of receptivity. We are also agents—reacting, experimenting, concerned with influencing the direction of our encounters in such a way that they will benefit and not harm. These actions involve us in peril: conflicts of ends will occur and, more than likely, new sorts of problems will arise as old ones are resolved. But this is not necessarily a bad thing. It is part of what it means to be an organism interacting with its environment. Dewey would agree with Schopenhauer: our world is one in which suffering is inescapable. But, where Schopenhauer would conclude from this fact that it would have been better not to have been born, Dewey, like Emerson and James, responds with meliorism.

Meliorism is the belief that our circumstances at a given moment, be they comparatively good or bad, can be improved. Such a view commends intelligent action in the sense that it encourages us to inquire into the amelioration of problems, individual and social, and the obstructions to their resolution. Such a view doesn't commit Dewey to a form of optimism. In fact, he explicitly rejects an optimistic orientation. In his words, meliorism "arouses confidence and a reasonable hopefulness as optimism does not. For the latter, in declaring that good is already realized in ultimate reality, tends to make us gloss over the evils that concretely exist."[43] For Dewey, optimism—with its view that our world is the best possible world—"co-operates with pessimism ... in benumbing sympathetic insight and intelligent effort in reform." Moreover, "it beckons men away from the world of relativity and change into the calm of the absolute and eternal."[44]

Here Dewey echoes William James. James wrote that "meliorism treats salvation as neither necessary nor impossible. It treats it as a possibility, which becomes more and more of a probability the more numerous the actual conditions of salvation become."[45] To put the point in Deweyan language, we can indeed reconstruct our experiences for the better—can secure and stabilize some of the goods within them—once we have grasped, through critical intelligence, the conditions that make for those experiences. But our efforts are not guaranteed. The world of action is a world of change, "a precarious and perilous place," which, when it is all said and done, retains its hazardous character, in spite of our intelligent efforts. The dangers may be modestly modified but hardly eliminated.[46] As Dewey writes in *Experience and Nature:*

> While philosophy has its source not in any special impulse or staked-off section of experience, but in the entire human predicament, this human situation falls wholly within nature. It reflects the traits of nature; it gives indisputable evidence that in nature itself qualities and relations, individualities and uniformities, finalities and efficacies, contingencies and necessities are inextricably bound. The harsh conflicts and happy coincidences of this interpenetration make experience what it consciously is; their manifest apparition creates doubt, forces inquiry, exacts choices, and imposes liability for the choices made.[47]

We can never claim that intelligence will secure our lives once and for all or "save us from ruin or destruction." The strangeness and unexpected aspects of nature will continuously interrupt, irritate, and exact choices from us. To think otherwise would be to turn our attention away from the facts of experience and suggest an unreasonable hopefulness that would lead away from the task of reconstruction.[48] To be sure, our conditions of living require "a certain intellectual pessimism, in the sense of a steadfast willingness to uncover sore points, to acknowledge and search for abuses, to note how presumed good often serves as a cloak for actual bad."[49] Ours is indeed a life of suffering. But suffering is only a part of our experiences. We must always be mindful of our capacity to act on our world.

If those efforts are frustrated (as perhaps they will be) or if they lead to other more complicated, nuanced problems (as they most assuredly will) such is the nature of our efforts to secure our world amid change. They are provisional and sometimes fail. But this fact should not lead us to turn our backs on this world or to believe that nonexistence is better than existence. Responses like these reflect a desire for certainty and ultimate guarantees.

Despite our best efforts, neither is possible nor, if we truly care about *this* world, desirable. Oliver Wendell Holmes states the position best, and Dewey quotes him at length in *Experience and Nature:*

> If we believe we came out of the universe, not it out of us, we must admit that we do not know what we are talking about when we speak of brute matter. We do know that a certain complex of energies can wag its tail and another can make syllogisms. These are among the powers of the unknown, and if, as may be, it has still greater powers that we cannot understand ... why should we not be content? Why should we employ the energy that is furnished to us by the cosmos to defy it and to shake our fist at the sky? It seems silly.... That the universe has in it more than we understand, that the private soldiers have not been told the plan of campaign, or even that there is one ... has no bearing on our conduct. We still shall fight—all of us because we want to live,

some, at least, because we want to realize our spontaneity and prove our powers, for the joy of it, and we may leave to the unknown the supposed final valuation of that which in any event has value to us. It is enough for us that the universe has produced us and has within it, as less than it, all that we believe and love.[50]

This is where Dewey's philosophy of action begins and why I believe it presupposes a view of tragedy. Because once we stop pondering God's intent or seeking to disclose that which purportedly lies behind the world of appearance, we are confronted with the tragic choices of fragile human beings seeking a bit of security in the here and now, and hoping, reasonably, for a better future for their children. His is a philosophy that begins with human agency and historical/natural limitations, accenting the fact that all we hold dear lies in this world, and that, with intelligence and a bit of luck, that's all we need to flourish.

But for Cornel West, Dewey fails, even with all his talk about contingency, to grapple seriously with tragedy and the problem of evil. West argues that although Dewey recognized, with Jefferson, "the irreducibility of individuality within participatory communities," and acknowledged, like Emerson, "the heroic action of ordinary folk in a world of radical contingency," he failed to "meet the challenge posed by Lincoln—namely, defining the relation of democratic ways of thought and life to a profound sense of evil."[51] For West, the only American philosopher to take seriously Lincoln's challenge was Josiah Royce. He even suggests that Royce's post-Kantian idealism can be read as a sustained meditation on the relation of evil to human agency.

Voluntarism, fallibilism, and experimentalism are central to both Dewey's instrumental pragmatism and Royce's absolute pragmatism. Both thinkers stress the importance of human will and practice. And as West notes, this emphasis leads to two basic claims in their philosophies: (1) that truth is a species of the good and (2) that the conception of the good is defined in relation to temporal consequences.[52]

For both thinkers, what we believe matters and what we do can make a difference in relation to our aims and purposes. Truth, then, has ethical consequences, and the future has ethical significance. West demonstrates the way in which both of these claims animate the absolute idealism of Royce and the instrumentalism of Dewey, and how each claim, particularly the second, prospective one, leads to the conclusion that all facts are fallible and that efforts to better our world are experimental. This, for West, is the common ground between Royce and Dewey—the view that "unique selves acting in and through participatory communities give ethical significance to an open, risk-ridden future.... The 'majesty of community' [Royce] and the 'the true spirituality of genuine doubting'[Dewey] combine to ensure that nothing blocks the Peircean road to inquiry."[53]

But when it comes to the fact of evil, West argues, Royce and Dewey go their separate ways. For West, the presence of evil affected Royce more than it did Dewey. This torturous struggle with evil and Lincoln's challenge attracted Royce to the work of Schopenhauer, and West sees the absence of references to Schopenhauer in Dewey's corpus as a failure. For Royce as for West, Dewey's faith in critical intelligence is woefully inadequate when confronted with a deep sense of evil, for the problem of evil demands of us a lifelong struggle against pessimism.

Royce attempted to hold on in a world of suffering and sorrow by way of his absolute idealism. He recognized that the irrevocable nature of our actions and the indeterminate character of the future made fulfillment at any present instant impossible. Yet Royce was "ready to accept the dear sorrow of possessing ideals and of taking [his] share of the divine task." For him, absolute reality ("the sort of reality that belongs to irrevocable deeds") and absolute truth ("the sort of truth that belongs to those opinions which, for a given purpose, counsel individual deeds, when the deeds in fact meet the purpose for which they were intended") grounded our actions in *this* world and made them sturdy. For West, though,

Royce's idealism went beyond worries about skepticism and epistemic relativism: reality and truth had to be absolute because they are "the last and only hope for giving meaning to the strenuous mood, for justifying the worthwhileness of our struggle to endure."[54] Without absolute truth and reality, pessimism is our only option.

At this point, West turns to a powerful moment in Royce's work in which he doubts his own response to the problem of evil.

> For I do not feel that I have yet quite expressed the full force of the deepest argument for pessimism, or the full seriousness of the eternal problem of evil.... Pessimism, in the true sense, isn't the doctrine of the merely peevish man, but of the man who to borrow a word of Hegel's, "has feared not for this moment or that in his life, but who has feared with all his nature; so that he has trembled through and through, and all that was most fixed in him has become shaken." There are experiences in life that do just this for us.... The worst

tragedy of the world is the tragedy of brute chance to which everything spiritual seems to be subject amongst us—the tragedy of the diabolical irrationality of so many among the foes of whatever is significant. An open enemy you can face. The temptation to do evil is indeed a necessity for spirituality. But one's own foolishness, one's ignorance, the cruel accidents of disease, the fatal misunderstandings that part friends and lovers, the chance mistakes that wreck nations:—these things we lament most bitterly, not because they are painful, but because they are farcical, distracting,—not foe-men worthy of the sword of the spirit, nor yet mere pangs of our finitude that we can easily learn to face courageously, as one can be indifferent to physical pain. No, these things do not make life merely painful to us; they make it hideously petty.[55]

For West, this constitutes recognition of a "deep," "profound" sense of evil, an intense grappling with its presence, which is entirely absent in Dewey's work.[56]

West believes that an acknowledgement of the profound reality of evil must infuse any meaning and value of democracy, and that Dewey simply fails to see that "the culture of democratic societies requires not only the civic virtues of participation, tolerance, openness, mutual respect and mobility, but also dramatic struggles with the two major culprits—disease and death—that defeat and cut off the joys of democratic citizenship."[57] Royce's insight is found, then, not in his absolute idealism—his quest for ultimate assurance—but, rather, in the recognition of evil that often leads us to seek that assurance. And such a recognition—stamped as it is with a Christian imprimatur—is required if we are to meet Lincoln's challenge.

Dewey would disagree. Evils are scaled down in his naturalistic philosophy. They are desires errant and frustrated: simply part of the vicissitudes of existence. To be sure, evils remain a powerful force in our lives—thwarting our efforts and often making our lives miserable and painful—but they are not thought of as a defect and aberration, as deviations from the perfect. For Dewey, the recognition of uncertainty displaces the assumption of an antecedent identity between the actual and ideal, along with all of the problems, particularly the problem of evil, that follow from it. Dewey's starting point, then, is quite different from Royce's. It is not one in which the ideal is already and eternally a property of the real. Ideals instead signal the possibility of modifying the current state of affairs; they take us back to Dewey's understanding of ideas as designations of operations and their consequences.[58] And as he put it in *The Quest for Certainty,* "The sense of incompetency and the sloth born of the desire for irresponsibility have combined to create an overwhelming longing for the ideal and rational as an antecedent possession for actuality, and consequently something upon which we can fall back for emotional support in times of trouble."[59] And, if that support fails us at the crucial moment, something to shake our fist at as we succumb to pessimism.

The problem of evil, for Dewey, is not a theological or metaphysical problem. It "is perceived to be the practical problem of reducing, alleviating, as far as may be removing, the evils of life," and the task of philosophy is to contribute "in however humble a way to methods that will assist us in discovering the causes of humanity's ills."[60] For Dewey, then, the world is neither wholly evil nor wholly good. It simply is what is, and *our* actions infuse it with meaning. Unlike Royce, Dewey does not begin with "bitter lament" over the "tragedy of brute chance." He simply acknowledges uncertainty and all that attends it as *the* constitutive feature of the world of action, arguing that our task is to act in this world as intelligently as possible in order to secure some consequences and avoid others.

This exposes us to the peril of evils. We may have experiences that make us "tremble through and through"—or even lead us to despair. But they would be *experiences,* not occasions for abstract lamentation over the failure of the universe. Not the result of ideals pitched too high, but moments of genuine defeat. Such moments concerned Dewey. He worried about despair, for he understood that to act is to risk defeat and that defeat can be debilitating. I read his passionate insistence on the need for critical intelligence as, at times, a desperate attempt to equip us with the tools to withstand such moments. Does this constitute an answer to Lincoln's challenge? To my mind, yes. If we understand that the world of action involves us in the peril of evils and that democracy is a product of our making, then we must define democracy in relation to that world and the uncertainty that attends it. Our democratic way of life is by no means guaranteed, nor is it perfect. The perennial problems of racism reveal as much. Democracy must be understood, then, apart from procedures and laws and seen as a regulative ideal toward which we strive (with all of the risks that striving entails).[61]

West remains unsatisfied for at least two reasons. First, his preoccupation with the problem of evil does not stem from a disconnection between the actual and ideal. He is more concerned with undeserved harm and suffering, and the inadequate grasp of this suffering (and the complex operations of power that produce it) by classical and contemporary pragmatists. Second, the fundamental challenge of evil to our democratic way of thought and life, in his view, takes the form of disease and death. Both of these facts of life defeat and cut short the joys of democratic citizenship.

The first reason is puzzling. When West claims that to be mindful of the operations of power is to confront the tragic, that is, "to confront the individual and collective experiences of evil with little expectation of ridding the world of all evil,"[62] he sounds a lot like Dewey. This is also the case when he claims elsewhere that "suffering is understood only as a reality to resist, an actuality to oppose. It can neither be submitted to in order to gain contemplative knowledge nor reified into an object of ironic attention. Rather it is a concrete state of affairs which produces discernible hurt and pain, hence requiring some sort of action."[63] What differentiates this view from Dewey's? What makes Royce's idealist formulation of the problem of evil more compelling? Perhaps it is Royce's struggle with Schopenhauerean pessimism—but this form of pessimism discloses a view of the ideal and actual that West, by his pragmatist lights, should reject. The point to be made here is that West leaves unattended the ambiguities and ambivalences in his understanding of evil and tragedy. And these problems are only complicated by his use of depth metaphors as standards of judgment on such matters (when he claims, for example, that classical pragmatists simply don't go "deep" enough when addressing the problem of evil).

Moreover, West makes a claim in his reading of Royce that, if we read it carefully, may say more about West than about Royce. He suggests that Royce was more concerned with justifying the worthwhileness of our struggle to endure than with skepticism and epistemic relativism. But surely these concerns are intimately related. Critics of relativism hold the view that unless something absolute stands behind the mess of our living, we have no reason to go on resisting evil. As Richard Rorty notes, "If evil is merely a lesser good, if all moral choice is a compromise between conflicting goods, then, they [critics of relativism] say, there is no point in moral struggle. The lives of those who have died resisting injustice become pointless."[64] For Dewey, however, this sort of handwringing is unnecessary. Rorty here states what I take to be Dewey's position quite well:

> To us pragmatists moral struggle is continuous with the struggle for existence, and no sharp break divides the unjust from the imprudent, the evil from the inexpedient. What matters for pragmatists is devising ways of diminishing human suffering and increasing human equality, increasing the ability of all human children to start life with an equal

chance of happiness. This goal is not written in the stars, and is no more an expression of what Kant called pure practical reason than it is the Will of God. It is a goal worth dying for, but it does not require backup from supernatural forces.[65]

There is no need, then, to justify the worthwhileness of our struggle to endure. The strenuous mood is maintained by our efforts, as Dewey writes, "to modify what exists so that it will take on a form possessed of specifiable traits."[66] In other words, the recognition of the possibilities of existence and our passionate devotion to the cause of these possibilities sustain the strenuous mood. We must see that Royce's desire to justify our efforts to endure emanates from his worrying about skepticism and epistemic relativism and the consequences of such views for our moral life.

As for the challenge of death and disease to our democratic life, Dewey's response would be pretty straightforward. At a certain level of abstraction, the inevitability of death constitutes a natural limitation. Organisms live and they die. It's a fact of nature: no mystery there. At another level, however, the issue becomes what we make of our time here. Death and disease may then be understood in concrete terms—for example, the fact that AIDS is destroying a generation of Africans or that violent death threatens African American males at rates disproportionate to other segments of the U.S. population. These facts bring the issues of disease and death down to earth as problems that impede our attempts at genuine democratic living.

I am sure West would claim that such a move does not speak to the individual struggle with disease and death—that the shudder evidenced in Royce's solitary moment is missing here. I will bracket my concerns about the existentialist overtones of West's objection only to make this point: that moving to the more abstract level does little to secure democratic forms of life and, more importantly, threatens those who ask such questions with debilitating despair or a sense of helplessness precisely because the alternatives they make available force us, in some way, to turn our backs on this world.[67] We then either give up on the possibility of our actions' effecting any significant change or we look to some other force that will, in the end, save us from ourselves. In the latter case, those of us concerned with bringing about radical democratic change must remember Dewey's admonition: "[We] will have to ask, as far as [we] nominally believe in the need for radical social change, whether what [we] accomplish when [we] point with one hand to the seriousness of present evils is undone when the other hand points away from man and nature for their remedy."[68]

Dewey's naturalism rejects what I take to be the Christian impulse informing West's conception of the tragic. Like Royce, West holds on to something like the drama of salvation to stave off a debilitating form of despair and dread. Dewey requires no such drama. Yet, I have maintained that he has a tragic sensibility, one that recognizes the ineliminable conflict of values that makes up our moral lives. By my reading, Dewey's view of moral experience begins with opposing goods and incompatible, but possibly justified, courses of action. He refuses to reconcile such conflicts and see harmony in tragic situations. He also refuses to be paralyzed in the face of tragedy. Unlike Schopenhauer, "the inseparable pain, the wretchedness and misery of mankind, the triumph of wickedness, the scornful mastery of chance, and the irretrievable fall of the good and the innocent"[69] do not produce in Dewey resignation but, rather, a will to engage the world with a reasonable hope that our actions *may* make our world better than it would otherwise be. What is at stake in all of this is not only what kind of person one is to become, but what kind of world is in the making.

Toni Morrison's Beloved, Tragedy, and Moral Experience

In arguing that Dewey's pragmatism is rooted in a tragic sensibility, I am not suggesting that he adequately grappled with what I take to be the tragedy at the heart of American democracy—the problem of racism. Unlike for example, Josiah Royce, who understood that the problem warranted a book-length treatment, Dewey never addressed racism as a central challenge to democracy. Obviously, he did not view it as a congenital ailment of American democracy. Racism understood as such would thwart the realization of his conception of democracy: he would have had no choice but to engage the problem philosophically. West's criticism does call attention to the fact that Dewey failed to address substantively "the blue note" of American history and its centrality to who we, as Americans, take ourselves to be—and this is deeply disturbing given the normative force of his work on democracy. But it doesn't follow that Dewey lacked a tragic vision. Had he offered a significant philosophical analysis of race in the United States, I believe that analysis would have made explicit the tragic dimensions of his moral and political philosophy.

In the last few pages of this chapter, I hope to reconstruct the view of tragedy I've outlined in my interpretation of Dewey in light of the brutal realities and choices that animate Toni Morrison's novel *Beloved.* My aim in reading the novel in this way is twofold: (1) to sketch, in a preliminary way, an example of a pragmatic view of tragedy that begins with tragic choices made within constraints imposed by the reality of white supremacy in the United States, and (2) to insist that our reflections on democracy in the United States begin by engaging the historical legacies of racism that threaten democracy's realization. I urge us—all of us—to look the facts of our racial experiences squarely in the face, to see the tragedy therein, and to go about intelligently guided experimentation with the goal of providing a better future for our children. Morrison's magisterial novel is, in my view, the best place to begin such a project.

Set in Cincinnati during Reconstruction, *Beloved* is a story about the psychical and physical devastation of slavery and the challenge of forging a self in its aftermath. Slavery has so wounded the characters of the novel that they cannot, no matter how they try, escape its effects. Sethe and Paul D work tirelessly to hold back the past, but they are haunted—literally, in Sethe's case—by the consequences and memories of slavery. In some ways, the novel makes the Nietzschean point that to live without forgetting is utterly impossible. As Nietzsche says: "There is a degree of insomnia, of rumination, of historical awareness, which injures and finally destroys a living thing, whether a man, a people, or a culture."[70] Indeed, we are confronted in the novel with Sethe's being consumed by an embodied past. We are also told that "this is not a story to pass on." *Beloved,* in my view, constitutes a profound insistence that the past does not count exclusively. But this knowledge and the possibilities of action that mark the epiphany of the novel are the fruit of the tragic choice at the heart of the story.

Sethe's decision to attempt to kill all of her children rather than allow them to be returned to slavery reflected her lived experiences at the Sweet Home plantation. She desired nothing more than to protect her children from the terror of slavery. To be sure, she wanted to shield them from physical violence, but more importantly, she wanted to safeguard them from assaults on their souls. Slavery and, by extension, white folks, in Sethe's view, "could take your whole self for anything that came to mind. Not just work, kill, or maim you, but dirty you. Dirty you so bad you wouldn't like yourself anymore. Dirty you so bad you forgot who you were and couldn't think it up" (215). Sethe's intimate knowledge of this experience led her to try to insure that her children would never experience such evil. Her back scarred with cherry blossoms, Schoolteacher's list of human and animal characteristics, and her violated insides served as constant reminders—historical burdens as it were—of slavery's assault on the soul.

But the historical burdens borne by Sethe, or for that matter any of the characters in the novel, are not presented simply to convey the horrible nature of slavery. Morrison's novel, as many critics have suggested, rewrites the traditional slave narrative by reconstructing what those stories silenced: the interior self of the slave. The descriptions of the past function, in some ways, to disclose the impulses and habits formed in the context of experience. Sethe's choice, then, is informed, in part, by a disposition shaped in the brutal context of Sweet Home. However, it is Sethe's freedom that ultimately transforms her choice from a melodramatic depiction of the evil of slavery to a tragic vision of the construction of a self in its aftermath. As Terry Otten writes:

> In projecting the inner life of her heroine, Morrison rescues the authentic self, making Sethe the victim of her own divided nature and thereby making her capable of choice and, ultimately, of achieving tragic stature. Sethe's crossing the river into freedom marks the climatic victory of the slave narrative and the beginning of the potential for tragic action.[71]

In explaining her choice to Paul D, Sethe reveals how freedom makes it possible to love unconditionally and to claim responsibility for her children.

Sethe says to Paul D: "Look like I loved em more after I got here. Or maybe I couldn't love em proper in Kentucky because they wasn't mine to love. But when I got here, when I jumped off the wagon—there was nobody in the world I couldn't love if I wanted to" (162). As Otten rightly notes, it is this ability and obligation to choose that marks the dividing line between melodrama and tragedy.[72] It sets Sethe's act of infanticide apart from all of the other acts mentioned in the novel. Sethe declares to Paul D, after she describes how freedom afforded her the opportunity to make a shift for her baby: "Well all I'm saying is that's a selfish pleasure I never had before. I couldn't let all that go back to where it was, and I couldn't let her nor any of em live under schoolteacher. That was out" (163).

Sethe's choice is between competing values, between incompatible, but morally justifiable, courses of action. In this sense, the novel exemplifies a pragmatic view of tragedy that takes seriously the blue note of American history. Otten has convincingly argued that *Beloved* "is more essentially Sophoclean than Euripidean"—in the sense that Creon and Antigone are, in Sophocles' plays, both morally justified in their actions. Morrison, who readily acknowledges the influence of Greek tragedy on her work, says that "this is not Medea who kills her children because she's mad at some dude, and she's going to get back at him. Here is something that is *huge* and *very* intimate."[73] As Otten argues:

> The novel sustains tragic focus in its depiction of conflict within character, in its obsession with the presentness of the past, in its movement — however circuitous—toward reenactment, in its ritualistic elements, and in its ultimate ambiguity mirroring the "victory in defeat, defeat in victory" that ends high tragedy.[74]

The Sophoclean dimension of *Beloved* links it to the pragmatic view of tragedy I've developed in my reading of Dewey. But, more importantly, it is the way Morrison handles Baby Suggs's response to Sethe's "rough" choice and renders Denver's actions to save her mother from the ghost of history that reveals a *distinctly pragmatic* sense of the tragic.

Baby Suggs initially offers a stunningly powerful conception of self-love that urges bodies and souls torn by the horrors of slavery to lay down the "heavy knives of defense against misery, regret, gall and hurt" (86), to see beyond the opaqueness of their brutal pasts, and to allow themselves to imagine a future. This requires, in Baby Suggs's view, the sanctification of the black body. They need to love that which had been reduced to a mere instrument of labor and see the spiritual worth that resides in them.

More than your eyes or feet. More than lungs that have yet to draw free air. More than your life holding womb and your life-giving private parts, here me now, love your heart. (89)

But Baby Suggs's message is rendered ambiguous by Morrison's narrative technique. For Baby Suggs, after witnessing the consequences of Sethe's choice, "repudiates her own message, finding it inadequate to express or explain the tragic action which lies at the heart of the novel."[75] As Morrison writes:

> Those white things have taken all I had or dreamed, she said, and broke my heartstrings too. There is no bad luck in the world but whitefolks.... Baby Suggs, holy, believed she had lied. There was no grace—imaginary or real—and no sunlit dance in the Clearing could change that. Her faith, her love, her imagination and her great big old heart began to collapse twenty-eight days after her daughter-in-law arrived. (89)

Baby Suggs's response to the evils of chattel slavery, as evidenced in the moral dilemma posed by Sethe's choice, is a lapse into a debilitating form of despair, what Morrison describes as marrow weariness—a form of existential fatigue that cuts not simply to the bone but through it. As Stamp Paid says, "God puzzled her and she was too ashamed of Him to say so" (177).

Baby Suggs's reply when Stamp Paid urges her to return to the Clearing and "say the word" reveal that her faith has been completely shaken. For her it is not simply a matter of God's failure to relieve the suffering of black folks, but rather the reality—her lived experience—of white folks coming into her yard. That reality and the choice it exacted made her tired. Stamp Paid, faced with a similar form of existential fatigue, "now, too late, understood her."

> The heart that pumped out love, the mouth that spoke the word, didn't count. They came in her yard anyway and she could not approve or condemn Sethe's choice. One or the other might have saved her, but beaten up by the claims of both, she went to bed. (180)

There *is* no grace, real or imaginary. There *is* only the fact that white people can treat black folk any way they choose. And, it seems to Baby Suggs, the only appropriate response to such a reality is resignation. But, again, Morrison's narrative technique complicates the conclusion. For, as Denver gathers up the courage to reenter the community to save her mother from the ghost of Beloved, Baby

Suggs's words provide her with the practical wisdom to risk herself. Ironically, this comes on the heels of an exchange (remembered by Denver) in which Baby Suggs tells Sethe, "Lay down your sword. This ain't a battle, it's a rout"(244). This appears to be a note of resignation, and Denver can't leave the porch. But then she hears clearly the words of Baby Suggs:

> You mean I never told you nothing about Carolina? About your daddy? You don't remember about how come I walk the way I do and about your mother's feet, not to speak of her back? I never told you all that? Is that why you can't walk down the steps? My Jesus my.
> But you said there was no defense.
> There ain't.
> Then what do I do?
> Know it, but go on out the yard. Go on. (244)

Here the past is thought of instrumentally: as the fruit of our undertakings that shapes our characters and informs our choices. Baby Suggs invokes the past to call Denver's attention to the pervasiveness of evil in the world—to the stream of experiences that make up the history of 124 Bluestone Road. She does this not to elicit resignation, but to urge Denver to act intelligently in the world: "Know it, but go on out the yard." The "it" refers to the pain and suffering that is constitutive of black experiences in the United States. It refers to those unspeakable things unspoken, the sublime of the black experience. I am reminded here of James Baldwin's description in *The Fire Next Time.*

This past, the Negro's past, of rope, fire, torture, castration, infanticide, rape; death and humiliation; fear by day and night, fear as deep as the marrow of the bone; doubt that he was worthy of life, since everyone around him denied it; ... rage, hatred, and murder, hatred for white men so deep that it often turned against him and his own, and made all love, all trust, all joy impossible—this past, this endless struggle to achieve and reveal and confirm a human identity, human authority, yet contains, for all its horror, something very beautiful.[76]

Baby Suggs's words, like Baldwin's, direct our attention to the perils of evil that permeate a world of action shaped by white supremacy. Nevertheless, she exhorts Denver to act.

Baby Suggs tells Denver, in effect, that she must come to terms with the death and suffering that is her past—she must come to terms with Sethe's choice—but she must also understand this history and the tragedy therein as part of the exigencies of life—dare I say the beauty of life? Tragedy is understood, then, as an ineliminable part of what it means to be a black agent in this world. On my reading, Baby Suggs's practical wisdom rewrites William James's formulation at the end of "The Will to Believe."

Act for the best, hope for the best, and take what comes.... If death ends all, we cannot meet death better.

Know it, but go on out the yard. Go on.

Beloved doesn't end with satisfactory outcomes guaranteed. At the end of the story, we are faced with broken human beings trying to piece together a life with one another. No grace still, real or imagined. Morrison's emphasis is on the possibility of a future, represented in Denver, and on Sethe's need to forget if she is to have a future. This emphasis extends the novel's insight beyond that of the individual. For what is at stake here is not only what kind of persons we will become, but what kind of world is in the making. In the end, I believe Morrison's novel brilliantly realizes what I have called the pragmatic view of tragedy: we must look the tragedy of our moral experiences squarely in the face and, with little certainty as to the outcomes, *humbly* act to make a better world for ourselves and our children. Her rendering of this point in terms of African American suffering insists that this racial dimension of life not be forgotten—that we, as Americans, never succumb to the illusion of innocence and the optimism that carries it forward. To hold this view requires of us an intimate knowledge of the tragic choices in relation to race that constitute American life, knowledge that will help us to act intelligently and to see how fragile we, as individuals and as a nation, truly are.

Conclusion

I have argued in this chapter that John Dewey's philosophy presupposes a tragic vision and that a pragmatic view of tragedy is one in which any situation properly called moral entails competing and conflicting values. Dewey sees conflict and uncertainty as constitutive and ineliminable features of our moral experience. For him, there are no guaranteed outcomes when we choose between conflicting values. We learn from tragedy that crude reductions of the complexity of our moral lives can lead to an exclusive attachment to one value and disregard for another.[77] Dewey, by contrast, commends a process of intelligently guided experimentation in a world we acknowledge is shot through with contingency.

We seek to secure our world, then, not by way of quests for certainty but rather by practical means, exposing our vulnerability as fragile, finite creatures to the perils of evil. To render Dewey's philosophy of action in sloganlike form: There is so much in the world that we cannot control. We should seek to control intelligently that which we can, bearing in mind that even when we succeed, the hazardous character of our world is only modestly modified, never eliminated. Intelligence, in this view, must be understood within the context of a generally humble orientation to the universe. In relation to all that is, we are small and our world is far from grand.

Yet Dewey failed to address the evils of white supremacy in his work. To be sure, his influence looms large among African Americans who have struggled to end racism in the United States.[78] But he himself never substantively engaged the problems of racism in any of his major work. Such an engagement would not only have offered powerful resources for thinking about certain conceptual problems plaguing African

American politics but would also have made explicit the tragic dimensions of American pragmatism. My reading of Toni Morrison's *Beloved* is an attempt to reconstruct a pragmatic view of the tragic in light of the devastating effects of white supremacy that continue to haunt American democracy. Slave narratives sought melodramatically to disclose the evil at the heart of American democracy. Morrison's reconstruction of those stories provides a glimpse into the tragic choices made and the consequences endured in the face of that evil. The tragic choices that we as a nation have made in regard to race—the butchering of precious ideals, as William James put it—have, ironically, made possible our present way of life. The knowledge that we gain from America's past can, however, equip us to engage intelligently the problems that prevent democracy's realization. By countering immodest claims of America's greatness and inevitable triumph with the brutal reality of broken black bodies and souls, that past, in all of its complicated beauty, humbly orients us to the world of action. *Beloved* is a story which insists that our reflections on the future of American democracy begin with the remarkable irony at its root. For me, this is the lesson the novel renders to Dewey and to pragmatism generally: if we are to think seriously about American democracy, we must come to terms with the tragedy of race and how it has shaped not only the life of the nation but also the choices of a blues people so deeply shaped by it. It is to those choices, so indelibly marked by quests for certainty and security amid the brutality of others, that I now turn.

2

"Black and Proud": Reconstructing Black Identity

Every choice sustains a double relation to the self. It reveals the existing self and it forms the future self.... But every choice is at the forking of the roads, and the path chosen shuts off certain opportunities and opens others. In committing oneself to a particular course, a person gives a lasting set to his being. Consequently, it is proper to say that in choosing this object rather than that, one is in reality choosing what kind of person or self one is going to be.

JOHN DEWEY, *Ethics* (1932)

An identity is questioned only when it is menaced, as when the mighty begin to fall, or when the wretched begin to rise, or when the stranger enters the gates, never, thereafter, to be a stranger.... Identity would seem to be the garment with which one covers the nakedness of the self: in which case, it is best that the garment be loose, a little like the robes of the desert, through which one's nakedness can always be felt, and, sometimes, discerned. This trust in one's nakedness is all that gives one the power to change one's robes.

JAMES BALDWIN, "The Devil Finds Work"

One striking consequence of the tragedy of race in the United States has been a preoccupation with identity formation among African Americans. Because most African Americans entered this fragile experiment in democracy as chattel, the question of who they take themselves to be has been intimately connected to a political and social reality that denied them recognition. African Americans historically stand in an uneasy relation to America, constantly faced with the choice, a tragic choice at times, of accepting America as home or rejecting the possibility of ever flourishing on these shores.

Ironically, the country itself, in its early years, struggled with the issue of its identity in relation to Europe. We need only recall Ralph Waldo Emerson's words in "American Scholar" (1837), where he urged an adolescent nation to declare intellectual independence, shake off its inferiority complex, and forge a form of life reflective of the new nation's distinctive landscape. Emerson powerfully declared in the opening of that address:

Our day of dependence, our long apprenticeship to the learning of other lands, draws to a close. The millions that around us are rushing into life, cannot always be fed on the sere remains of foreign harvests. Events, actions arise, that must be sung, that will sing themselves. Who can doubt, that poetry will revive and lead in a new age, as the star in the constellation Harp, which now flames in our zenith, astronomers announce, shall one day be the pole-star for a thousand years?[1]

Walt Whitman took it upon himself to answer Emerson's call, and his poetry sung of America. But African Americans were forced to create themselves amid the absurdity of a nation committed, at once, to freedom and unfreedom. Theirs was a blue note, an unstable chord that called attention to the unbridled chaos at the heart of American democracy. That African Americans have been, for the most part, successful in these attempts at self-creation is testimony to the enormous power of their creative energies.

Nonetheless, questions of black identity remain. How should African Americans understand themselves as individuals and as a group in relation to a nation that historically denied them recognition? With whom should they identify, and on what basis—blood, language, customs, inheritance? What are we to make of our country's past in light of the successes of the civil rights movement and the expansion of a black middle class? A lot is at stake when we discuss racial identity in the

United States. And one thing is certain: conceptions of black identity continue to animate the political choices of many African Americans, prompting concerns about how such ideas might affect efforts to secure justice in our democracy. We are horrified by the prospect that differences that make no difference serve as the basis for exclusion and a lack of moral concern for others. We worry that identities, wrongly understood, may blind us to a central lesson of tragedy—that they may, by denying the complexity of our moral lives, lead to obsession with one value to the exclusion of others.

How we think about black identity matters, particularly when we hold the view that our beliefs about the world have ethical significance. For when persons act in the name of a particular identity they often presume that there is a supreme end that defines and justifies their desires and purposes—that their actions and dispositions form the basis for widespread approbation and that they are obligatory and legitimate. How we think about black identity, then, affects how we as African Americans understand notions of virtue, right, and the good: who we take ourselves to be, how we conceive of our obligations to those we consider "one of us," and how we orient ourselves to "others." It matters, then, if one person believes that races are fictions, while another believes there is an African culture that properly orients African-descended peoples throughout the world. Both of these views wield a tremendous amount of influence, not only in the U.S. academy, but also in the arena of politics. In this chapter, I critically examine a particular view of black identity, one which assumes that notions of obligation to the race and the desires and purposes of African American individuals derive from and depend upon a view of who we take ourselves to be, independent of the choices we make. I do this with an eye fixed intensely on the task of reconstructing the way many African Americans think of their ethical lives in relation to their political choices.

I maintain that notions of virtue, right, and good flow, as John Dewey says, from independent springs, such that each has an equally legitimate basis and all can pull us in different and, sometimes, conflicting directions.[2] This makes moral decision a real problem and gives ethical judgment and moral discernment their vitality. Of course, my claim points to the tragic dimensions of the world of action—that we often find ourselves confronted with competing goods as we act. It also locates the notions of character development and moral progress in our ability to make "delicate distinctions" in the face of uncertainty. Truly moral decisions are not settled by reference to some fixed and unchanging racial identity. Indeed, our individual and collective identities are, in part, a consequence of our moral decisions.

My concern here is not whether races are real. Reality is a denotative term: it designates everything that happens. Lies are as real as trees. Arguments that races are not real or that black identities are incoherent because they are based on false premises do not move me. For my purposes the issue of whether races are real is beside the point. My principal concern lies with the social practices that constitute the use of a shared language, a context within which race talk matters deeply. Even if one disagrees with my naïve realism, one can talk about utterances that involve race language; the truth or falsity of the utterances is not our only concern. Our concern may instead involve the appropriateness or correctness of such language use, and an utterance can be true *and* inappropriate.[3] I am not suggesting that the objective status of races is not an interesting question, but it is not the *only* question.

I am also not interested in defending an essentialist conception of race or of black identity. Talk of racial essences is at best a bad way of talking about particular experiences; at worst it encourages misguided quests for certainty that aim to secure us from the contingency that is an inherent part of our lives. My intention is to offer a pragmatic way of thinking about black identity that takes seriously the problem-solving activity intrinsic to being a moral agent. My emphasis, then, will be on our capacity as black individuals to judge the respective claims of duty and desire as they arise in concrete experience, understanding that in some cases they may indeed conflict. We will still speak of black identity but will attempt not to overextend its reach.

When someone utters a sentence such as "I am an African American" in the context of a debate about public policy, she is not disclosing something that was previously internal; instead, her words indicate to those around her that, in discussing this particular topic with her, another set of issues must be taken into account. Richard Rorty makes the point best:

> Such sentences are not used to report events going on within the Cartesian Theatre which is a person's consciousness. They are simply tools for coordinating our behavior with those of others. This is not to say that one can "reduce" mental states such as beliefs and desires to physiological or behavioural states. It is merely to say that there is no point in asking whether a belief represents reality, either mental reality or physical reality, accurately. That is, for

pragmatists, not only a bad question, but the root of much wasted philosophical energy.[4]

The question, then, is not whether our beliefs about race and racial identities represent reality, but for what purposes it would be useful to hold such beliefs and to invoke them as crucial aspects of our identities.

In what follows I sketch two ways of understanding black identity—what I call an archeological approach and a pragmatic historicist approach—in each case focusing on its ethical dimensions.[5] I argue that the pragmatic approach better enables us to understand the complex ethical choices that attend any talk about black identity. I further draw out the implications for contemporary debates about black identity of what I have called elsewhere a pragmatic tradition of racial advocacy, which emerged in the early nineteenth century as African Americans drew on the biblical story of Exodus to articulate a sense of peoplehood and racial obligation.[6] In the end, I suggest that we have approached the issue of black identity from the wrong direction: it is not simply a question of who we are determining how we act in the world. Rather, the choices we make in the face of problems and meddlesome circumstances turn out to be our lives, requiring of us continual cultivation of our ability to make delicate distinctions.

Approaches to Black Identity

THE ARCHEOLOGICAL APPROACH

We can think of black identity in terms of a specific form of life that binds a group of individuals to one another—a sort of collective true self. This form is distinct from that of other peoples—perhaps different in its conception of knowledge, in its understanding of beauty, and in its formulation of the moral and ethical norms that ought to guide action in the world. In this view, black identity reflects the common historical experiences and shared vocabularies "which provide us, as one people, with stable, unchanging and continuous frames of reference and meaning, beneath the shifting divisions and vicissitudes of our actual history."[7] This singular constellation is the essence of the people and constitutive of who we are as individuals.

In *Identity in Democracy*, Amy Gutmann describes a view of cultural identity groups in which culture represents a way of life that is comprehensive: it "constitutes and constrains the identities (and therefore the lives) of its members by providing them with a common language, history, institutions of socialization, range of occupations, lifestyles, distinctive literary and artistic traditions, architectural styles, music, dress, ceremonies and holidays, and customs that are shared by an intergenerational community that occupies a distinctive territory."[8] Gutmann discusses African Americans mainly in her chapter on processes of ascription. I suspect she does not consider them a cultural identity group because they do not occupy a distinctive territory. But black identity is no less complexly articulated. It may involve racial as well as cultural or political dimensions, depending in part on the ends to which it is invoked.[9]

When articulated as a particular form of black nationalist politics, for example, black identity is much like the cultural identity group Gutmann talks about. The black nation provides the boundaries within which we think of our political ambitions (territorial or cultural sovereignty for example), who we are (racial consanguinity), how we understand our relation to people outside the group, and, perhaps most important, how we understand our obligations to one another. Here the notions of good and obligation proceed out of our understanding of the racial self. In other words, for black nationalists of a certain sort, black identities and the culture out of which they take shape provide a comprehensive context within which its members make choices.[10]

Let me focus this view by reference to a historical example. Cultural nationalists (of various sorts) in the era of black power argued that African

Americans have a specific cultural inheritance. We are African. We have a value system that in spite of the "perceived" rupture of the transatlantic slave trade continues to distinguish us from Europeans and animate our choices. If these values fail to inform our actions, at least on a conscious level, the failure only indicates the effects of white supremacy: we have been robbed of our cultural inheritance. Our aim, then, should be to reconstruct, as best as we can, a form of life that reflects the true way of being African in the world. Maulana Karenga, founder of the Us organization, developed an elaborate cultural theory of blackness, which he called Kawaida theory. Karenga argued that, through a complex set of ritual practices, African Americans could reconnect with their past—with a proper way of being African in the world—and that this reconnection would facilitate both healthier relationships with others and a more revolutionary politics.

Karenga's view was only one expression of a position that informed numerous political projects of the period. Many believed that African

American freedom required a revolution of black minds. Black individuals needed to remove the psychological chains of white supremacy and embrace a consciousness that reflected a more authentic way of being in the world—a world, as Karenga was fond of saying, in which blackness would become our ultimate reality. This position assumed what can be called an expressivist conception of the racial self. For Karenga and many others, African Americans were self-determining agents primarily because there was something unique about them *as* black people. This uniqueness determined their relations with "others" and defined their obligations to the race. If a black individual failed to connect with this inner something and with those similarly situated, she would fail in effect to live the life that is uniquely hers. The same was true for African Americans in general. If black people in the United States failed to embrace their cultural inheritance—their unique form of life—then they would fail to live in a way that was truly theirs.

From Martin Delany to Marcus Garvey, such views of identity have informed political action. In some significant ways, this view—which assumes that despite many differences black Americans share a sense of who black people are, and that a set of concomitant beliefs is sufficient to settle most problems that they confront—continues to be a powerful force in our political and cultural imaginations. Advocates of Afrocentrism, for example, hold that most of the problems that confront African Americans would be resolved if we only lived an authentically African life or, as Molefe Asante would say, a properly centered existence.[11] My intuition is that most arguments seeking to debunk black identity talk as hokum in fact reflect deep disagreements with this particular formulation of black identity and the politics that support it.

According to this archeological approach, black identity is concerned with uncovering our true selves and inferring from that discovery what we must do. Black identity is interpreted here in terms of reality and appearance.

There is a *real* way of being black and a *false* way. Something out there is essentially black, and when we lose our way, as some of us have as result of white supremacy, we need only find "it" and all will be well.

I should not be too glib. The impulse underlying this approach does have roots in the experience of white supremacy. Frantz Fanon, writing in the context of colonial struggles, located the reasons for this approach in "passionate research directed by the secret hope of discovering beyond the misery of today, beyond self-contempt, resignation and abjuration, some very beautiful and splendid era whose existence rehabilitates us both in regard to ourselves and others."[12] Thus archeological projects often entail constructing monumental histories, which answer a psychological need to respond to collective humiliation, to lash back and not accept certain conditions of living. The conception of the self informing these projects is often fixed, an unchanging reference for deliberation. Given this premise, either one acts like a true black person—one who understands who she is—or one doesn't. It is not *really* possible to experience genuine conflict or uncertainty about how one should act as a black person; all the distinctions have already been made.

A problem arises, however, when we postulate one single factor—the racial self—as an explanation for the moral lives of black people. The uncertainty and conflict that are characteristic of any situation properly called moral are obscured. The complexity that marks, for example, political decision making is reduced to a simple question of fidelity to one's cultural inheritance: will one be authentically black or an Uncle Tom? Problems may involve issues of gender, class, sexuality, religious preference, geographic difference, or the difficulties of falling in love, but all can be resolved by an appeal to the good and to the notions of obligation that flow from an authentic way of being black in the world. Such simplifications of problematic situations reflect—and promote—a loss of the capacity to discriminate and to make delicate distinctions. The fact that we are often unsure of the right and just approach, and ignorant of the consequences of our actions, is lost. Moreover, our individuality is compromised as this idea of black identity, as Kwame Anthony Appiah rightly worries, "goes imperial" and implicates itself in cases where judgments and choices should instead be made with an eye to the particular forces impinging on us at the time.

My position should not, however, be seen as similar to the views put forward by someone like John McWhorter, whom I mention only as a kind of stand-in for a lay position that seeks, however clumsily, a different way of understanding the complexity of contemporary identity talk and black politics. McWhorter, in particular, takes issue with conceptions of blackness that constrain black individuality and limit our capacity to describe the complexity of the lives of African Americans. He insists that much of race talk among African Americans today trades on a culture of defeatism in which ideas of victimology and anti-intellectualism, along with a "questionable" leadership class, obscure the actual lives of black individuals.[13] In his view, race no longer stands as *the* explanatory category of the situation of African Americans. Instead, he appeals to a vibrant American tradition of self-help and moral perfectionism that accounts for the kinds of lives we want to lead and should lead in terms of our individual choices and efforts. Once we rid ourselves of bad ways of thinking about race and black identity, McWhorter maintains, we can embrace a "deracialized" paradigm of living. He never quite says what this might look like—perhaps a naïve version of humanism.

Responding with cries of "race traitor" or "neocon shill" will not get us far toward determining the stakes of the argument. McWhorter rightly notes that our moment demands we show greater discernment when using race to talk about problems confronting black individuals. However, he overstates his case when he claims that race language and appeals to black identity function principally as tools of victimology. This view reveals an all-or-nothing approach to the category: either such appeals capture fully the experiences of African Americans or they are mere fictions, doing more harm than good.

McWhorter's position is, in some ways, a bad (perhaps very bad) version of efforts to respond to the "imperial implications" of an essentialist view of black identity. The typical response to this view has been to deconstruct race, claim that the notion is an arbitrary social construct, and problematize the way we think about racial identity. We have become quite familiar with some of the arguments: that we should focus on real forces like the operations of capital and not on ideological notions like race; that goods and services should be distributed on the basis of merit, not on the basis of racial identity; and perhaps the most widely held, that our belief in race is a necessary condition for the existence of racism and that getting rid of race language will help us end racism once and for all.[14] In the admirable effort to break loose from the stranglehold of bad ways of thinking about race and black identity, many critics have overcompensated, and not provided adequate arguments to support their moves. The classic example of this is the early work of Kwame Anthony Appiah, in which he argues that race language is necessarily racist. I have nothing substantive to add to the many responses to his work. I would only suggest that to avoid some of his more controversial conclusions we must realize that black identity *has been* and *can be* thought of in different ways, that our moral lives as black individuals are not reducible to one single explanatory principle and, most importantly, that race language and racial identities are, at bottom, suggestions about the terms in which deliberations about particular moral questions are best conducted.

PRAGMATIC HISTORICIST APPROACH

The pragmatic view of identity does not hold that identity is about discovery. Rather, identities are seen as *consequences* of human activity—specifically, our problem-solving activity.[15] In this view, character and conduct are interrelated and mutually dependent. The self is not some stable, unchanging frame of reference; rather, it is an organization of habits that is *relatively* stable and enduring. These habits—formed, at least in part, from previous experiences and always subject to modification as we act—constitute our character.[16] Or, as Dewey writes, "Character is the interpenetration of habits. If each habit existed in an insulated compartment and operated without affecting or being affected by others, character would not exist."[17] No self stands still; it is, for better or worse, constantly becoming, and "it is in the *quality* of that becoming that virtue resides."[18] Moreover, our understanding of the beliefs, choices, and actions that rely on these habits arises in the context of bringing these experiences to consciousness in narrative—the history of the self. What we have done and are doing, and the stories we weave about these experiences, are absolutely critical for a pragmatic view of black identity.

Unlike Tommie Shelby, I do not deny the relevance or centrality of black identity to black political struggle.

Shelby argues powerfully in *We Who Are Dark* for a position he calls pragmatic black nationalism—"the view that black solidarity is merely a contingent strategy for creating freedom and social equality for blacks, a pragmatic yet principled approach to achieve racial justice."[19] In making his argument, Shelby rejects a standard claim that African American politics requires, if it is to be successful, a notion of collective identity. He notes that such views often result in a reification of race and a conception of black life that obscures relevant differences among African Americans and frustrates individual freedom. In his view, the shared experiences of antiblack racism are sufficient for our efforts to secure racial justice. Black identity talk is simply not necessary.

But Shelby fails to take seriously what a pragmatic view of black identity might suggest. The term *pragmatic,* as he uses it, seems to have only heuristic value and not to refer to a set of philosophical commitments. Shelby would have us believe that our identities are not particularly relevant to how we engage in struggles for racial justice. But if identities are the products of our efforts to overcome problems, then the content and consequences of our efforts impact the content of our character. We need not discard identity talk, then, but simply to reconstruct the term in light of our pragmatic commitments. The kinds of dispositions requisite for the kind of society both of us desire are, in part, formed in the context of political struggles. To the extent that character and conduct are intimately interrelated and mutually dependent, identities matter. The problem is with a certain view of collective identity, one that Shelby puts forward and rightly distrusts. This view motivates political practices and justifies political choices on the basis, more often than not, of an already fixed conception of black identity. But individual and collective identity can be thought of differently. Black identities and the identities of those who struggle for racial justice are as much the products of principled struggle as they are the motivation for that struggle. Who we take ourselves to be—that is, how we understand ourselves as moral agents—often guides how we engage in politics, and the sorts of choices we make while engaging in politics fundamentally shape who we take ourselves to be. Identity talk matters, then, because of its ethical and moral implications for *and* beyond politics.

Shelby also denies Laurence Thomas's claim that genuine cooperation among African Americans requires a group narrative, that is, "a set of stories which defines values and entirely positive goals, which specifies a set of fixed points of historical significance, and which defines a set of ennobling rituals to be regularly performed."[20] Such a narrative promotes mutual trust, which in turn informs solidaristic efforts to secure freedom and justice. Shelby rejects Thomas's view on the grounds that genuine cooperation is a rare occurrence in African American politics. He also takes issue with Thomas's claim that mutual trust can be formed only through participation in group narratives. We need not agree with the particulars of Thomas's position, however, to agree that narrative is critical to character formation: that the kinds of stories we tell ourselves help orient us—habituate us even—to the world and our fellows. Character formation should be a crucial component of political struggle: it is not enough simply to fight for justice; one must reflect that commitment in one's character. Otherwise we end up with individuals like Robert Mugabe, who fought in the name of justice but failed to exhibit it in his life. What I want to suggest is that we think about black identity in a truly pragmatic way, insisting on its importance for character formation and avoiding the narrow racial essentialism that Shelby rightly holds at arm's length.

I have argued elsewhere that in the early nineteenth century a pragmatic view of racial advocacy informed the use of race language as well as ideas of black identity. Through analogical readings of the Exodus story, African Americans were able, not only able to construct a collective identity, but also to avoid the essentialist trap of reducing the ethical and moral lives of African Americans to a fixed conception of the racial self. Analogical readings of Exodus not only emplotted the varied experiences of African Americans, they also placed a premium, given the story's religious roots, on a certain ethical stance. The aim in invoking Exodus was less to gain land or identify blood relations than to guarantee blessings through righteousness.

Race talk remained. But race was not understood as a biological category or some version of a metaphysics of presence. It was instead a sociological category, which singled out those who were prone to be treated a certain way or vulnerable to certain kinds of experiences. In this context, appropriations of the Exodus story functioned in part as a way or style of constructing black identity in early nineteenth-century America. The story located black identity talk in the common social heritage of slavery and discrimination—the environment within which African American problem-solving activity took place and the habits that constituted what many took to be black identity were formed.

My particular reading of the Exodus story aimed to offer a plausible historical account of a form of racial politics that does not presuppose an essentialist conception of race. Too often contemporary discussions of racial politics run aground precisely because the participants assume a narrow field of meanings as to what race and black identity might signify for African Americans. Bad stories usually present bad options, which often lead us to act as if we are bad people and to be preoccupied with things of dubious importance. We have told a bad story about racial politics in America. *Exodus!* was my attempt to offer a different narrative—a historically inflected account of an alternative way of thinking about race-based politics.

The early-nineteenth-century debate among African American leaders over the use of race language, for example, provides an interesting alternative to our contemporary, rather limited deliberations about racial essentialism and color blindness.[21] William Whipper, the president of the American Moral Reform Society (AMRS), rejected the use of race language because, in his view, it was inextricably bound to the justificatory language of slavery and the denial of citizenship rights. For him, any talk of race—even for positive self-identification or to describe the specific treatment accorded a particular segment of the U.S. population—only reinforced that language's insidious hold on our moral imaginations. In addition, he argued that if white Americans were to be condemned for their use of racial designations, then African Americans, to be morally consistent, should also reject the language of race. In the end, Whipper claimed that race talk could serve only evil purposes, for it blinded Americans, white and black, to our common humanity:

> That the colored people are equally guilty, by aiding in perpetuating these distinctions, because they cultivate a spirit of selfishness, at war with their dearest interests, and the spirit of common humanity—while they render themselves inconsistent by repudiating in others the practice of principles they themselves support and sustain. (*Colored American*, March 29, 1838, p. 38)

Whipper's argument resembles many contemporary statements about the problems of identity politics. Some hold that appeals to race rest on bad biology and render the moral lives of those who embrace the idea incoherent. Others hold that identity groups constrain individuals, narrowing the range of their moral concern to members of the group, and, as such, are antithetical to democracy.

The response in 1838 to Whipper is instructive. Samuel Cornish, the editor of the *Colored American,* for example, cited the specific circumstances of African Americans in the United States, arguing that "our condition in the community is a peculiar one, that we need SPECIAL EFFORTS and special organization, to meet our wants and to obtain and maintain our rights." This was neither a chauvinistic appeal to the intrinsic value of race language or a denial of any claim to American citizenship but, instead, an assertion of the pragmatic value of race language in addressing the problems of a society fundamentally committed to racist practices.

Perhaps the most sophisticated response came in a letter from William Watkins to the 1838 convention of the American Moral Reform Society. Watkins argued for a kind of contextualism and an understanding of language as grounded in the particular practices of everyday life. The assumption that doing away with racial language would somehow end racial prejudice, he wrote, betrayed a peculiar view of how language worked. Race was not a matter of essential differences between human beings; it was instead an aspect of language deeply embedded in the customs and habits of American society. Abandoning race language would in itself do nothing to uproot the custom of racial difference and prejudice in the United States or to alleviate the condition of African Americans.[22] Race language could indeed be useful in so far as it helped African Americans, in William James's terms, "get into satisfactory relation with other parts of their experiences, to summarize them and get about among them by way of conceptual shortcuts."[23] Race mattered, then, not only because of processes of ascription—the identification and singling out for particular treatment of certain individuals—but also because it was a tool that could be used in problem solving.

Black identities emerge within complexly organized interactions. They result, in part, from efforts to respond to a world that continually exacts choices from us, not from appeals to an idea of the self that exists outside the vagaries of human activity. Nor does moral obligation proceed from nonempirical principles. A pragmatic understanding of black identity, then, shifts the way we think about our moral obligation to "the race."

I am well aware that our identities are shaped, in part, by a past and a set of stories in which our individual actions have had little say. But as Dewey writes in his *Ethics:* "Except as the outcome of arrested development, there is no such thing as a fixed, ready-made, finished self. Every living self causes acts and is itself caused in return by what it does. All voluntary action is a remaking of self, since it creates new desires, instigates new modes of endeavor, brings to light new conditions which institute new ends."[24] I do not take Dewey to be denying the idea of continuity between who we take ourselves to be in time A as opposed to time B, for the stories we weave about our choices and beliefs, our pains and joys, provide a semblance of continuity. As he writes, "Our personal identity is found in the thread of continuous development which binds together these changes."[25] Any notion of black identity, then, must be understood within the social contexts in which individuals who view themselves as black act.

Obligations are also forged in the context of our doings and sufferings as we come to understand our relation to others. The pragmatic historicist view, however, denies the legitimacy of claims that black people are morally obligated to one another simply because they are black. This seems an indefensible position, based on specious racial reasoning, which inevitably fails to throw us back into the world of experience. Moreover, easy appeals to racial solidarity often obscure the hard work required to mobilize actual individuals to redress perceived wrongs.

The pragmatic view of black identity instead understands moral obligation in terms of *we-intentions;* in our efforts to secure some consequences and avoid others we develop a sense that some other person is one of us (not, that is, one of "them," who support a society premised on white supremacist practices). Such obligations do not proceed from some mystical idea of black solidarity or belonging but, rather, reflect efforts to secure some consequences and avoid others. These efforts often involve conjoint activity. We join with others who face similar unjust treatment (or who do not face such treatment but are nevertheless committed to justice), and we resist that treatment together.[26]

What is striking about this formulation is that it is thoroughly embedded in the world of action. Here ideas of racial solidarity and obligation are not predicated on some conception of blackness that hovers above the messiness of our living. Instead, the varied (racial) problems of our way of life result in the *strategic* subordination of differences in relation to the commonality of particular problems. We find ourselves at given moments speaking to the fact that we are black (a fact that has resulted in a certain kind of treatment) as opposed to our many other identities (being a woman, poor, gay, etc.). The pragmatic view of black identity holds, then, that racial solidarity and obligation are local, in the sense that both, like identity talk in general, are bound up in the context in which they take form. Our ability to distinguish that specificity (or context) determines, to some degree, the effectiveness of efforts to respond to the problem faced. In other words, our diagnosis of the problem guides the direction of our response.

For Robert Gooding-Williams, this view is not pragmatic enough, in that it simply shifts the issue from a prepolitical idea of the racial self to an equally problematic notion of "commonly shared problems"—another form of racial essentialism. In Gooding-Williams's view, any appeal—including my own—to commonly shared problems fails precisely because, in the post–civil rights age, what some African Americans view as a "racial problem" others don't consider a problem at all.

My point here is that, especially in our post–Jim Crow or post–civil rights era, we should not take for granted, and will find it ever more dubious to take for granted, that there are problems that an overwhelming majority of (let alone all) blacks see as palpably present and that an overwhelming majority (let alone all) see as palpably demanding collective mobilization. More and more, blacks will disagree about the existence, nature, significance and scope of antiblack racism, and their disagreements will be complicated by disputes relating to such issues as black feminism, the legitimacy of homosexual unions, and the appropriateness of interracial intimacies.

In light of this, the idea of racial solidarity has to result from "collective action" and democratic debate about needs—debates that involve efforts to persuade others that certain matters are in fact problems. Racial solidarity has to be forged in "the crucible of politics," not by appeals to "common problems that clearly and plainly manifest themselves prior to the pragmatic engagement of politics."[27]

But this criticism seems a bit odd. In *Exodus!* I invoked the notion of palpably shared problems in a passage that follows my effort to hold off an essentialist reading of black identity:

> The idea of a common condition and by extension a common interest, however, is another concern. A problem *may* be a shared one for black individuals. We *may* all agree that slavery is wrong or that lynching is evil. But that fact does not lead to the conclusion that we have identical interests or that we will agree on a course of action.... The issue is not common interests or an agreed-on course of action. Rather, it is the common problem that necessitates conjoint action, actions that may vary, given the different conceptions of the good that animate them, but are nevertheless connected by their

efforts to respond to a palpably shared problem.[28]

The point is that African American politics comprises a variety of positions. I *assume* that certain problems are seen as shared—at least in the easy cases of slavery and lynching. But even in regard to these cases I recognize that agreement is not necessarily the case and qualify my statement with the auxiliary verb *may*. The importance of politics in all of its complexity is deployed here to hold off a certain narrow conception of black politics. I go on to say that the "aim is to allow for a plurality of action and to build forms of overlapping consensus with an eye toward problem-solving and not with the view that there is but one conception of the good to be recognized by all black people precisely because they are black."

Obviously, problems are not common problems prior to political deliberation. By way of inquiry we come to see certain problems as shared. Such conclusions are not antecedent to our actions but, rather, are the fruits of our efforts to orient ourselves effectively in relation to particular experiences. I should note, however, that *inquiry not only results in determinations that we might share problems, but also allows us to assess the relative merit of a claim that denies the idea of a commonly shared problem.* Gooding-Williams rightly notes that in the post–Jim Crow or post–civil rights era a number, let's say a third, of African Americans might believe that there are no substantive obstacles to their living a middle-class life in America. Some, like Ward Connerly, even argue that race no longer impedes upward mobility. But to my mind this is an empirical question—a claim to be tested in experience.

To simply acknowledge that African Americans hold different assumptions or draw varied conclusions about their life-chances in the United States does not end the conversation. It is fairly obvious that individuals can be wrong in their views of racism. I can imagine, for example, a few black slaveholders arguing for the merits of the institution of slavery. Other commitments may blind them to the racial and unjust dimensions of slavery. If someone were to claim that banks do not discriminate on the basis of race when they issue loans to Americans, or deny that, on occasion, law enforcement officers engage in a kind of policing that singles out black drivers unjustly, data could be cited to contradict their assertion. What is needed in this instance—and Gooding-Williams is right in this regard—is a vibrant conversation and debate. Race language can serve in these deliberations (though not necessarily) as a useful tool for delineating problems and generating effective resolutions. My aim, contrary to what Gooding-Williams takes my argument to be, is to locate the processes of black identity formation in these efforts and to highlight the messy politics such efforts always involve.

I should note that race language and black identity talk "work" in another, more positive, sense as well.[29] They invoke narratives, stories of a community's sojourn. I would personally find it difficult to tell the story of the horrors of lynching or the triumphs of the civil rights movement without the language of race. Indeed, the word singles out some events, places, and personalities that are constitutive of what can be called "black" communities and the identities of individuals who inhabit them. The stories that go along with these communities often, though not always, habituate black individuals to respond to situations in particular ways. I am well aware of the potential negative consequences of narratives about community. Romantic reconstructions of an African past that are patriarchal and heterosexist are just one example among many of the pernicious ways communal narratives can police individual identities. But I remain convinced that the quality of individuality depends on the types of communities in which we live, which in turn depends on the kinds of stories we tell.[30]

Charles Taylor writes about this issue more generally in terms of a horizon of important questions: the ideal of individuality and the notion of self-choice so central to it, he says, "supposes that there are *other* issues of significance beyond self-choice."[31]

These other issues form the background of things that matter; they help define the significance of the formation of our identities and habituate us in one direction or another. The use of race language among African Americans often invokes the specific pain and suffering, joy and triumph that is definitive of experiences as a community in the United States. To discard that language would be tantamount to removing our capacity to tell *that* story—a story so critical to whom many of us take ourselves to be. To use Taylor's language, it would, in effect, bracket out a background of things that matter.

I can imagine a number of counters to an argument such as this. Some might compare race to phlogiston, a hypothetical substance once thought to be an element of all combustible material; when material burns or iron rusts, the theory went, phlogiston is released. An account of phlogiston, our critic might argue, is essential to any history of chemistry. But no chemist today would say that phlogiston is real. In the late eighteenth century, Antoine Lavoisier demonstrated that the active element in burning and rusting is oxygen, a theory we hold to this day. Phlogiston doesn't exist—earlier chemists were simply mistaken. So too with race. Of course, race language is essential to any account of African American history. But races are merely fictions—those who say otherwise are simply mistaken. Here, though, some argument needs to be given for what constitutes the real. There are *different reals within experience,* and race should be viewed in terms of Dewey's pragmatic instrumentalism, which holds that real objects are nothing but the things it pays us to have names for in certain schemes of interactions.[32] In this view, races are as real as football fields, dollar bills, or head-negroes-in-charge. If they are proven to rest on bad science, like phlogiston, it doesn't make them any less real. As Dewey notes, "the experience has changed; that is the thing experienced has changed—not that an unreality has given place to a reality, nor that some transcendental (unexperienced) Reality has changed, not that truth has changed, but just and only the concrete reality experienced has changed."[33] The point is simply that race language or black identity talk can not be escorted offstage because of some questionable conception of the real.

But even this quick defense of race and, by extension, the particular view of black identity I am commending, requires something else: that, for me, these ideas are *live* options. That is, they appeal to me as real possibilities. If I ask you to believe, for example, that, *under certain circumstances,* black solidarity is essential to the flourishing of black individuals and to the idea of justice, and that notion "makes no electric connection," as William James puts it, and "refuses to scintillate with any credibility at all," then the idea is completely dead for you. The fact that an idea can be live for some and dead for others, however, shows that its deadness or liveness are not intrinsic properties but issues of our individual temperaments.[34] They are measured by our willingness to act and, in some cases, to act irrevocably. This view holds off, I believe, the complaint that ideas of black identity end up as forms of conscription, drafting reluctant individuals into their fold or labeling those who refuse to join or choose to leave as either race-dodgers or AWOL.

Conclusion

In the end, the pragmatic view of black identity rests on two nodal points. First, race language and black identities are descriptions of certain schemes of interaction that help us get into satisfactory relation with other parts of our experience. They are tools to be used in our problem-solving activity. For example, race language is the best means of describing racial profiling, a form of policing that singles out black individuals (or members of some other groups) for a particular kind of treatment, and unless folk are willing to give up the ability to describe such practices they will have to concede that race language must remain in our conceptual toolbox. But this does not mean that all discussions of problems involving African Americans are best conducted with the term *race*. We must cultivate our ability to see that some problems are best described otherwise. Failure to do so narrows our political options and suggests a hardening of our individual capacity of discrimination, which too often blinds us to the uncertainty and conflict characteristic of any situation properly called moral. Such blindness inevitably affects our character—we can become obsessed with narrow notions of "the race"—and denies the lessons of the pragmatic view of tragedy outlined in chapter 1 by seeking security in the certainty of race and black identity.

Second, black identity is, in part, a consequence of the kinds of stories we tell about our beliefs, choices, and actions in the context of problem-solving activity. When we decide that the use of race language is appropriate to describe a particular event—like racial profiling—that event is made sense of against the background of other events that matter, like the historical tensions between police departments and black communities. This background of things that matter shapes our characters and informs our conduct; it amounts to a reservoir of experiences that is indispensable to any effort to invade successfully the future. Such descriptions of the past disclose the impulses and habits formed in the context of experiences that carry us one way or another.

This pragmatic way of thinking about black identity shifts the discussion in at least two ways: (1) we move from the idea that obligation and good are determined in relation to a fixed racial self to the idea of solidarity and identity formation in the face of particular problems (a solidarity that is constantly remade, given the shifting nature of problems), and (2) this view evades the narrow debates about whether or not races are real, and instead insists that we look the facts of racialized experiences in the United States squarely in the face. There we find, usually on the other side of the tracks, America's darker souls struggling to create themselves and to sing America.

What's striking is that the sound always has at its root a blue note reflective of the limit conditions of the world of action and of an insistence, building on the words of Baby Suggs, to act and create anyway. Race, the idea of black identity, and the extraordinary history they reference remain live hypotheses. To be sure, America's history of white supremacy has produced particularly charged conceptions of black identity and history. But for those of us who struggle to imagine a post-soul politics in the aftermath of the sixties revolution, it is necessary that we think about these issues more clearly. Once we do, perhaps we can get on with the business of finding better ways of talking about the complexities of black lives and of responding intelligently to the actual problems we face.

3

"Ethiopia Shall Stretch Forth Her Hands unto God": The Problem of History in Black Theology

To say "I think, hope and love" is to say in effect that genesis is not the last word; instead of throwing the blame or the credit for the belief, affection and expectation upon nature, one's family, church, or state, one declares one's self to be henceforth a partner.

JOHN DEWEY, Experience and Nature

People are trapped in history and history is trapped in them.

JAMES BALDWIN, "Strangers in the Village"

Religious language has been a critical resource in the construction of black identity. From the Christian slaves' identification with the Exodus story to the religious views of the Nation of Islam, African Americans have given voice—through various religious traditions—to their own sense of peoplehood, secured for themselves a common history, and imagined a future for their children. These efforts have occurred within the context of a society that has historically denied African Americans access to the benefits and burdens of full inclusion in American democratic life. The religious imagination of African Americans has been especially important in the struggles against the dehumanizing effects of those practices.

Too often our views about black identity stem from assumptions about common historical experiences and shared vocabularies that fix our frames of reference without regard to the shifts and changes that make up our actual lives. This singularity of reference and meaning is seen as the essence of black folk, determining how we understand ourselves in relation to others, the scope and extent of our political aspirations, and—perhaps most importantly—the manner in which we conceive of our obligations to one another. But identities are more complicated than this sort of account suggests. I argued in chapter 2 that identities are made. They are formed and reformed as we experience forces that encroach on us and exact choices that shape who we are and will become. Identity is less about essences and more about the *consequences* of human interaction: the product of our beliefs, choices, and actions as we engage our world.

Invocations of religious languages in African Americans' struggles against white supremacy have produced particularly charged conceptions of identity and history. Political struggles have often been inscribed within religious narratives, and aspirations for freedom—what Robin Kelley refers to as "freedom dreams"—have been formulated as divinely sanctioned ends.[1] Uses of the Exodus story constitute just one example of the extraordinary religious imagination of those caught on the underside of this fragile experiment in democracy. From invocations of Psalms 68:31 to reconstructions of Judaism and Islam, many African Americans have imagined themselves and their struggles in terms of salvific history, an arena in which God works on behalf of his chosen people. David Walker's 1828 *Appeal* asks:

> But has not the Lord an oppressed and suffering people among them? Does the Lord condescend to hear their cries and see their tears in consequence of oppression? Will he let the oppressors rest comfortably and happy always? Will he not cause the very children of the oppressors to rise up against them, and oftimes to put them to death? God works in many ways his wonders to perform.[2]

Walker's *Appeal* and the efforts of many other African Americans bring a sense of the sacred to the construction of identities and the idea of a black community. The political implications of these uses of religious language vary from Martin Luther King Jr. to Malcolm X, from Cornel West to Louis Farrakhan. But in every instance religious stories have provided an interpretive framework within which experiences can be made sense of and, for some, hope can be sustained.

This is particularly true of the black theological project—that extraordinary but flawed effort on the part of theologians like James Cone to recast Christianity as essentially a religion of black liberation. In this chapter, I address what I call the "problem of History" informing much of the work of black liberation theologians. To be sure, one of the significant contributions of black liberation theology has been its historicist turn.[3] Liberation theologians understand the centrality of historical processes to any form of political praxis. This understanding involves more than an assertion about God's activity in history; it also insists on the importance of historical consciousness to theological reflection. Thick description then becomes a critical tool in understanding God's relation to African Americans.

The problem, at its root, involves the presumption of a continuous history of African Americans. Much like advocates of the archeological approach to black identity, discussed in chapter 2, black liberation theologians often posit History—in a sense I'll mark with a capital- *H* —as a soulful or spiritual event and as the site for the production of an authentic black, and in this case Christian, subject. James Cone says as much in his brilliant text *God of the Oppressed:*

> Indeed our survival and liberation depend upon our recognition of the truth when it is spoken and lived by the people. If we cannot recognize the truth, then it cannot liberate us from untruth. To know the truth is to appropriate it, for it is not mainly reflection and theory. Truth is divine action entering our lives and creating the human action of liberation. Truth enables us to dance and live to the rhythm of freedom in our lives as we struggle to be who we are.

Therefore to speak truth we black theologians must set forth the authentic experience of blackness.[4]

In this sense, History has more gravitas than the various artifacts we have produced over time. It stands as an arbiter of who is worthy or pious and who has access to the Kingdom; it contains the Truth that "enables us to dance and live to the rhythm of freedom." Black theologians' invocations of history, then, seem to fall unwittingly into "the transcendentalist trap of making historical consciousness the new candidate for grounding" theological claims.[5] Instead of revisable accounts and experimental tinkering, the turn to black history often reinforces a kind of dogmatism and bad racialist thinking.

Terms like *race* and *nation* are "more-than" categories. More than general descriptors for individuals who hold particular characteristics in common, they seem, recalling Schelling or Hegel, more real than the individuals they describe. We come to understand who we are in relation to a more-than that is obviously greater than ourselves—that determines our values, defines (in part) our purposes, and constitutes that for which we must suffer and, if necessary, die. In the end, all that we are and will become, if anything, is bound up with a *pious* relation to the whole. Indeed, black individuals and, I suppose, their relationships with God are literally unintelligible apart from the whole—the race.

History, in this view, constitutes a reservoir of meanings that form the basis of a kind of black piety, where we express loyalty to the sources of our existence (God, black ancestors, communities, a tradition of struggle), which make us who we are and provide us with tools to become who we are destined to be. Black individuals, then, are told of their indebtedness to the race and the necessity of solidarity with others with whom they may have no immediate relation, and that their individual importance resides in the extent to which they identify with these sometimes imponderable relationships.

The expressions of loyalty this view of history entails often involve blind deference to authority. By contrast, pragmatism, as I understand it, insists on the moral and ethical significance of historical work. Pragmatism urges us to see that our beliefs about the world—the kinds of stories we tell about our conduct and ourselves in historical crises—have ethical significance, motivating choices that shape the world we live in as well as the people we take ourselves to be. Its historicism helps us to understand that beliefs, choices, and action all arise in the context of the constant activity of bringing the past to consciousness in narrative. We turn to the past, then, not out of blind deference, but in order to open up future possibilities. And piety, in this view, refers to habits of character, not to essentialist characterizations of racial selves.

These insights have particular significance for black theology. In presenting this view, I begin with a brief sketch of three trends within black theology with a particular focus on the work of James Cone. I then examine ways in which the historical experiences of African Americans are used to ground some theological claims and the problems that arise from this use. More specifically, I locate black theology in its historical moment as a response to the secular rants of black power. I argue that black theology has constituted a form of apologetics insofar as it has sought to justify its relevance to various forms of black militancy. I end by offering two possible philosophical resources, Nietzschean and Deweyan, for responding to the problem as I have outlined it, concluding, as expected, that my version of pragmatism offers the most appropriate way to answer the problematic invocations of history by some black theologians.

Trends in Black Theology

Black theology consists in at least three dominant trends. The first is classical black theology. With the publication of James Cone's *Black Theology and Black Power* (1969) and *A Black Theology of Liberation* (1970),[6] a series of heated academic debates about the relation between the historical experiences of black people in the United States and their faith in God were begun. Scholars explored the experiences of living in a white supremacist culture in order to shed light on the essential meanings of African American religious conviction. Partly in response to the eversecularizing momentum of the black power movement, classical black theologians translated, in effect, a particular understanding of the prophetic Christian tradition of African Americans into an idiom of black power and, in the process, underscored the importance of social context for theological reflection.[7]

The second trend takes up the issue of social context and emphasizes the importance of narrative and the framework of Afrocentrism. Works by narrativist and centrist black theologians like Dwight Hopkins and Peter Paris extend the classical black theologians' turn to social contexts by delving even deeper into black cultural sources. Victor Anderson describes this effort as a hermeneutics of return, that is, "a narrative return to distinctively black sources for the purpose of establishing and reassuring the legitimacy of black theology in a postrevolutionary context."[8] With this turn to narrative, so these particular theologians argue, we are able to see the *continuity* between black theological reflection in the context of slavery and Jim Crow and the black theological project in our current moment.

This narrative turn and black theology in general are challenged and deepened by a third trend, the contributions of black women theologians and historians who highlight the gendered character of the story. The works of Jacqueline Grant, Delores Williams, Evelyn Brooks Higginbotham, and Katie Cannon (just to name a few) stand as grand correctives of the black theological project. By turning to the historical roles of black women in the religious life of black America, womanist theologians and historians unsettle the standard and often patriarchal accounts of African American religion by emphasizing and foregrounding the experiences of black women. They do so, however, in relation to a culture that is not simply racist but sexist as well—a challenge that implicates white *and* black America.

There is an underlying similarity between these three trends. Each attempts to square its theological efforts with the historical and social experiences of African Americans. This, I believe, is a genetic preoccupation. Classical black theologians place historical processes and political aims at the heart of their theological projects. Their reflections begin with a radical skepticism about white interpretations of the gospel that, implicitly or explicitly, justify white supremacist practices. They respond by offering counterinterpretations that transform received understandings of biblical texts into a message based in a social context and directed to those caught on the underside of American life.[9] Histories of black experiences and biblical interpretation, then, constitute the twin premises of black theological reflection. The claim that God is in fact on our side and acts on our behalf is linked in a symbiotic relationship to historical processes and political aspirations for liberation.

The subsequent trends have attempted to deepen this linkage. The work of the narrativist/centrist theologians is grounded in the desire to tell a continuous story of how African Americans have come to terms with their circumstances and their beliefs. Womanist theologians complicate this narrative by pointing to fissures and breaks—specifically along the lines of gender—in the story. Both, like classical black theology, underscore the importance of history.

But what exactly is the version of African American history that informs much of the black theological project? How can we locate it? Victor Anderson suggests that much of the historical work of black theology presupposes a conception of black culture and heroic genius defined by the terms of white supremacist ideology. For him, black theology is undermined by its conception of African American subjects, the history it tells of these people and their activities, and, finally, the radical oppositional character of its project. Such a point of departure results in not only what Anderson calls a crisis theology but a theology in a crisis of legitimation. That is to say, if we understand the experiences of African Americans only in terms of their suffering and their struggles for freedom, then once that suffering is no more black theology no longer seems relevant or viable. In both cases, the ideology of white supremacy—the reason for the suffering *and* the struggle—circumscribes black existence and theological reflection.

But something about this criticism doesn't seem right. Black liberation theologians take themselves to be addressing the difficulty of being both black *and* Christian.[10] The reality of being black foregrounds the ways in which race has overdetermined what Christianity might mean in the United States and in the world. But God intervenes here, and the powerful message and life of Jesus Christ, it is argued, stand as a profound negation of these political realities. As such, black theologians are not necessarily *completely* beholden to the political consequences of white supremacist practices. To claim that they were would be to deny the power of God and to accord undue authority to the proponents of white supremacy. Understood in this way, then, black theology is not reducible to a form of antiracist political praxis—which would be tantamount to conflating Christianity with radical politics. Instead, black theologians address the political realities that prevent individuals, black or otherwise, from fully expressing their God-given humanity. As James Cone proclaims in *Black Theology and Black Power:*

> Black people know that they comprise less than 12 percent of the total American population and are proportionately much weaker with respect to economic, political, and military power.... *But having tasted freedom through an identification with God's intention for humanity,* they will stop at nothing in expressing distaste for white power.... This willingness to die for human dignity is not novel. Indeed, it stands at the heart of Christianity.[11]

One could say that ethical concerns about justice have a central place in black theological reflection and that keeping track of unjust practices constitutes an important dimension of what it means to be a Christian. This view signals the more universalist dimension of black liberation theology, for a concern for justice easily extends to a concern about forms of oppression not reducible to racism—to, for example, criticisms of capitalism, patriarchy, and homophobia. For theologians who are descendants of slaves, justice is never a bad idea *precisely because they serve a just God.* [12]

Anderson's criticism downplays this dimension of black theology and instead focuses on its opposition to white supremacy. This oppositional orientation, however, derives from a certain conception of God and what he demands of us. If this conception of God derived solely from an opposition to white supremacy, black theology would indeed find itself in the crisis of legitimation Anderson describes. If, however, we emphasize the Christian side of the challenge of being black and

Christian in the United States, the notion of opposition looks very different and, in my view, less problematic. One need only think of, for example, Henry Highland Garnet's 1848 *Address to the Slaves.* Garnet argued that submission to slavery constituted a sin against God or, to put the point more baldly, that if the slave loved God, she had to rebel. Certainly it is the view of God that urges opposition here not the other way around.

But Anderson is right to worry about the views of history, culture, and identity that inform how black theologians think about the black side of the difficulty of being black and Christian. His worries, however, are best directed toward the ways black theologians have taken up the discourse of African American historical experience and how a particular historical moment, in the late 1960s and early 1970s, shaped their view. My intention here is not to disparage classical black theologians for being products of their historical moment. We all are, in part, products of our histories. My aim is rather to highlight certain assumptions about African American historical experiences that frustrate the efforts of many contemporary proponents of black theology.

We can easily locate the view of historical experience in black theology, and particularly classical black theology, in the context of the black power movement.[13] In some respects, black theology can be seen as a response to the criticisms of black Christian practice made by various proponents of black nationalism, persons with increasingly secular commitments. We need only think of the Black Panther Party and its use of Mao's Red Book or the romanticization and deification of African culture among cultural nationalist groups like Us as examples of the increasing marginalization of African American Christianity in black political life during this period.[14]

Maulana Karenga's Us organization, for example, offered an elaborate counter to Christian conceptions of piety. Through the creation of a cultural theory, called Kawaida, and ritual practices, like Kwanzaa, Karenga invented a tradition aimed at forging a new kind of black political subjectivity, one steeped in "African values" instead of "Western" ones. For him, echoing Frantz Fanon, the black revolution was, in part, a struggle for the minds of black people. As I mentioned in chapter 2, many self-identified black nationalists of this period held the view that a revolution or decolonization of the mind was a prerequisite for the success of the black revolution. African Americans had to shake off the shackles of psychological bondage by rejecting Western values. We had to see our bodies as beautiful and to refuse the power of a white normative gaze in determining our self-worth. Self-determination involved, then, a profoundly powerful invocation of self-love over and against historical arguments and justifications for the degradation and devaluing of black bodies.[15]

The call to reject Western values included, for some, a rejection of the white Christian God. For many black activists of the period, Christianity was a tool of oppression—a means to divert African Americans' attention from the prevailing realities of their conditions of living to some "bye and bye, pie in the sky." Moreover, purveyors of the gospel were seen by many as hucksters out to line their pockets at the expense of needy communities. Images of Reverend "Ike" and the politically conservative John H. Jackson, president of the National Baptist Convention, U.S.A., only hardened such judgments.

These realities stood alongside genuine efforts by many black Christians to reconcile their faith with the new militancy of the black power movement. Martin Luther King Jr. offered a particular vision of how to be a Christian and to struggle for freedom. His calls for love and his insistence on redemptive suffering oriented the black freedom struggle in a particular way. The tone of the children of Malcolm X, however, was more strident and less forgiving. In response to the wave of criticisms directed at Stokely Carmichael and the Student Nonviolent Coordinating Committee for their uncompromising cry of "Black power" at a 1966 march in Greenville, Mississippi, a few black clergymen, primarily from northern cities, published a full-page ad defending use of the phrase in the July 31, 1966, *New York Times:*

As black men who were long ago forced out of the white church to create and to wield "black power," we fail to understand the emotional quality of the outcry of some clergy against the use of the term today. It is not enough to answer that integration is the solution. For it is precisely the nature of the operation of power under some forms of integration which is being challenged.... Without the capacity to participate with power—i.e., to have some organized political and economic strength to really influence people with whom one interacts—integration is not meaningful.... We regard as sheer hypocrisy or as a blind and dangerous illusion the view that opposes love to power. Love should be a controlling element in power, but what love opposes is precisely the misuse and abuse of power, not power itself. So long as white Christian churchmen continue to moralize and misinterpret Christian love, so will justice continue to be subverted in this land.[16]

The clergymen make two striking moves: First, they locate the origins of black power in the historic emergence of independent black denominations; in their view, the black church constitutes *the* institutional manifestation of black power. Second, they reject the notion that love and power are diametrically opposed; to embrace black power does not necessarily constitute a rejection of King's philosophy. Instead, as King would later echo in *Where Do We Go from Here?,* they argue that "love should be a controlling element of power" (a formulation reminiscent of the venerable Walter Rauschenbusch). These two formulations form the foundation of black liberation theology's embrace of the politics of black power. It is against the backdrop of such attempts to reconcile Christian commitments with the politics of black power, the development of alternative forms of black piety, and strident criticisms of white and black Christianity that black liberation theology emerged.

James Cone's first book, *Black Theology and Black Power,* stands as a wonderful example of the resulting effort at translation. He writes:

> Black Power and black religion are inseparable. Both seek to free black people from white racism. It is impossible for Black Power to be effective without taking into consideration man's religious nature. It is impossible for black religion to be truly related to the condition of black people and to the message of Jesus Christ without emphasizing the basic tenets of Black Power. Therefore, Black Theology seeks to make black religion a religion of Black Power.[17]

Cone recognized that many questioned the relevance of black Christianity to black power, and he countered with the startling (perhaps desperate) claim that "the message of Black Power is the message of Christ." As he would later argue in *The Spirituals and the Blues:* "Contrary to popular opinion, the spirituals are not evidence that black people reconciled themselves with human slavery. On the contrary, they are black freedom songs which emphasize black liberation as consistent with divine revelation. For this reason it is most appropriate for black people to sing them in this 'new' age of Black Power."[18] Obviously, some held contrary views.

Indeed, black theology can be read as a form of apologetics—an attempt, much like the liberal Protestantism of old, to justify its existence in response to the new clerics of black life. As Cone writes:

> Let me admit that the black slaves' picture of the world is not to be defended as a viable scientific analysis of reality; that their image of the Promised Land, where "the streets are pearl and the gates are gold," is not the best way of communicating to contemporary Black Power advocates with their stress on political liberation by any means necessary: that a new black theological language is needed if black religion is going to be involved in the historical strivings of black people in America and the Third World.[19]

I should say that classical black theologians were not and are not necessarily self-identified black nationalists, for in some respects nationalism of any sort can be seen by the Christian as a form of idolatry. But it is precisely in the effort to remain relevant as the circumstances of black insurgency changed in the late 1960s and early 1970s that classical black theologians found themselves caught in the webs of a black nationalist imaginary, and particularly its account of African American historical experience.

Cone understood his theological project, in part, as *existentially* bridging the gap between the then current lives of black folk and the ministry of Jesus as revealed in the Bible. This involved an embrace of the rhetoric of black power, and the timbre and tone of his theological claims reflect the sound of the period:

It is the power to love oneself precisely because one is black and a readiness to die if whites try to make one behave otherwise. It is the sound of James Brown singing,

"I'm Black and I'm Proud" and Aretha Franklin demanding "respect." The black experience is catching the spirit of blackness and loving it. It is hearing black preachers speak of God's love in spite of the filthy ghetto, and black congregations responding Amen, which means that they realize that ghetto existence is not the result of divine decree but of white inhumanity.[20]

Indeed this is an idiom of black power: utterances predicated on an oppositional stance to white racism that affirm the worth of black selves.

Cone argues that black power affirms the basic human dignity of black persons. We come to revel in our blackness—the very feature of our existence that has served as the basis for our negation. We cherish our own image and, as in the extraordinary love poem that is *Beloved,* we begin to love our beautiful black selves. But Cone goes a step further: God's love for us contradicts the realities of our conditions of living. We become self-determining agents insofar as we see ourselves as children of a just God: the existential state of *nobodiness* so central to the practices of white supremacy is denied and a sense of *somebodiness* is affirmed. Here God talk echoes, and justifies, the politics of transvaluation so central to the black power era. Of course, this formulation is not new. We hear it in the voices of Christian slaves in the antebellum South. Cone, however, declares it in the fiery rhetoric of black power.

In the context of the black freedom struggle, the rhetoric of black power—with its condemnation of white society and its affirmation of black self-worth—enabled the expression of disillusionment and despair and articulated a critique of the middle-class focus of civil rights reform. In one sense, we see in the politics of the sixties and seventies a formal expression among many black folk that racial segregation and terror must end, backed by the argument that black folk are self-determining agents. Among many black nationalists, of course, the language of nation, bound up with a certain understanding of race, was the crucial tool of expression. That language, with its redemptive promise, served as a resource for personal identity construction and collective solidarity.[21] However, it also often obscured the tensions and differences among African Americans. Specifically, the class differences that called the black power movement into being were caught under the thumb of modern statecraft and one of its primary tools: national history (that is, a particular story about the collective meaning and purposes of black individuals). And in some ways, the efforts of black liberation theologians to translate prophetic black Christianity into the idiom of black power resulted in its embrace of that history.

At least two critical assumptions lie behind particular versions of black nationalist historiography in the United States. First, that black people can only reach freedom by *cultivating their peculiar national identity.* [22] With this assumption, History takes on a different hue. It consists of black people (or, more than likely, black men) who see themselves as acting in accordance with tradition, fulfilling their sacred duties, and defending their ways of life against encroachment. In one version of the story, such men are viewed as heroic figures who make possible an expression of our national (read: racial) genius. The second assumption involves *the subversion of the present by the past.* Tradition and History make possible heroic efforts that, to echo the early writings of Friedrich Nietzsche, deny the vitality of the present. To get a sense of this particular view, we need only think of appeals to the forms of life of ancient Egypt as a remedy for our current ills. Here Tradition and History are presumed to contain wisdom far beyond our current capacities. Our relation to our ancestors and to future generations constitutes a larger purpose which extends beyond any fragile individual: we are but fragments of a greater whole. And it is through our relation to Tradition and History—and the answers they provide—that we are oriented appropriately to our fellows and to problems that confront our people.

At this juncture we can begin to see the "historical malady" that plagues the black theological project. In their rejection of biblical interpretations that supported white supremacy, black theologians turned to the historical experiences of black Christians to ground their own perceptions of the texts. But, how they understood that history was of vital importance. Like many activists of the black power era, these theologians presupposed a problematic conception of black identity and history. Reflecting on the theological significance of the spirituals, Cone demonstrates his commitment to such a view of history:

> Black history is the stuff out of which the black spirituals were created. But the "stuff" of black history includes more than the bare historical facts of slavery. Black history is an experience, a soulful event. And to understand it is to know the Being of a people who had to "feel their way along the course of American slavery," enduring the stresses and strains of human servitude but not without a song. *Black history is a spiritual!* [23]

Metaphysical claims are collapsed here into ontological claims and the result, despite Cone's protestations, is a reification of blackness. Tradition and History, far wiser than we will ever be, have settled the problems of our living in advance of our experience. The meanings of African American historical experiences are thus oversimplified. The complexity of individual African American lives denied. Such a view of history can deny us the power of reflexive thought about ourselves and our interactions with the world, the exercise of which informs daily, sometimes tragic, choices and recognizes the contingency and indeterminacy at the heart of action.

In my view, three difficulties—descriptive, theoretical, and existential—attend such accounts. The descriptive problematic involves the plotline of the story. I am reminded here of James Baldwin and Ralph Ellison's criticisms of Richard Wright. Both worried that Wright's representations of black life betrayed the complexity of African American existence. The same can be said of stories of African American experience that are mainly about liberation and presuppose a subject in constant struggle. There is much more to our living than simply resisting white supremacy. Moreover, the singular focus often results in a relatively coherent account in which the internal fissures of black communities are obscured. Suffering and resistance then subordinate all other considerations—even the differential experience of that suffering and the different aims of resistance.

The theoretical problematic refers to the Christian dimension of the problem of being both black and Christian. Like Anderson, I worry that God talk among black theologians, at least in their worst moments, functions merely as a source of the strenuous mood, serving simply to justify and sanctify a particular political orientation—even though it is precisely in our relation to God and His relation to us that we resist oppression.[24]

Lastly, the existential problematic again entails a simplification of the complexity of African American lives. The existential involves how to live, how to hope, and how to love. But if our lives are reduced simply to struggle and our stories presume an understanding of black agency as *always already* political, then the various ways we have come to love and hope are cast into the shadows as we obsess about politics, narrowly understood, and as History orients us retrospectively instead of prospectively. We end up, despite our best intentions, ignoring the sheer joy of black life and unwittingly reducing our capacity to reflect and act in light of the hardships of our actual lives. Perhaps, more importantly, "our ability to make delicate distinctions" is lost as History settles beforehand the difficult existential questions "Who am I?" "How should I live?" and "What should I do?"

How, then, do we rescue historical awareness in black theology from black power's cultural metaphysics? How do we avoid the use of the past in order to subvert the present?

Nietzsche, Dewey, and Black Theology

We must first recognize that history, as the perspectivalism of Friedrich Nietzsche and the philosophical historicism of John Dewey suggest, must serve us. In our effort to understand the different ways African Americans have attempted to solve crises, and to better equip ourselves to respond to challenges, we turn to, echoing Samuel Beckett, the "mess" of their doings and sufferings. This turn imposes constraints by emphasizing historical limits and the transient nature of social practices. But it also makes social analysis and cultural criticism an indispensable part of our historical work—work that accounts for the present *and* projects a future.

Our character and capacity to act freely result not only from a past which shapes and informs who we are but also from the kinds of stories we tell ourselves about that past. In responding to the demands of life we situate ourselves by telling stories—stories not of abstracted concepts (race or nation) but of people, situated in circumstances, struggling to respond to those circumstances with the tools at hand.[25] By doing so, we make possible informed moral action. The stories we tell ourselves about the past make up the background of things that matter and form a part of what Alasdair MacIntyre refers to as a stage we did not design, upon which we find ourselves involved in actions not necessarily of our making.

Tradition and history do not settle matters in advance. We do not stand before them with nothing left for us to do, with our character already decisively shaped. As the early Nietzsche asks regarding such an orientation to history: "What is left to do for the historically educated man, the modern fanatic of process...? He has nothing to do but to continue to live as he has lived, to continue to love what he has loved, to continue to hate what he has hated, and to continue to read the newspaper which he has read; for him there is only one sin—to live differently than he has lived."[26] Tradition and history, in this account, are viewed instead as the background of relatively unquestioned values, beliefs, and commitments that inform our actions. We stand in pious relation to that background but not in blind deference to its authority, for it is always subject to revision or rejection. We look to the past, in other words, not retrospectively, in an attitude of reverence and supplication, but prospectively, seeking to equip ourselves to live vitally and to secure a better world for our children.

Nietzsche and Dewey make similar points about the role of history in our lives, albeit with different aims. For Nietzsche, history, if it is to serve life, must be transformed into art: our relation to the past must not be as "incarnate compendia" but as creators and inventors in the face of open possibility. For Dewey, if we are to understand our current situations, crises, and problems, we must have a historical consciousness that highlights the conditioned character of our lives. Both views, I believe, can help the black theological project break loose from the "problem of history."

In "On the Advantage and Disadvantage of History for Life," Nietzsche critiques what he sees as the defect of his time. He believes that his age suffers from historical fever inasmuch as his contemporaries failed to find the proper balance between remembering and forgetting. For Nietzsche, human beings are separated from animals in part because we are burdened by the past. We live historically. But in order to live full lives, in his view, we must cultivate an ability to live unhistorically: we must find the strength to be enclosed within our own limited horizon. We must, if we are to experience happiness, be able to forget (as well as to remember) at the right moment.[27] To live an utterly historical existence would be like being forcibly deprived of sleep. I alluded to this point in my discussion of Toni Morrison's *Beloved* in chapter 1. Sethe's inability to forget revealed that we must cultivate this ability. Nietzsche puts it succinctly:

> It is possible to live with almost no memory, even to live happily as the animals shows; but without

forgetting, it is quite impossible to live at all. Or, to say it more simply yet: *there is a degree of insomnia, of rumination, of historical sense which injures every living thing and finally destroys it, be it a man, a people or a culture.* [28]

A completely historical existence arrests action: we are overwhelmed by the constant state of becoming that surrounds us, and this uncertainty stifles our ability to will and desire. A balance is required, if we are to flourish, between the historical and the unhistorical.

But, in proper balance, history is important to life. Nietzsche writes of three kinds of history that can serve life. First, monumental history provides models of excellence; by presenting the lives of great men and past events, it informs us that greatness was, at least at one time, possible and may be possible again. Second, antiquarian history preserves and venerates the past. It imbues specific ways of living with the love of tradition. The antiquarian historian, through his veneration of the past, "gives thanks for his own existence. By tending with loving hands what has long survived he intends to preserve the conditions in which he grew up for those who will come after him—and so he serves life."[29] Finally, critical history engages the men and events of the past to judge and in the end condemn them. This kind of history allows us to see the injustices of the past in order to eliminate them in our present lives. As Nietzsche states:

> He must have the strength, and use it from time to time, to shatter and dissolve something to enable him to live: this he achieves by dragging it to the bar of judgment, interrogating it meticulously and finally condemning it; every past, however, is worth condemning—for that is how matters happen to stand with human affairs: human violence and weakness have always contributed strongly to shaping them. It is not justice which here sits in judgment; even less is it mercy which here pronounces judgment: but life alone, that dark,

driving, insatiably self-desiring power.[30]

For Nietzsche, each kind of history is useful only on its own soil. When we aspire to greatness, we turn to monumental history; if we want to preserve and venerate our customs, we cherish the past as antiquarians; and if we are burdened or oppressed in the present, we need critical history. If any of these forms of history are carelessly used, great damage can be done, for "the critic without need, the antiquarian without reverence, and the connoisseur of the great who has not the ability to achieve the great are such growths which have been alienated from their native soil and therefore have degenerated and shot up as weeds."[31]

Each of the forms of history, then, can also do disservice to life. Monumental history can block the way to an expression of our genius. We may become so enamored of past men and moments that we are blind to our own greatness. Those who hate the present may masquerade in monumental drag, using their admiration for the great and powerful of the past to hide their true disdain for themselves—acting as if their motto were "Let the dead bury the living." Antiquarian history can likewise smother the present. When we revere and praise things primarily because they are old, the past is not so much preserved as embalmed, and true piety withers away. The danger of critical history is, perhaps, just the opposite: everything old becomes necessarily bad.

What guards against each of these misuses is history whose aim is life. We need history to show us how and when to forget, when to lay down our crosses so that life might be liberated and we can flourish. For Nietzsche, only world-historical men can do this—figures who have learned to live unhistorically and superhistorically. By unhistorical, he means having the skill and power to forget, to retreat within their limited horizons. By superhistorical, he means responsive to those forces that would turn one away from a constant state of becoming, which arrests action, toward "that which gives existence its eternal and unchanging character, toward art and religion."[32] Objective or scientific history cannot do justice to these world-historical figures. Only creative persons, individuals capable of creating new horizons, forms within which future generations can live and flourish, can write such history. Historians who fail to achieve this numb our creative energies, lead us to look to the past for all that is valuable, and "undermine that impulse to heroic exertion that might give a peculiarly human, if only transient, meaning to an absurd world."[33]

We need not embrace the subjectivism and the antidemocratic sentiments at the heart of Nietzsche's account to grasp his central insight into how we should view history. For Nietzsche, history must not be approached as a site that contains all of the answers for living. When viewed in this way it too often absolves us of the responsibility to address imaginatively the complexities of our current moment. Our sight steadily fixes on the past, like eyes fixed on Gorgon, and turns us to stone—leaving our current moment to wither from neglect. Nietzsche makes this point powerfully:

Draw about yourselves the fence of a great and embracing hope, a hopeful striving. Form an image for yourselves to which the future ought to correspond and forget the superstition that you are epigoni. You have enough to ponder and invent by pondering that future life; but do not ask history to show the How? and Wherewith?[34]

History, then, should not be invoked to fortify our actions with the supposed certainty of past doings and sufferings. Instead, to use Emerson's wonderfully rich formulation, we draw circles around our inheritance, with history providing the instrumentalities to invade the future with a little more than luck. We understand more fully why certain features of our lives have lapsed into incoherence, how varying and competing approaches impact our form of life, and how the choices, beliefs, and actions of our fellows, as well as impinging events, turn us around and cast us off in new directions.[35] We stand not as servants to History but as historically conditioned organisms transacting with environments, for weal or woe, in the hope of securing a better life.

Most black theologians, I believe, would readily agree with the thrust of this account, and would find it odd that I would suggest otherwise. For them, the end-in-view is to secure a better life for those caught on the underside of the modern project, and the historical turn only deepens a form of political praxis aimed at achieving that end. My problem rests not so much with the turn to history as with how that history is imagined and invoked. The historiography of black power saturates the black theological project, as I have already suggested, and orients it to the past in problematic ways. Many proponents of Black Power have found themselves looking to the past in search of greatness, or venerating all that is old to the detriment of the new or attempting, a posteriori, to invent a past for themselves—one they would prefer to the past from which they actually are descended. Each of these approaches to history makes us, contrary to our best intentions, passive servants and retrospective in our orientation.[36]

James Baldwin spoke to these tendencies in *The Fire Next Time.* Although he understood the rage at the heart of the Nation of Islam and sought to render that rage intelligible to those who found it incomprehensible, Baldwin rejected the Nation's invented past:

> The paradox—and a fearful paradox it is—is that the American Negro can have no future anywhere, on any continent, as long as he is unwilling to accept his past. *To accept one's past—one's history—is not the same thing as drowning in it; it is learning how to use it.* An invented past can never be used; it cracks and crumbles under the pressures of life like clay in a season of drought.[37]

For Baldwin, the "beauty" of African American history orients us to task of transforming our circumstances. We cannot deny that beauty by grasping for security in the idols of race and nation or by retreating into the cave of History to ponder shadows. Instead, we must look the facts of our experiences squarely in the face. And it is here that pragmatism offers its resources.

John Dewey's seminal essay "The Need for a Recovery of Philosophy," critiques not so much the failure of his age as the scholasticism and conservatism of professional philosophy.[38] Dewey believes that modern philosophy suffers from cultural and social irrelevance because its major preoccupation (securing the epistemological remedy to our subject-object ailments) yields bad ways of thinking about experience. Consequently, he believes, philosophy fails to speak to our everyday doings and sufferings.

Dewey aims, then, to emancipate philosophy from a "too intimate and exclusive attachment to traditional problems" in order to make what philosophers do—that is, to envision, imagine, and reflect—useful in dealing with our problems. This may at first seem unrelated to the problem of history in black theology, but it is precisely in Dewey's discussion of experience, and the notion of contingency that it presupposes, that the idea of history serving us takes on added significance. As Dewey writes in *Democracy and Education:* "Past events cannot be separated from the living present and retain meaning. The true starting point of history is always some present situation with its problems."[39]

Dewey contrasts traditional conceptions of experience with notions he views as more congenial to present conditions. In the views he dismisses, experience is regarded as, above all, concerned with knowledge, a psychical thing in which the past counts exclusively and reference to precedent is believed to be its essence. The empirical tradition, then, is committed to particularism. Connections and continuities are supposed to be foreign to experience, and experience and thought are antithetical terms.[40] Each of these orthodox views of experience deepens the subject-object problematic at the heart of modern philosophy.

Dewey responds by arguing that knowing can be properly understood only as a functional activity in the context of experience. We think or inquire *within experience,* for inquiry arises as we encounter difficult problems or meddlesome circumstances. Understood in this way, experience includes both the act of experiencing and the experience, what William James referred to as the double-barreled sense of the word. "Like its congeners, life and history," Dewey writes, "[experience] includes *what* men do and suffer, *what* they strive for, love, believe and endure, and also *how* men act and are acted upon, the ways in which they do and suffer, desire and enjoy, see, believe, imagine—in short, processes of *experiencing*." [41] As such, experience cannot be reduced to simply a psychical thing. The problem, then, is not whether there is epistemic justification for the existence of a world outside our ideas but, rather, how we go about dealing and coping intelligently with our environment.[42]

For Dewey, such activity necessarily entails a degree of randomness, because, as I suggested in chapter 1, "any reaction is a venture; it involves risk." But to the extent that we generate the foresight to anticipate future consequences in our present doings and sufferings, we engage in intelligent activity. He therefore rejects the notion that "the past exclusively counts." Experience, for Dewey, is prospective; it is as much about projection and anticipation as it is about recollection and memory. Dewey warns us to be suspicious of *eulogistic predicates:* invocations of permanence, essence, totality, *verum et bonum,* and the like lead to an artificial simplification of our lives.[43] Echoing in some ways Nietzsche, Dewey argues: "If [the past] were wholly gone and done with, there would be only one reasonable attitude towards it. Let the dead bury the dead."[44]

This connection to the future is the primary basis for critical intelligence—the primary basis, that is, for insisting on our *active* presence in the world. Critical intelligence is forward-looking, and only by ignoring this, Dewey argues, "does it become a mere means for an end already given. The latter is servile, even when the end is labeled moral, religious or esthetic."[45] This prospective orientation presupposes that connections and relations are constitutive of our experiences and that we can infer from these experiences standards and norms that will help us in the future.

In the orthodox view of experience, our doings and sufferings provide us no guidance for moral and social behavior. Dewey argues, however, that it is through critical examination of our experiences that we are able to articulate our obligations intelligently and to decide, without guarantee of success, what is best for us to do under specific circumstances. Let me quote in full a passage that, up to now, I have only referred to in fragments:

> Experience is primarily a process of undergoing: a process of standing something; of suffering and passion, of affection, in the literal sense of these words. The organism has to endure, to undergo, the consequences of its own actions.... Experience, in other words, is a matter of simultaneous doings and sufferings. Our undergoings are experiments in varying the course of events; our active tryings are trials and tests of ourselves.[46]

What is interesting about Dewey's conception of experience is not only his rejection of modern philosophy's obsession with the "given," but the role history assumes in our lives once we take his conception of experience seriously.

To be sure, the background of things that matter—of relatively unquestioned beliefs and values—informs our actions. It habituates us in particular ways and offers answers to many of the problems we may face. We cannot disavow this inheritance; it certainly shapes our character and informs who we are. We can no more choose, as Jeffrey Stout wryly notes, whatever moral principle pleases us than a scientist can accept whatever theory she wishes were true: "Moral and theoretical decisions are alike constrained by the values and norms of a living inheritance within which even the changes we call revolutionary leave nearly everything in place."[47] We cannot reject the past wholesale or assume, to borrow Thomas Nagel's phrase, a view from nowhere.

But sometimes our habits and beliefs fail us. In the course of our transactions with our environment—transactions that result in the irritation of doubt—our experiences may lead us to conclude that some of our inherited beliefs are not for us. We then tinker and experiment and, as we grope for resolution, we determine, as best as we can, when it is appropriate to forget and when to remember. Dewey says as much when he writes, "Dismembering is a positively necessary part of remembering. But the resulting disject membra are in no sense experience as it was or is; they are simple elements held apart, and yet tentatively implicated together."[48]

Toni Morrison's novel *Beloved* powerfully captures this point and insists that the past does not count exclusively. An embodied past literally consumes Sethe, and it is in the wisdom of Baby Suggs's ghost that Denver finds the courage to leave 124 and seek help from others. Forgetting and remembering stand in dialectical relation as the fragile, broken selves that populate the novel struggle to imagine a future implicated in a terrifying past and present. Morrison writes:

They forgot her like a bad dream. After they made up their tales, shaped and decorated them, those that saw her that day on the porch quickly and deliberately forgot her. It took longer for those who had spoken to her, lived with her, fallen in love with her, to forget, until they realized they couldn't remember or repeat a single thing she said, and began to believe that, other than what they themselves were thinking, she hadn't said anything at all. So, in the end, they forgot her too. Remembering seemed unwise.... It was not a story to pass on.[49]

To accept our past is not to drown in it. Instead, history offers those caught on the underside of life resources to forge a self amid the absurd and to hope, despite the odds, for a better tomorrow.[50]

In this pragmatic view, then, history is understood quite differently. Not only its subject matter changes but also the role it plays in our lives. To begin with, historical actors are not seen as stable, continuous subjects. We are constantly changing because our environments are always changing, for better or for worse. Any kind of stability depends upon actions chosen intelligently with the aim of securing the values we cherish. Moreover, history is not a dispassionate detailing of past facts or a mere elaboration of different points of view. Rather, history helps us by illuminating our present predicaments. David Mandell is right when he argues that "determining the worth of an idea, concept, or institution often requires first recovering the original context in which it was developed. In order to have a sense of its adequacy to the present, it is important to know what problems it was originally designed to solve."[51] History, then, is instrumental in our efforts to alter the state of things. Dewey, like Baldwin, states the point powerfully:

> Imaginative recovery of the bygone is indispensable to successful invasion of the future, but its status is that of an instrument. To ignore its import is the sign of an undisciplined agent; but to isolate the past, dwelling

upon it for its own sake and giving it the eulogistic name of knowledge, is to substitute reminiscence of old-age for effective intelligence.[52]

What we have here, unlike with Nietzsche's account, is not history as heroic autobiography but, instead, history as an instrument in the struggle of organisms to hold on and, perhaps, to flourish in an environment that sometimes facilitates and sometimes obstructs their actions. No recourse to monumental or antiquarian history, just a historical awareness of the conditioned character of our actions.

With such a pragmatic conception of experience, the black theological project can escape the problem of history. The focus remains "the doings and sufferings" of black people, but how we understand these particular organisms and the environment with which they interact fundamentally changes. In this view, criticism of the radical oppositional character of black theology loses a bit of its punch. If we take the experiences of African Americans seriously as we engage in theological reflection, then we must take seriously their struggle to end white supremacy. Racial identity and struggle remain extraordinarily relevant to our efforts, but our understanding of them changes. Specifically, the two assumptions of the historiography of black power are dropped: we do not have recourse to a continuous history of African Americans, nor do we view history as a tool to subvert the present.

I recognize the attractiveness of such views. They secure us in a world where insecurity abounds, where we are valued less than others, where our babies seem destined for jail or the crackhouse—where tragedy abounds. Such views let us know that the human adventure is not a pointless exercise in which death alone awaits us at the end. Indeed, the sheer terror of the contingency of life and its tragic implications send us frantically running for the security of History, Tradition, permanence, totality, real essence, or God. We understand that a world shot through with the evil of white supremacy deeply affects how we live, but we must also understand that our beliefs, choices, and actions shape both that world and the people we take ourselves to be. As Dewey writes, "To note contingency in connection with a concrete situation of life is that fear of the Lord which is at least the beginning of wisdom."[53] Again, Morrison deepens the statement: we must "know it, but go on out the yard." In this view, our historical work is, in a significant sense, moral work. It is an attempt to inform our actions through the kinds of stories we tell ourselves with more than a little luck, because all is not settled. No longer beholden to the superstition that we are epigoni, we have much still to do, and how we understand that "doing" matters greatly.

4

Agency, Slavery, and African American Christianity

Hope and aspiration, belief in the supremacy of good in spite of all evil, belief in the realizability of good in spite of all obstacles, are necessary aspirations in the life of virtue. The good can never be demonstrated to the senses, nor be proved by calculations of personal profit. It involves a radical venture of the will in the interest of what is unseen and prudentially incalculable.

JOHN DEWEY, *Ethics*

I have seen the lightning flash, I've heard the thunder roll, I've felt sin breakers dashing trying to conquer my soul. But I heard the voice of Jesus saying still to fight on. He promised never to leave me, never to leave me alone.

NEGRO SPIRITUAL

If the concept of God has any validity or any use, it can only be to make us larger, freer, and more loving. If God cannot do this, then it is time we got rid of Him.

JAMES BALDWIN, *The Fire Next Time*

Whether history is seen as relating stories of our genius and triumphs over obstacles or as sanctioning practices that demean or subordinate persons or groups not considered one of us, much is at stake. The kinds of stories we tell ourselves about past experiences indelibly shape our characters and orient us to our fellows and to our world in particular ways.

Of course, histories are not simply justifications for the subordination of others or chauvinistic celebrations of invented pasts and open-ended futures. Such reductions are relevant, however, in situations where individuals and groups do not merely find themselves captured by certain narratives but are in fact the victims of brutal practices. Here historical considerations are intimately and inextricably bound up with existential and political concerns. The fact that African Americans had to create themselves in the context of a society that denied them moral standing and subjected them to arbitrary and deliberate violence exacerbated the anguish that is typically associated with creating meaning for one's life in an uncertain world. Indeed, attempts to live, love, and hope—the existential problematic—were constrained by the absurdity of the condition of being black in America. I am reminded here of W.E.B. DuBois's provocative question: "How does it feel to be a problem?" The reality of being a problem people also obviously shaped political action, which varied from arguments for the inclusion of African Americans in American society to calls for an independent nation-state. In both efforts directed toward self-creation and the context of political activism, the horrors of white supremacy in the United States have made history a crucial battleground. Too often American history has denied the active presence of African Americans, whom slavery supposedly reduced to "sambos." Freedom, and agency—so the story went—was the possession of white folks.

Appeals to African American experiences have aided in the battle to undermine such narratives. Those experiences reveal an active subject, a rational agent working to secure her freedom. Indeed, agency in the everyday doings and sufferings of black people *had* to be demonstrated in order to affirm the long-denied humanity of African Americans. History has mattered (and still matters) in the making of black selves and in the struggle against those structures that would obstruct such efforts.

In this chapter, I examine how the trope of agency colors the histories of American slavery and shapes accounts of the role and function of African American Christianity within that relation of domination. My aim here is to develop more fully the descriptive and existential problematic discussed in chapter 3 in order to reveal the deleterious consequences that follow from reductionist accounts of agency. American slavery and black Christianity are my point of entry to this discussion because they remain important and contested sites in accounts of African American agency. How we tell their stories, as I have suggested, indelibly marks how we conceive of their role and place in our current practice. In *Generations of Captivity*, for example, Ira Berlin insists that "the slaves' history—like all human history—was made not only by what was done to them but also by what they did for themselves."[1] The various ways slaves retooled families amid radical disruption and forged a distinctive black Christian practice while white Christians often held them in bondage constitute, in Berlin's view, examples of the extraordinary agency of a subject people and complicate in a wonderfully provocative way the history of American slavery.

I want to take up Berlin's insistence on the agency of the slave within the context of this totalizing system of domination. I do so in light of Albert Raboteau's magisterial book *Slave*

Religion. [2] Both of these texts, albeit in very different ways, are preoccupied with resisting accounts of slavery that reduce slaves to mere objects—simply extensions of their master's will. The character of heteronomous slaves, in those tellings, gives way to an account of "subordinated agents" struggling to establish the conditions for the possibility of freedom. Ironically, Christianity plays a central role in that effort.[3]

My interest in the topic stems, in part, from a preoccupation with what can be called a phenomenology of black agency—that is, an effort to describe and think about the complex ways African Americans, as a subjugated people, have negotiated the realities of their conditions of living in the United States. To be sure, the term *agency* has a range of associations: from ideas of the will to rational choice, freedom, motivation, and selfhood. We can think of agency, for example, in the language of Donald Davidson, Charles Taylor, Pierre Bourdieu, or Judith Butler—each theorist offers a different account. But sustained attention needs to be given to the various ways the concept is invoked in studies of African Americans. Too often an unproblematized invocation of agency as political resistance stands in for any detailed account of that resistance or of what we might mean by this elusive term.

In this chapter I put forward a view of agency that reflects my commitment to evading the "structure and agency" problematic. Human organisms act and are acted upon. As such, the idea of individuals acting freely is qualified (not displaced) by Darwinian insights about a world that encroaches on us daily, exacting choices and constraining our abilities to act.

I begin by making explicit the relation between the pragmatic view of experience, laid out in earlier chapters, and the idea of agency. I suggest that Dewey's reconstruction of experience overcomes the sorts of worries that many feminists have voiced about the concept and leaves room for a notion of agency that *can* be politically robust. I then turn to Berlin and Raboteau. Through a reading of both authors, I take up the vexing issue of positing

African American Christianity as an instance of "slave agency." The question driving this account is this: How do we avoid the claim that the appropriation of Christianity by slaves was, in fact, an accommodation to slavery? An answer to the question requires a thicker account of the "religious meanings" of the slaves' conversion (a subject most historians dare not broach). In the course of exploring this issue I offer a brief historical account of the evolution of Christianity among African American slaves during the early part of the nineteenth century.

Experience and Black Agency

In chapter 3, I argued against a conception of history that offers a particular understanding of African American experience as the ground for black theological claims. Such a view, I maintained, does not result in revisable accounts and experimental tinkering but instead reinforces bad racialist thinking. Moreover, I argued that such a view orients us to African

American history retrospectively, urging us to look to the past as a source of settled answers, not as a resource to invade the future. I should note the irony here. Appeals to African American historical experience purportedly work to demonstrate the agency of a subject people, but the resultant orientation to those experiences has too often constrained our imaginations—political, moral, or otherwise. My invocation of a pragmatic conception of experience aims, then, to take seriously the doings and sufferings of African Americans without denying the complexity of black living or appealing to a static tradition. Experience, in my view, captures the transactional nature of our engagement with our environs and insists that we are relationally constituted—that who we are and will become involve the kinds of choices made, actions taken, and beliefs held in the context of the world in all of its complexity. We are indeed agent-patients.

I am well aware that my use of the concept of experience raises a number of worrisome questions. Richard Rorty, for example, has vehemently argued that pragmatists should trade in talk of experience for talk of language, because "experience" carries with it the very metaphysical pretensions pragmatists rightly dismiss. Rorty also claims that Dewey was better off insisting that we rid ourselves of the problematic distinction between appearance and reality, not by way of a reconstructed notion of experience, but by offering instead a distinction between beliefs useful for differing purposes. For him, Dewey's appeal to "misdescribed experience" and his efforts to provide a "ground-map of the province of criticism" reveal the problematic residue of empiricism informing his thinking. Rorty holds instead that the greatness of Dewey's work

> lies in the sheer provocativeness of its suggestions about how to slough off our intellectual past, and about how to treat that past as material for *playful* experimentation rather than imposing tasks and responsibilities upon us. Dewey's work helps us put aside that spirit of seriousness which artists traditionally lack and philosophers

are traditionally supposed to maintain. *For the spirit of seriousness can only exist in an intellectual world in which human life is an attempt to attain an end beyond life, an escape from freedom into the atemporal.* [4] It seems to me, however, that much more must be said about Dewey's experimentalism and the importance of inquiry in order to ascertain the kind of work that the concept of experience is doing for him. I do not want to rehearse the vast commentary on this point here,[5] but I should say that Rorty's rating of playful experimentation over and against the spirit of seriousness smacks of a kind of smugness and arrogance that Dewey's concept of experience cautions against. Experience, Dewey writes, "reminds us that the world which is lived, suffered and enjoyed as well as logically thought of, has the last word in all human inquiries and surmises."[6] At the heart of the concept is the contingency that calls forth and constrains action, orienting us humbly to problems confronted and, all too often, left unresolved.

Rorty might respond by saying that while his formulation may indeed reek of the arrogance of an ironist, he is nevertheless right in his criticisms of Dewey. For the essential problem with Dewey's use of experience is his effort to make "true" a predicate of experience instead of a predicate of sentences. I could concede Rorty's point, but relatively little of significance for Dewey's overall view is at stake here. I do want to suggest, and Rorty would agree, that language is important for Dewey (particularly given what he says about it in *Experience and Nature*). However, Dewey would adamantly reject the view that language leaves us with simply "playful experimentation" or with Rorty's characterization of seriousness as a longing "to escape freedom into the atemporal." This claim says more about Rorty's orientation and his strong reading of Dewey than the sort of position Dewey actually commended. Playful experimentation is the tool of Rorty's romantic ironist, not Dewey's intelligent inquirer. In the end, for

Dewey, once we give up the quest for certainty we are thrust into the world of experience, and critical intelligence aids in our constant negotiation of its complexities. It is a world in which concerns about truth and correspondence constitute only a small fraction of our doings and sufferings, and distinctions between the playful and serious distract more than clarify. His aim is to clear the underbrush—to unblock the path for everyday, ordinary people to transform their world.

Despite my resistance to Rorty's criticisms I recognize the perils of invoking the concept of experience—particularly in the name of marginalized groups. Joan Wallach Scott, for example, in her important essay "The Evidence of Experience," challenges appeals to experience in efforts to recover and represent the lives of those rendered invisible in orthodox histories. The concept, in her view, presupposes the identities of such groups or persons as self-evident and natural. Moreover, she claims, appeals to the evidence of experience in these sorts of accounts "locate resistance outside of its discursive context and reify agency as inherent attributes of individuals."[7] We become more concerned with making the experience of groups or persons visible than with accounting for the various ways those experiences are produced. Such appeals fail to recognize the extent to which they are captured by the very linguistic practices they seek to undermine. For Scott, "It is precisely this kind of appeal to experience as uncontestable evidence—as a foundation on which analysis is based—that weakens the critical thrust of histories of difference." She goes on to claim that "by remaining within the epistemological frame of orthodox history, these studies lose the possibility of examining those assumptions and practices that excluded considerations of difference in the first place."[8] The concept of experience, then, reveals a commitment to a kind of empiricism that leaves unexamined—because it simply posits the fact of difference—the various ways difference is produced, how it operates, and how it constitutes the manner in which we see and act in the world. To avoid this problem, the historian must understand experience as a discursively constituted and highly contested category—not an unproblematic given that allows her to make visible those rendered invisible by standard histories. This opens up a critical examination of what Scott refers to as the ideological system itself, along with the binary categories (homosexual/heterosexual, man/woman, black/white) that it uses in representing identities.

Scott insists, and rightly so, that we remain mindful of the political dimensions of historical inquiry. Easy appeals to experience and the ostensibly self-evident identities of persons who have experiences short-circuit critical consideration of the political contexts that shape us and our world. This view seemingly locates politics elsewhere, and too often the result is bad descriptions that fail to reveal the complex ways in which identities are produced and how they operate. What is needed instead is a genealogy (in Michel Foucault's sense of the word) of experience.

I am certainly sympathetic to Scott's position. She rightly worries about characterizations of experience that fail to examine carefully the conditions that determine how experience relates to knowledge, presume a tendentious unity among members of a particular group (e.g., women, African Americans, or homosexuals), and insist that agency is an inherent attribute of individuals.[9] I hope I have demonstrated in the previous chapters that Dewey offers resources for thinking about experience that evades each of these concerns. His transactionalism insists on the relation of our actions with contexts that shape and impede or facilitate our efforts to secure desired ends. Appeals to experience in subaltern histories, then, do not settle matters by, say, evidencing the fact of difference; rather, experience constitutes the arena within which differences acquire salience and meaning. With this in mind, Dewey reconstructs what we mean by knowledge and insists that solidarities are made and remade in the context of problem-solving activity. Here, as I mentioned in chapter 1, knowledge is understood as the fruit of undertakings that seek to resolve problematic situations. It proceeds after the pattern provided by experimental inquiry, not upon the groundwork of ideas framed prior to our experience. Agency remains. We are indeed constantly negotiating an environment that demands much of us, and it is in Dewey's insistence that we do so intelligently that his pragmatism reveals its critical and moral imperative.

Much hangs on what we mean by agency here. Scott and feminists like Judith Butler worry, among other things, that appeals to agency too often presume intention and motive as the source of our actions. Butler in particular denies the fact of a rational agent antecedent to action ("an individual's will or intention"), insisting instead that our choices "draw upon and reengage conventions which have gained their power precisely through a sedimented iterability." Performative agency then marks the various ways our actions are simultaneously produced and constrained by linguistic processes. It is in light of this claim that Butler declares that "there is no opposition to power which is not itself part of the very workings of power ... agency is implicated in what it opposes."[10]

I have grown a bit weary of this sort of claim. Admittedly, it acquires much of *its* own power in the context of those who would deny the insight—individuals committed to a certain version of a bourgeois liberal subject. But I believe one could concede the claim that opposition to power is implicated in the very workings of power without giving up too much or taking on the rather burdensome view of language Butler's position presupposes. Pragmatists, particularly Deweyan pragmatists, do not hold the view that a rational agent exists apart from experience. In fact, we have traded in a conception of rationality for that of intelligence, which involves directed attempts to secure certain aims and to avoid others. We understand that the goods we seek take on significance for us in light of the particular demands of our environment. Experience, rightly understood, avoids, then, the traps that a position like Butler's aims to rectify.

By my pragmatist lights, giving priority to experience signals a conception of agency profoundly implicated in the vicissitudes of life. Experienced situations are of two types: some take place with a minimum of regulation and foresight; others occur, in part, as the result of intelligent action. Both types are "had, undergone, enjoyed or suffered," but they are distinguishable to the degree that the former reflect the dispensation of fortune or providence, while the latter constitute "the funded outcome of operations." Intelligently guided action, then, reflects our efforts to modify our conditions of living within the context of a particular problem. Here Dewey rejects explicitly the view of mind as a spectator apart from the world, knowing "by means of an equipment of powers complete within itself, and merely exercised upon an antecedent external material equally complete in itself." Instead, we find ourselves in the midst of indefinite interactions in a world that is neither fixed nor complete "but is capable of direction to new and different results through mediation of intentional operations."[11]

For Dewey action is an inherent part of what it means to be an organism transacting with one's environment. But action as such is not necessarily *intelligent.* This requires directed operations performed in the modification of conditions.

> In the end men do what they can do. They refrain from doing what they cannot do. They do what their own specific powers in conjunction with the limitations and resources of the environment permit. The effective control of their powers is not through precepts, but through the regulation of their conditions. If this regulation is to be not merely physical or coercive, but moral, it must consist of the intelligent selection and determination of the environments in which we act.[12]

It is not enough, then, to assert the mere fact of human agency. Rather, we must insist on the necessity of intelligently guided action as we confront a precarious and unstable world. For Dewey, this precariousness—what I referred to in chapter 1 as contingency with tragic implications—is a necessary condition for freedom, in the sense that a world complete and exact offers no place for freedom.

It is important to note that for Dewey the specificity of agency emerges within the particular situation. We have little recourse to preordained characterizations of our actions. Perhaps the problem, at least for those of us who write about African Americans, rests with a view that, whatever the particular situation, always presents agency as politically liberatory. That is to say, we invoke the trope of agency, as Walter Johnson has so brilliantly argued, as a way of defending the humanity of a subject people—as a way of holding off the claim that they were mere pawns in the actions of men.[13] Saidiya Hartman's powerful study of racial subjugation and the formation of African American identity in the nineteenth century demonstrates clearly the problems inherent to such a view.[14] Expressions of black agency during this period, she argues, were in many ways expressions of processes—the products of what Michel

Foucault terms "normalizing discipline"—that reproduced black subjection. African American appeals, for example, to discourses of rights, liberty, and equality only buttressed conceptions of the subject that aided in their domination. Slaves and former slaves were viewed simultaneously as property *and* as persons. As property, they were seen as beasts of burden and treated accordingly. As persons, they were held responsible and culpable for their actions in ways that reinforced their subservience. Both facilitated the terror and violence of black subordination.[15] Hartman's study cautions against any assumption that black agency in this period, whether at the level of everyday practices or in explicit claims for liberal freedom, was necessarily liberatory. In fact, she powerfully demonstrates the claim that African American subject formation and the performance of that subjectivity were always already colored by and implicated in the operations of power it purportedly opposed.

Again, we could concede this claim and still commend a conception of agency that is potentially politically robust, and hold onto the notions of individuality, liberty, and equality that Hartman seemingly wants to dispense with. Her underlying antihumanism and subsequent suspicion of the central tropes of liberalism presuppose a conception of human agents that pragmatists simply reject.[16]

Still, I take Hartman's general point, as well as Scott's and Butler's, seriously: talk of agency (particularly when attributed to groups on the margins of societies) requires a nuanced understanding of the forces that constrain us. Failure to attend to these nuances can easily result in flat descriptions and romantic characterizations of our choices, beliefs, and actions that deny we are both agents and patients. This problem is evidenced quite clearly in the ways some scholars of African American religion have taken up the question of the role of Christianity in the lives of African American slaves.[17] The claim has been that African American Christianity exemplifies the agency of the slave. And of course, it does. The problem is that this agency is often presumed to be oriented toward a liberatory praxis, a view that denies what Saba Mahmood describes as the different modalities of agency.[18]

For Mahmood, the conception of agency is too often theorized within the terms of subversion and resistance, leaving unexamined the various "projects, discourses, and desires" that escape these terms. As she puts it:

> If the ability to effect change in the world and in oneself is historically and culturally specific (both in terms of what constitutes "change" and the means by which it is effected), then the meaning and sense of agency cannot be fixed in advance, but must emerge through an analysis of the particular concepts that enable specific modes of being, responsibility, and effectivity. Viewed in this way, what may appear to be a case of deplorable passivity and docility from a progressivist point of view, may actually be a form of agency—but one that can be understood only from within the

discourses and structures of subordination that create the conditions of its enactment.[19]

Mahmood understands her project as, in some ways, expanding the insights of Judith Butler by avoiding the traps of thinking about agency in solely an agonistic and dualistic way. Instead she seeks to dislodge the notion of agency from a preordained teleology of emancipatory politics—the point of which, I take it, is to open up the possibility of talking about agency in terms of something other than volition and resistance.

What I find particularly useful about Mahmood's account is not her debate with other poststructuralists but, rather, her insistence on detaching agency from progressive politics. Her fundamental claim is that various modalities of action take place under specific conditions that inform, shape, and constrain them. If we focus solely on the interiority of the self, we lose sight of this crucial dimension of the domain of action. Her turn to Aristotle, and Michel Foucault's appropriation of him, seeks to reassert the primacy of actual practices in the formation of dispositions and character. Her aim is not to affirm the universality of virtue ethics but to insist that we think of ethics as local and bound up with determinate techniques and discourses through which highly specific ethical-moral subjects come to be formed.[20]

My reading of Dewey intersects with Mahmood's account. Dewey's view that agency emerges within particular situations allows for different modalities of agency and opens up space for the analysis of the kinds of religious practices that escape the rather narrow terms of submission and resistance. To attribute to agency a specified form and content prior to the actual experiences is to abjure the active work individuals do in intelligently transforming situations.[21] Such a view blinds us of the need to commend, on occasion, a certain form of action to our fellows, because we presume that it is already instantiated. More specifically, the insistence of linking black agency to a form of emancipatory politics has often blocked the way to a more nuanced understanding of the role and function of African American Christianity in the context of slavery. The result has flattened the description of the complexity of African American religious life as well as the existential dilemmas African American individuals have faced.

Ira Berlin and the Place of African American Christianity

In *Generations of Captivity,* Ira Berlin offers, among other things, a striking account of the transformation of American slavery during the nineteenth century. With his typical acuity, Berlin describes the changes wrought during this period, what he calls the migration generation, which fundamentally reoriented master and slave and signaled, yet again, the dynamism of the peculiar institution. Against the backdrop of the continued development of the nation-state, the emergence of new labor disciplines associated with the ascendance of cotton, and the terror of the domestic trafficking of black bodies, African

American slaves (and free persons) found existential resources to negotiate the horrors of their enslavement and subordination.

Berlin argues that the transformation of American slavery unleashed during the Age of Revolution was greatly accelerated between 1810 and 1861. In particular, the domestic slave trade resulted in the massive transfer of black bodies across the continent and the consolidation of the plantation revolution. What Berlin refers to as the "Second Middle Passage" involved the forced movement of well over a million black slaves, driven by the cotton and sugar revolutions in the southern interior that would eventuate in powerful slave societies.[22] That these events would fundamentally shape American society does not go unremarked: slaveholding interests would eventually come to dominate America's body politic. But perhaps more importantly, this forced movement disrupted forms of social organization that had developed among slaves and produced a distinctive discourse about them. Families were split apart. Men and women were sold with little regard to networks of care forged under the earlier kind of labor discipline. Black slaves were forced to march, chained one to the other, to a more brutal form of enslavement. And those involved in the trade generated a vocabulary for talking, representing, and thinking about the bodies sold. As Berlin notes:

> The internal slave trade became the largest enterprise in the South outside of the plantation itself, and probably the most advanced in its employment of modern transportation, finance, and publicity. It developed its own language: prime hands, bucks, breeding wenches, and fancy girls. Its routes, running counter to the freedom trails that fugitive slaves followed north, were similarly dotted by safe houses—pens, jails, and yards that provided resting places for slave traders as well as temporary warehouses for slaves. In all, the slave trade, with its hubs and regional centers, its spurs and circuits, reached into every cranny of southern society. Few

southerners, white or black, were untouched.[23]

In this view, the Second Middle Passage was a constitutive element of an emergent regime of truth central to the migration generation—that is, a way of talking, thinking, and representing that organized and regulated relations of power between masters and slaves, slaveholders and nonslaveholders.

What is striking about Berlin's account is the way he figures slaves as simultaneously the objects of physical and discursive violence *and* as progenitors of ways of thinking that eventually play a role in undermining the effectiveness of that violence. To be sure, the Second Middle Passage was a wretched experience. A profound sense of degradation and desperation attended those snatched from their love ones. But Berlin goes to great lengths to show that the domestic slave trade was also a site for the production of new forms of solidarity. "Many who survived the transcontinental trek formed strong bonds of friendship akin to those forged by shipmates on the voyage across the Atlantic. Indeed the

Second Middle Passage itself became a site for remaking African American society."[24] This solidarity took shape not only in the efforts to forge new family units (even as memories of loved ones and life on the seaboard persisted) but also in the communion made possible by Christian fellowship.

The latter point highlights an interesting convergence: at the very moment African Americans were subjected to the disrupting discipline of the Second Middle Passage they converted in large numbers to Christianity. How are we to account for this? Berlin suggests that "the trauma of the Second Middle Passage and the cotton revolution sensitized transplanted slaves to the evangelicals' message." Displaced men and women were eager to find existential resources to forge a new way of being-in-the-world in light of the prevailing conditions. Berlin goes on to claim that "responding to the evangelical message, they found new meaning in the emotional deliverance of conversion and the baptismal rituals of the church. In turning their lives over to Christ, the deportees took control of their destiny."[25] In other words, slaves' sense of themselves (perhaps as moral agents), fashioned within a particular form of life, was shattered when the institutional moorings of that life were removed as a result of the Second Middle Passage. Slaves then drew on new languages to orient themselves to the brutal realities of their conditions of living, and Christianity, in Berlin's view, offered such a language. The suggestion is that what would become an organized religious life originated as a means by which a coherent social life could be structured by slaves in the southern interior.

This is indeed a provocative thesis. But, of course, the process of African American conversion brings into view another dimension of the transition faced by the migration generation: the changing nature of the religious landscape and its relation to the institution of slavery. If we are to take seriously the importance of African American Christianity to the migration generation, we need to account more fully for the context and religious meaning of their conversion (and, perhaps, for how the Second Middle Passage fits within these broader processes).

We know that early efforts to convert African slaves to Christianity often failed. Many of the slaves simply did not speak English well enough to understand Christian instruction. Moreover, slaveholders often resisted missionary efforts, fearing that Christianity would undermine the very practice of slavery. Peter Kalm, a Swedish traveler to America in the late 1740s, captured this fear:

It is likewise greatly to be pitied, that the masters of these negroes in most of the English colonies take little care of their spiritual welfare, and let them live on in their Pagan darkness. There are even some, who would we be very ill pleased at, and would by all means hinder their negroes from being instructed in the doctrines of Christianity; to this they are partly led by the conceit of its being shameful, to have a spiritual brother or sister among so despicable a people; partly by thinking that they should not be able to keep their negroes so meanly afterwards; and partly through fear of the negroes growing too proud, on seeing themselves upon a level with their masters in religious matters.[26]

It must be noted as well that many slaves rejected Christianity out of hand as the religion of those who held them in bondage. One would be hard pressed not to recognize the hypocrisy of slaveholders and clergy who embraced Christian doctrine while, as was sometimes the case in South Carolina, requiring slaves to take an oath before being baptized:

You declare in the presence of God and before this Congregation that you do not ask for the holy baptism out of any design to free yourself from the Duty and Obedience that you owe to your Master while you live, but merely for the good of Your Soul and to partake of the Graces and Blessings promised to the members of the Church of Jesus Christ.[27]

African Americans converted to Christianity in significant numbers during the so-called Great Revivals of the eighteenth and early nineteenth centuries. These gatherings emphasized individual experience, ecstatic worship, and a belief that all were equal before God. The revivals constituted the primary vehicles by which everyday, ordinary individuals reshaped Christianity in the image of the common folk: religious leaders were to be unpretentious; the experience of God's grace was declared to be available to anyone, without mediation; religious instruction was to avoid obscurantism; and churches were placed in the hands of those who attended them. One of the distinctive features of the revolutionary generation was thus the democratization of the emerging nation's religious life, which resulted in a fascinating fragmentation of the religious landscape.[28]

During this period we find an explosion of popular religious formations informed by the democratic ethos of Jeffersonian and Jacksonian political movements, as well as by millennialist traditions.[29] African American conversion to Christianity takes place within this reconfiguring of American religious life and must be seen within this broader pattern if we are to understand how it "riffs" on the gaps and excesses of the so-called democratization of Christianity. Indeed, African Americans found themselves in these revivals, sitting alongside white Christians, enraptured by the power of God's word and the immediate experience of his presence.

To be sure, this emphasis on immediate experience, the resemblances of worship services to African forms of religious expression, the licensing of black preachers, and the initial condemnation of slavery by Baptists and Methodist resulted in the conversion of large numbers of African Americans.[30]

The Methodist General Conferences of clergy and lay leaders strongly condemned slavery in 1780, 1783, and 1784. They prohibited their ministers from owning slaves and eventually extended that prohibition to the membership in general. The Methodist conference of 1787 urged preachers to work diligently on behalf of African Americans, "for the spiritual benefit and salvation of the negroes." The General Committee of Virginia Baptists also condemned slavery in 1789 "as a violent deprivation of the rights of nature."[31] But the egalitarian impulses of the revolutionary era soon gave way to the logic of the plantation. As these once marginal religious formations became more mainstream, they fractured over the issue of slavery, foreshadowing what would happen to the nation in 1861.[32] Ironically, then, at the very moment when African Americans forged a distinctive Christian witness, many evangelical, white Christians revealed what Kenneth Burke has called a "trained incapacity"[33] and failed to address the contradictions between slavery and their commitment to a democratized faith. Nevertheless, the context of African American conversion must be read in terms of the broader efforts by ordinary religious folk to rend the gospel from the hands of Anglican overseers.

The horizon within which African Americans engaged in this work, of course, was that of slavery and racial proscription. In the southern interior, black Christianity took the form of the invisible institution. On the southern seaboard, black religious expression was more visible but constantly policed by a fearful white gaze. In the North, we begin to see independent black denominations, a material indication of their communities' maturation. In each instance, a generalizable understanding of Christianity was voiced. African Americans, particularly those in bondage, found in the Christian gospel as it was preached during the Great Revivals liberating possibilities—both in their personal experiences of conversion and in a vocabulary that enabled them to escape the psychical effects of slavery. Many Christian slaves came to see themselves as a unique—even a chosen—people with a particular moral sense, capable, thanks to their distinctive relationship to God, of distinguishing intuitively the wrongness of slavery and racial discrimination and the rightness of their common complaint. This connection with God allowed them to step outside of the master-slave relationship, which defined them as a mere extensions of a white master's will, and to see themselves as self-determining agents.

To tell the story of the development of African American Christianity is, in some significant sense, to tell the history of American religion. Throughout this period, it remained ambivalently, yet intimately, connected to white America. The ambivalence flowed from the marginal status of African Americans—the fact that their invocations of democracy and Christianity were shadowed by the spectre of slavery and white supremacy. Given this context, the appropriation of Christianity was both enabling and an accommodation in its political outlook. It made possible a critical insurgent politics but also contained the more radical possibilities of that politics.[34]

I mention this not only to qualify my description of African American Christianity during this period, but also to trouble an invocation of slave religion as an unproblematic example of black negotiation of the totalizing system of slavery. Obviously, I concede to Berlin the significance of African American Christianity to this period of slavery. But Berlin does not quite show us *how* the embrace of Christian doctrine might have substantively aided the slave in negotiating her subordination. What is it about slave religion that enables us to read it as a resource for the slave—as an act of agency on the part of the perceived heteronomous subject? I have attempted in the last few pages to gesture toward a possible answer, but much more needs to be said. As it stands, neither an assertion of the fact of black Christianity nor an assertion of its existential and political implications can escape the reading offered by someone like Orlando Patterson.

In Patterson's view, "The slaves found in fundamentalist Christianity paths to the satisfaction of their own needs, creating the strong commitment to Christianity that has persisted to this day." They created an institution that offered "release and relief" from the horrors of slavery. But Patterson goes on to emphasize

> that the religion they experienced was the same as their

masters' in all its essential doctrines and cultic aspects, that while the spirituals they sang may have had a double meaning with secular implications, it is grossly distorting of the historical facts to claim that they were covertly revolutionary in their intent; and, most important of all, it is irresponsible to deny that however well religion may have served the slaves, in the final analysis it did entail a form of accommodation to the system.[35]

In the end, Patterson argues, slave religion fortified the domination inherent in the relationship between masters and slaves. No *fundamental* adjustment was made in that relation as a result of conversion. In fact, one might go as far as to say that the "release and relief" from the agonies of slavery and the modicum of dignity before God and each other that conversion made possible worked to solidify the slave's accommodation to the new labor discipline of the southern interior.

Patterson argues here against a certain historiography addressing the reach of African American agency. Many historians of the sixties and seventies rejected the claims of the likes of U. B. Phillips, Kenneth Stamp, and Stanley Elkins and sought to demonstrate that the slave was not a "prepolitical" or simply a "sambo." Slaves created, in fact, relatively autonomous lives. And the agency inherent in those efforts was often read in *political* terms—hence Patterson's reference to the so-called revolutionary implications of slave conversion.

For Berlin, *negotiation* is the key word; slaves, he indicates, were not passive objects. I am not suggesting that his invocation of the slave's agency constitutes a claim for the revolutionary implications of slave religion. But I take it that he means something much stronger than that slaves adjusted and adapted to the changing realities of their conditions. Let me quote at length a passage from the introduction to *Generations of Captivity:*

> Slaveholders severely circumscribed the lives of enslaved people, but they never fully defined them. The slaves' history—like all human history—was made not only

by what was done to them but also by what they did for themselves.... All of which is to say that slavery, though originally imposed and maintained by violence, was negotiated. Although disfranchised, slaves were not politically inert, and their politics—even absent an independent institutional basis—was as active as any. The ongoing context forced slaveowners and slaves, even as they confronted one another as deadly enemies, to concede a degree of legitimacy to their opponent. No matter how reluctantly given—or, more likely, extracted—such concessions were difficult for either party to acknowledge. Masters presumed their own absolute sovereignty, and slaves never relinquished the right to control their own destiny. But no matter how adamant the denials, nearly every interaction of master and slave forced such recognition, for the web of interconnections necessitated a coexistence that fostered grudging cooperation as well as open contestation.[36]

Slavery was not only a relation defined by violent, coercive power. It was also a hegemonic relation—echoing Eugene Genovese here—in which the consent of the dominated was constantly won and rewon. Or, as Berlin puts it, "The ongoing context forced the slaveowner and the slave ... *to concede a degree of legitimacy to their opponent."* Such a formulation opens up space for a wider (and more plausible) account of the experiences of the slave that make the interface of slaveholder and slave an inevitable site of ideological contestation. To be sure, domination is reproduced—but always under varying and transforming conditions. The underlying assumptions of Patterson's view simply miss this point altogether.[37] Berlin *can,* then, posit *the fact* of African American Christianity as a consequence of ideological contestation and not merely as an accommodation to slavery. The question remains, however, in what way this was the case, and how can we avoid the trap of linking the slaves' effort to a preordained teleology of emancipatory politics. Albert Raboteau's

Slave Religion gestures toward an answer.

African American Conversion and Slave Religion

Raboteau's pathbreaking study of slave religion still stands as the definitive work on the subject. The text opens with three quotations, each providing a key insight into the overall intent of the book:

It is our duty to proceed from what is near to what is distant, from what is known to that which is known to that which is less known, to gather the traditions from those who have reported them, to correct them as much as possible and to leave the rest as it is, in order to make our work help anyone who seeks truth and loves wisdom.

ABU'L-RAYHAN MUHAMMAD AL-BIRUNI
(973–1050)

Lord! Lord! Baby, I hope yo' young fo'ks will never know what slavery is, an' will never suffer as yo' foreparents. O God! God! I'm livin' to tel' de tale to yo', honey. Yes, Jesus, yo've spared me.

MINNIE FULKES, FORMER SLAVE

We are bound to search the intelligible actions of men, for some indications of their inner significance.

THOMAS MERTON

With each quotation, Raboteau announces that his study is, in some significant sense, an act of piety, a demonstration of his indebtedness to the sources of his being. He aims to acknowledge this by providing space for the slaves to "speak their truths," in part by making extensive use of slave narratives throughout the text. Minnie Fulkes's statement, for example, in referring to the horror of slavery and to passing on the story, alerts the reader to the fact that the book will present something more than a dispassionate detailing of the facts of slave religion. Indeed, much more is at stake here. I want to suggest that *Slave Religion* is not merely a historical account of the evolution of Christianity among African Americans. A theological argument is embedded in the historical details (the Merton quotation is an important clue to this dimension of the book).

Raboteau makes the case implicitly throughout the text that we ought to regard these Christian slaves as akin to the early Christians: that their earnest articulations of their faith in God under captive conditions offer a profound example of Christian witness. Moreover, as the Merton quotation suggests, the reader is urged to witness the significance of God's power and grace in the lives of these subject peoples. If Raboteau is indeed concerned with making visible the agency of those rendered invisible, that agency is always mediated by a divine agency.

In this sense, Raboteau takes up in 1978 the sort of concerns that later animated Amy Hollywood's brilliant essay "Gender, Agency, and the Divine in Religious Historiography."[38]

Hollywood struggles with how to write histories of medieval Christian women who produced religious writings and claimed to receive their authority directly from God. Expressing a concern that recalls Mahmood's, she questions how historians might square the driving force behind much of subaltern histories—a preoccupation with agency and authority—with the attribution of deeds to a supernatural agency. In short, what do we, as historians, make of God talk in our stories? Hollywood finds resources to tackle this concern in Dipesh Chakrabarty but, at the conclusion of her essay, poses some profound questions that, I believe, Raboteau had answered in his history of slave religion: "Should we assume that agency, as understood within secular historiography, is the only way in which to think about politics (either in the past or in the present)? ... If it is not, what happens to the very demand to make the other an agent of history that dominates the projects of subaltern and feminist history themselves?"[39] Raboteau answers the former question with a resounding no, demonstrating that the lives of Christian slaves often seep beyond the boundaries of politics, narrowly construed, that so often dominate subaltern histories.

Raboteau's account of conversion and its "inner significance" for the slave provides the beginning of an answer to the question I posed earlier to Berlin. Raboteau recounts a notion of "spiritual agency" among the slaves that opened up space for the possible articulation of freedom. This spiritual agency was not reducible to political realities (although it certainly affected them), but was bound up with the insight of those eighteenth- and nineteenth-century evangelicals who insisted that God's presence was "capillary": his spirit flowed throughout the entire body of the believer, reorienting her to the world and to herself.

In the chapter "Catechesis and Conversion," Raboteau details the difficulties and challenges faced by white missionaries in their efforts to convert the slaves to Christianity. I have already mentioned some of those challenges. What is interesting, however, is what resulted from the eventual success of their efforts. Raboteau writes:

> Catechesis moved in two directions. The slaves were taught the prayers, doctrines, and rites of Christianity, but as the missionaries realized, the slaves had to somehow understand the meaning of Christian belief and ritual if instruction was to become more than mere parroting. And here the whites had limited control. For the slaves brought their cultural past to the task of translating and interpreting the doctrinal words and ritual gestures of Christianity. Therefore the meaning which the missionary wished the slaves to receive and the meaning which the slaves actually found (or, better, made) were not the same.[40]

On the one hand, the gap between the intended meaning of the utterance and its reception became a space for innovation and creative play. An indeterminacy marked the missionary enterprise and was essential to the appropriation and potential subversion of dominant interpretations of the gospel.[41] On the other hand, the trained incapacity of many white Christians to distinguish their commitment to the gospel from their commitment to white supremacy meant that they turned to the gospel for the resources for rebuke, refutation, and reclamation. The rest of Raboteau's book proceeds on the basis of this delineation: the heresy of white Christianity and the efforts on the part of the slave to reclaim, as Howard Thurman noted, the religion profaned in his midst. The effort of reclamation was made possible by the very nature of Protestant evangelicalism:

It was in the nature of Protestant evangelicalism to de-emphasize the role of mediations between person and God.... At the core of this piety was the Reformation insight that salvation was based not on external observances and personal merit, nor on the intercession of church and clergy but on the relationship of the individual to the sovereign will of God. With this view of the religious life the person inevitably turned inward and searched his or her own heart to discern the work of God's spirit there.[42]

Obviously, the experience of conversion held tremendous implications for the life of the slave. The slave was made anew, transformed by the reordering presence of God. Her embrace of Christianity then reflected a fundamental transformation of the spirit. As a result, God's presence in the slaves' lives, Raboteau would have us believe, short-circuited the ultimate power of the master-slave relationship. The slave was now beholden to a master who was no respector of persons. This insight informs Raboteau's effort to disrupt an account of slave agency as necessarily a political act. Raboteau's use of the example of a slave known as Praying Jacob illustrates the power of the slaves' spiritual agency.

[Praying Jacob] was a slave in the state of Maryland. His master was very cruel to his slaves. Jacob's rule was to Pray three times a day, at just such an hour of the day; no matter what work was or where he might be, he would stop and go and pray. His master has been to him and point his gun at him, and told him if he did not cease praying he would blow out his brains. Jacob would finish his prayer and then tell his master to shoot in welcome—your loss will be my gain—I have two masters, one on earth and one in heaven—master Jesus in heaven, and master Saunders on earth. I have a soul and a body; the body belongs to you, master Saunders, and the soul to Jesus.[43]

Praying Jacob's power derived from a supernatural concern that led him to extol a kind of independence from his master. Otherworldliness precipitated a form of rebelliousness, but that agency was bound up with submission to divine agency. Such a formulation runs counter to the efforts of many black liberation theologians to render the power of African American Christianity in principally political terms.[44]

The conversion experience equipped the slaves with the resources to imagine themselves as agents in the world. That is to say, the reordering presence of God in the lives of Christian slaves made possible a sense of individual and communal value that rejected the dehumanizing effects of slavery. Material representations of this sense of self—in the form of prayer meetings, sermons, and song—provided the existential armor to endure the terror of slavery. Raboteau's answer to the question about how the embrace of Christian doctrine substantively aided the slave thus involves an exploration (and an interpretation) of the theological innovations of African American Christianity, not so much to ascertain the truth-value of its claims as to examine the way such beliefs and practices informed the lives of those who held and engaged with them.

But there is another dimension to this account. Raboteau believes that the conversion of the slave made possible momentary breakthroughs between slave and slave owner. Here *a common grammar of faith* emerged that often challenged, in spiritual if not necessarily political terms, the slave regime of truth. The example of the slave Morte demonstrates the potential power of this grammar of faith. After recounting his conversion experience, Morte brings his master to tears and subsequently preaches to him and his family. Raboteau writes of this moment:

> Unfortunately, we don't know what Morte thought about the significance of his power, spiritual and momentary though it may have been, over his master. Nor do we know what his fellow slaves thought when they saw Morte breaking up the rocky ground of the white folks' hearts. However, the spectacle of a slave reducing his master and his master's family and friends to tears by preaching to them of their enslavement to sin certainly suggests that despite the iron rule of slavery, religion could bend human relationships into some interesting shapes.[45]

The reference to "iron rule" and to openings within it takes us to the heart of one of the main concerns of this chapter. For Raboteau, African American conversion, rightly understood, resists reduction to structural determination.

To make this claim forcefully, however, requires that we take seriously the religious meanings of the experiences themselves. We could certainly raise questions about Raboteau's descriptive reductionism and whether his account actually provides an adequate explanation of the slaves' experiences. But for the limited purposes of this chapter, I am content to insist, with him, that closer attention be given to the "religion" of the slave—in part, because such attention will disrupt the stale dualisms of domination and resistance (and, perhaps, signification and resignification) that inform accounts of agency in general and implicitly guide descriptions of slave agency in particular. Moreover, it might also result in more nuanced accounts of African American religious experiences.

My general aim in this chapter has been to insist on the complexity of African American religious life and to resist naïve attempts to reduce that complexity to an easily manageable political reality—a tendency that is, I believe, typical of this country's melodramatic approach to the problems of race. I am of the firm belief that appeals to a fixed and stable notion of black identity, to a conception of history as a storehouse stocked with answers to all of our problems, or appeals to an idea of black agency that presumes our inclination to resist limit our imaginations and in various ways blunt our capacity to modify our conditions of living, precisely because each denies the active work we do in the face of problematic situations. Such appeals too often direct our attention to antecedent and not consequent phenomena. They seek to tame the potential chaos of contingency but end up obscuring the moral imperative that we act intelligently and earn our deaths by passionately embracing the conundrum of life. In short, bad thinking about African American history, identity, and agency compromises what James Baldwin referred to as all of that beauty—those funded experiences, colored in a dark shade of blue, that enable us to invade the future with a bit more than luck.

5

Explicating Black Nationalism

We seek psychic security from within our inherited divisions ... while gazing out upon our fellows with a mixed attitude of fear, suspicion and terror. We repress an underlying anxiety aroused by the awareness that we are representative not only of one but of several overlapping and constantly shifting categories, and we stress our affiliation with that segment of the corporate culture which has emerged out of our parent's past—racial, cultural, religion—and which we assume, on the basis of such magical talismans as our mother's milk or father's beard, that we "know."

RALPH ELLISON, *Going to the Territory* l

> An identity would seem to be arrived at by the way in which the person faces and uses his experience.
>
> JAMES BALDWIN, *No Name in the Street*

I have reached a point in my argument where I must address explicitly the nationalist politics of the black power era. I do so not with the intent of bashing the shortcomings of black nationalism during the 1960s and 1970s. I do not hold the view, for example, that the black power era represents a moment of decline in the black freedom struggle, where the powerful and persuasive moral claims of Martin Luther King Jr. gave way to the polemics of violence. The works of Robin D.G. Kelley, Nikhil Singh, Timothy Tyson, and a host of others have provided a different periodization of the black freedom struggle, which complicates this narrative by locating the tendencies of black power in earlier periods.[1] Tyson, for example, points to the efforts of Robert Williams, president of the Monroe, North Carolina, chapter of the NAACP, whose rhetoric of self-defense and self-determination in the early 1950s reveal how such sentiments informed African American political struggle long before Stokely Carmichael's fateful "Black power" cry in 1966.

I do hold the view, however, that much of the politics of the black power era was premised on problematic conceptions of black identity, history, and agency such as I have addressed in the previous chapters. In chapter 4, for example, I sought to trouble conceptions of black agency that presuppose a teleology of emancipatory politics. My aim was not to deny the notion of black agency but to insist, given my pragmatic commitments, that agency be viewed as an emergent property of particular situations. We ought not to offer a phenomenology of black agency as inclined, in advance of the contexts within which it is exercised, to resist oppression and to seek freedom. To do so narrows, often in the name of unspecified ideological commitments, our descriptions of what African Americans actually do. This is particularly relevant for characterizations of African American religious life.

I made this point about description explicit in my earlier discussions of black identity and history. In each instance, I invoked specific political formulations associated with some variant of black nationalist politics as examples of bad ways of thinking about political and moral matters. Black identity, I argued, should not be thought of as the findings of an archeological project aimed at discovering, once and for all, who we really are. And African American history should not be viewed as a reservoir of meanings that singularly and prior to individual experience determines who we are and provides us with the tools to become who we are destined to be. These formulations, I maintained, amount to what can be called black quests for certainty detached from the messy realities of African Americans' actual beliefs, choices, and actions. Such seeming certainty often entails a crude reduction of the moral complexity of the moral lives of African Americans and an attachment to one value to the exclusion of others. In other words, black quests for certainty too often deny the lessons of tragedy and produce melodramatic politics.

But some attention needs to be paid to what we mean when we describe the nationalist politics of the black power era, for those descriptions often impede a fuller understanding of African American political behavior. To be sure, black nationalism remains a hotly contested concept. We all know that the nationalist politics of black power suggest a form of militancy that is somehow different from sit-ins or marches. Some of us associate the phrase with violence, remembering H. Rap Brown's ominous call: "Burn, baby, burn!" Others equate black nationalism with some form of separatism or view it simply as a counter to integration. Those of us who abhor violence and valorize the courage of those who participated in the sit-ins and marches vehemently disagree with a certain kind of militancy. And not a few of us reject outright the idea of leaving the United States: we are American citizens and America is our home.

Important issues are often obscured in the course of these debates. One might wonder, given the heated nature of the exchanges, whether the interlocutors are even discussing the same subject. Certainly, most African Americans, regardless of their political orientation, work within a long tradition concerned with the nature of racism. And the controversies are all limited by the historical conditions in which African Americans live. But the ambiguity and disparate careers of the words that inform these exchanges, along with the lack of attention to those careers and ambiguity, tend to obscure the nature of the disagreements. In many cases, a preoccupation with the term *black nationalism* diverts attention from the questions at hand and narrows the debate to an exchange about labels. Typically when a person describes herself as a black nationalist she announces in effect that the political stakes (and temperature) of the conversation have been significantly raised. Hostile debates result, but not substantive dialogue.

My aim in this chapter is quite limited. Attention is given to two related ways in which present discussions about the nationalist politics of the black power era obscure the complex motivations, meanings and outcomes of this historical period and blind us to the ways in which this complexity influences how we live our lives and talk about racial matters today. First, I argue that much more careful thought needs to be given to how we define black nationalism. How do we distinguish between black nationalism and its siblings? What are its essential features, and how should the phrase be used? In many cases, I would say, the term simply gets in the way and distracts from adequate accounts of the way many African Americans have responded to their conditions of living. Second, I argue that most studies of the politics of this period have confused descriptive and normative claims. Agreement or disagreement with black nationalisms shapes descriptions of the political project and results too often in either a celebratory embrace of a particular ideology or a hypercritical account of its politics. Both of these issues, the problem of definition and problem of valuation, are dimensions of the broader problem of description. Both block the way to vivid description of the actions and events that comprise the black power era.

I intend to show that the problems of description outlined here are best avoided by my pragmatic approach, which accomplishes several things: (1) It evades the definitional problematic through explication by elimination, replacing the phrase "black nationalism" and instead assessing critically the practices with which it has been associated. (2) It addresses the problem of valuation by treating "black power" as a shorthand for a number of political formations with different and often competing conceptions of the good. And (3) it promotes intellectual instrumentalities that can better equip us to understand and respond to contemporary issues of race and racism in the United States.[2] Geertzian thick description is required if we are to understand this persistent form of black political activity and its relevance to our current moment.[3] Many scholars are now undertaking just this kind of work.[4] I add my *pragmatic* voice to theirs in an effort to disrupt the easy shorthand that bad thinking about black identity, history, and agency can be attributed to the bad politics of black power. Such labels do little to clarify the political judgments and choices of African Americans; explication by elimination, as I will show, reveals a much more interesting political landscape. My task, then, is simply to clear a bit of the theoretical underbrush in order to aid this descriptive work and to open up space for more innovative forms of black political engagement in the twenty-first century.

The Problem of Definition

How do we identify a black nationalist? One need only glance at a few anthologies about black nationalism to notice that the label has been applied to political projects and personalities with varying aims and ends. Scholars have attempted to capture this diversity by describing particular projects as revolutionary, cultural, religious, educational, strong, weak, and so on. But the first question is still how we decide who or what is nationalist. One possible point of departure can be found in the claim that black nationalism "put[s] the discourses of race and nation together, by projecting an imagined community—a people—for whom blackness serves as an emblem."[5] This view assumes that there is something all black people share as black people. But there are any number of ways in which to think about this basic assumption.

Some definitions of black nationalism, for example, posit a biological basis for national belonging. Here, the word *nation* points to a common biological or ontological essence among black people. Drawing an analogy with a biological organism, this view sees the nation as the essential unit in which the black individual's nature is fully realized. Another view holds that the character of a nation is environmentally determined: that there is something about a people's place of origin that determines the essential features of the nation. Still other views invoke the phrase to refer to a community with shared ends or aspirations. These ends may vary: some communities may seek recognition as sovereign political units; others desire some form of self-determination, control over community resources, or, perhaps, a return to a place of origin. These views may also overlap. They range from a kind of piety—a recognition of sources upon which the existence of black people depends—to a means for imagining a future toward which black people aspire.[6] And any of these views of black nationalism can be thought of in economic, political, and cultural terms.

Let me offer an example of this particular problem of definition. Wilson J. Moses, one of the more insightful scholars of black nationalism in the United States, defines black nationalism according to established criteria for defining nationalisms generally. He argues in the introduction to *Classical Black Nationalism: From the American Revolution to Marcus Garvey* that black nationalism in the period between 1850 and 1925 "may be defined as the effort of African Americans to create a sovereign nation-state and formulate an ideological basis for a concept of a national culture."[7] Attempts to define black nationalism as simply the development of sentiments of unity among peoples of African descent in the United States will fail, he maintains, precisely because such views are too broad to be meaningful. Rather, "The essential feature of classical black nationalism is its goal of creating a black nation-state or empire with absolute control over a specific geographical territory, and sufficient economic and military power to defend it."[8]

Moses provides what might be called a *strict* definition of black nationalism. For a political practice to be appropriately described as an example of black nationalism, it must meet, in his view, certain necessary and sufficient conditions. The goal of possessing a sovereign state, for example, is a sufficient condition, a position consistent with standard accounts of European nationalism. This goal might presuppose a particular conception of the racial self in which group members presume a common history, beliefs, and kinship that substantiate their claim to constitute a separate and distinct people entitled to possession of a self-governing state. In fact, Moses deems this second point a distinctive feature of nationalisms in general. The idea of the nation-state, in his view, cloaks a more sinister notion of racial consanguinity, a belief in and "a commitment to the conservation of racial or genetic purity, a myth of commonality and purity of blood. The nation is seen as an organic segment of humanity, and like the family, an ordinance of God, whose members own a common ancestry and ties of ethnic kinship."[9] The most sinister feature of black nationalism, then, and Moses believes this is true of every instance of nationalism, lies precisely in the concept of the racial self.

But I take it that a number of political efforts during the black power era—efforts that have been described as nationalist—would fall outside of Moses's definition. The Black Panther

Party, for example, even in its earliest formulations did not view its emancipatory efforts in terms of an embrace of and an effort to preserve some essentialized black identity nor did it argue for a separate, sovereign state. Indeed, one need only take a cursory glance at *Black Power,* the classic book by Kwame Ture (Stokely Carmichael) and Charles Hamilton, to get a sense of the narrowness of Moses's definition. To be sure, Ture and Hamilton analogized the plight of African Americans to that of colonized people around the world and, in doing so, assumed the manicheanism of Frantz Fanon's powerful account in *The Wretched of the Earth.* But in the hands of Ture and Hamilton that manicheanism did not result in a call for all-out revolution in pursuit of a sovereign state; instead, they called for a form of interest group politics predicated upon a particular understanding of how groups in the United States compete for scarce resources and benefits. Theirs was a form of pluralistic politics based upon a fundamental transformation in the psychology of African Americans and a particular idea of what constituted political modernization for a subjugated people.

The example demonstrates the limitations inherent in strict definitions of black nationalism. Too often the messiness of the politics (what some may describe as confusion) seeps beyond the boundaries of definitional exactness. What of those elements in the modern Black Convention Movement, for example, that resisted a certain way of thinking about black people, their communities, and their problems? How those differences came to a head in the Gary Convention of 1972 revealed a fractious grouping of nationalists with different conceptions of the good and, I would suggest, different understandings of the utility of appeals to collective identity.[10] Many were self-described nationalist. And we could take them at their word.

In fact, that could be a criterion for distinguishing black nationalism from its siblings. We might identify the project as nationalist if its proponents describe themselves as such. William Van DeBurg offers this approach as a rule of thumb:

Since most people are known primarily by their deeds, if someone looks, speaks, writes, and acts like a nationalist, others may be justified in treating them as such until compelling evidence to the contrary is produced. As is the case with the racial self-identification section on census questionnaires, each of us in a sense *becomes* what we claim to be. Unfortunately, there is no foolproof litmus test for use in nationalist accreditation.[11]

Here Van DeBurg provides what might be called a *loose* definition of black nationalism. This view seeks to evade the definitional problematic by simply assenting to groups' and individuals' self-identification. Surely it is reasonable to assume that only a person committed to the politics of black nationalism would describe himself as a nationalist.

But this too can generate problems, and Van DeBurg acknowledges as much when he states that there is no foolproof test. Certainly people can misdescribe their politics or, worse, engage in self-deception. Imagine someone describing himself as a black nationalist. I take him at his word. But I notice in his behavior that he acts more like a Republican. He voted for George W. Bush and argues vehemently for something called family values. In all that he does in the matter of politics, he appears Republican. Van DeBurg would say that compelling evidence should lead us to conclude that he was simply mistaken. But this presupposes a set of ready-to-hand criteria for identifying the activity of black nationalists—perhaps he means something other than what we assume the term implies. Perhaps it was just an exaggerated expression of his commitment to an antiracist politics. The plurality of groups calling themselves nationalist motivates, in part, the need for a loose definition but also militates against establishing unambiguous criteria.

Let me make this example a bit more concrete. Eugene Rivers, pastor of the Azusa Christian Community and cofounder of the Boston TenPoint Coalition, describes himself as a black nationalist. He is a provocative figure who came to national prominence because of his efforts to respond to gang violence in his local neighborhood and his community empowerment programs. When asked in a 2005 interview what he meant by the term *black nationalism,* Rivers drew on some familiar tropes. "A black nationalist," he maintained, "is someone who is committed to black people as a people and the development and control of institutions that advance the interest of black people primarily although not necessarily exclusively."[12] This formulation presupposes that African Americans are a people and not a race, a distinction that enables him to avoid the trappings of a narrow racial essentialism (he believes race talk is a manifestation of white racist talk) and makes available a number of ways to imagine peoplehood and the attendant obligations.

But when the interviewer asked how he reconciled his self-description as a black nationalist concerned with bettering things for black people with the fact that he has worked closely with the right-wing Bush administration, Rivers offered an unusual response:

Foreign policy. My relationship with white America is a foreign policy question.... Black America has a foreign policy [toward] white America. You don't get it. I'm not joking. This is a black nation for real. That's counterintuitive to you because there's all this black nationalist talk, but no one has really thought through what all these implications really are. I just dropped something on you and it went "Wheeew"[gestures over his head]. I ain't mad. I'll talk to anybody—get the brilliance. Nixon went to China. If Nixon goes to China ... I talk to Bush because I have 35 million people in my country whose interests have to be advocated for.[13]

We may perceive Rivers's behavior (meeting with Bush and supporting the administration's faith-based initiatives) as contrary to our understanding of black nationalism, but he has ready-to-hand a justification consistent with a certain understanding of what black nationalism involves. One could compare his actions, for example, with Marcus Garvey's and Malcolm X's meetings with the KKK. Both justified their actions as being consistent with the interests of black America. Obviously sounding and looking like a black nationalist aren't in themselves sufficient.

We cannot rely simply on self-description, nor can we reduce black nationalism to an essential characteristic. To my mind, the endless variations on the basic themes of black nationalism make it difficult, if not impossible, to say exactly what black nationalism is. And this is not necessarily a bad thing. Too often, scholarly efforts to use a set criterion to distinguish black nationalism from other political ideologies fall into rather ahistorical accounts of messy politics. If the term is to be helpful at all, one must go instead into the thicket of historical description, where the criterion is whether or not the term *black nationalism* "aids us in finding our way around the discursive terrain we occupy, which is partly a matter of knowing how to cope with the ambiguities one is likely to encounter there."[14] In other words, one can set aside the question of whether black nationalism has been correctly defined, and ask instead whether the varied practices singled out by the term are worth debate and investigation.

A Bad Question: What Is Black Nationalism?

In the second lecture of his 1907 book *Pragmatism,* William James describes a heated argument among friends. The dispute centered on a squirrel clinging to one side of a tree and a human being imagined as standing on the tree's opposite side. As the person attempted to catch a glimpse of the squirrel, the animal moved quickly, keeping the tree between them. The question was whether or not, in circling the tree, the person actually goes around the squirrel. The dispute seemed interminable, but James's response is instructive. He writes that it all depends on what is meant by "going round the squirrel." *That* is the crucial question. "You are both right and both wrong," James writes, "according as you conceive the verb 'to go round' in one practical fashion or the other."[15] This example illustrates the pragmatic method, a method of settling what might otherwise seem interminable metaphysical disputes, and it does so by interpreting the relevant issues in light of their respective practical consequences.

I mention James's formulation here only to frame how we might evade the problems of definition that plague accounts of black nationalism. Many proposed definitions aim to settle, once and for all, what black nationalism means. But we know that any number of views can stand in for the meaning of black nationalism. It might prove more useful to take up the actual practices that are identified by the term. We could then explicate the phrase "black nationalism" by elimination. W. V. Quine writes about explication as follows:

> We do not claim synonymy. We do not claim to make clear and explicit what the users of the

unclear expression had unconsciously in mind all along. We do not expose hidden meanings, as the words analysis and explication would suggest; we supply lacks. We fix on the particular functions of the unclear expression that make it worth troubling about, and then devise a substitute, clear and couched in terms to our liking, that fills those functions. Beyond those conditions of partial agreement, dictated by our interests and purposes, any traits of the explicans come under the head of "don't cares."[16]

Explication does not necessarily involve claims about the essence of a term like *black nationalism;* rather, it can be seen as exchanging terms that give us trouble for others that are less troublesome. These sorts of explications, if they are good ones, help us take up familiar accounts that often confuse us and translate them in ways that are better suited to our own aims and ends.[17]

For example, one could say that any group that suffers from the history of oppression that characterizes the African American sojourn in the United States would be preoccupied with protection, recognition, and association—protection from arbitrary and deliberate racial violence, recognition of their humanity in the face of state-sanctioned apartheid, and the comfort and solace of association with those who are similarly situated.[18] Much of what is associated with black nationalism can be thought of as a reflection on these three notions. The question of protection might involve a claim that we should control the legitimate use of force given its illegitimate application in relation to African Americans. The goal might find expression in the desire for a sovereign, independent nationstate or a number of different claims about how best to protect ourselves: by appealing to the moral conscience of our fellow citizens, by holding the state accountable to its stated commitments to principles of justice, by claiming the right of self-defense, or by insisting that those who are subject to violence close ranks and seek security in the form of, for example, insular neighborhoods.

Demands for recognition in light of state-sanctioned apartheid might take the form of broad-based claims to American citizenship or they may take the form of racial pride, insofar as that pride affirms the dignity and humanity of an otherwise degraded people. Similarly, the need of association with others who are subject to racist treatment might lead to formulations concerning the necessity of those associations in the face of racist practices, to unquestioned loyalty to those who face similar treatment, or to arguments instead for the idea of a beloved community bound by solidarity and a commitment to justice.

It seems to me that this approach—tracing the practical effects of particular formulations in light of specific concerns—is more fruitful than pursuing the more general question about the meaning of black nationalism. If appeals to racial solidarity are read as responses to particular practices instead of as necessary features of a theoretical term, then perhaps we might better negotiate the messiness of African American political struggle.

"Theoretical terms," as Jeffrey Stout powerfully states, "should serve interests and purposes, not the other way around. Humpty Dumpty had it right. Explication as elimination is one way to achieve mastery over words that fail to behave when set within a theory. Like the stern principal, we expel the unruly in the hope of facing fewer problems. The only appropriate test is entirely pragmatic."[19]

The Problem of Valuation

The second problem of description involves judgments as to the merits of nationalist politics. This problematic evidences itself in two distinctive tendencies: (1) celebratory accounts and (2) hypercritical accounts. Celebratory accounts, driven by ideological presuppositions associated with black nationalism (in whatever guise), purport to tell the story of 1960s and 1970s radicalism and to demonstrate its relevance for contemporary problems. The works of Molefi Asante and Maulana Karenga stand as examples of this kind of historiography, which celebrates, I believe, uncritically the rise of black consciousness and its particular construction of race-based politics. In contrast, hypercritical accounts begin with a negative valuation of the aims of black nationalist politics (in whatever guise). These works emphasize the limitations of a certain kind of race-based politics, but rarely provide a nuanced account of black power and black nationalism as a complicated historical formation with a number of different strands and political outcomes. In both types of accounts ambiguity as to what actually constitutes black nationalism is lost. Each is an expression of problematic racial reasoning, an unbalanced view of the period—either sentimental or hard-hearted. And this is a bad thing.

I want to focus on hypercritical accounts, however. They seem to have the more insidious effect on our understanding of this crucial historical moment precisely because they often hide under the cover of "objective" analysis and escape characterization as simply ideological defenses of black nationalism. In his book *Amiri Baraka:*

The Politics and Art of a Black Intellectual, for example, Jerry Watts presents a biting account of Amiri Baraka's difficulty, as evidenced throughout his amazing career, in "negotiating an ever-evolving political and intellectual worldview that could simultaneously facilitate tactical political and social thinking, authorize but discipline the articulation of black rage, mediate erratic feelings of estrangement from Black America, and nurture the psychic space necessary for him to realize his creative, artistic talents."[20] A daunting task indeed, but Watts offers an interesting portrait of Baraka's efforts. In his view, Baraka fails miserably, principally because of his crudeness and simplemindedness as a political thinker. In the end, Baraka's politics evinced a disdain for everyday, ordinary people and was, despite its rhetorical flourishes of rage, a politics predicated on white patronage. As Watts writes (with a level of disdain that is worth noting):

> One cannot grasp the limitations of the Baraka-led black nationalist appeals of the 1960s and 1970s

without recognizing that these projects rested on the ability and desire to project a militant black face to a supposedly timid white America and, in doing so, to convince whites and other blacks that black nationalists secretly possessed a serious political game plan and would act on it if not appeased. Image was every thing. Behind all the "hate whitey" rhetoric, Baraka and his colleagues were modern-day black clients in search of white patrons.[21]

This analysis is indebted, of course, to Martin Kilson and Adolph Reed. Both view predominate forms of black nationalism during this period as ideologies of economic and status mobility for aspiring black elites. I do not want to tackle the merits of this claim or the particulars of Watts's account of Baraka's political and artistic achievements. Both are in need of qualification, and I think Komozi Woodward's book, *A Nation within a Nation: Amiri Baraka (Leroi Jones) and Black Power Politics* does much of that work. But what strikes me about Watts's analysis is his synecdochic account of Baraka. Indeed Baraka's black nationalism is made to stand for various nationalist projects of the black power era. Watts's assessment of Baraka's crudeness as a political thinker is thus easily extended to black nationalism generally. For Watts, the black nationalist moment was "mired in parochialism, ethnic/cathartic/therapeutic cheerleading, and sectarianism" and produced relatively little of lasting intellectual and artistic value.[22]

Throughout this account, Baraka's failures are attributed to failures of his political ideology. Black nationalism of whatever sort is simply bad. In fact, Watts notes, "Like all nationalism, black nationalism is predicated on a reified consciousness. In this instance, all blacks are thought to share a collective interest as a result of their blackness."[23] (I am not convinced that only proponents of black nationalism hold this view. It often manifests itself in what can be called black commonsense politics). Watts obviously disagrees with black nationalism, and this disagreement dominates his characterization of a very complicated and messy political moment. His analytical tools simply do not help him to find his way around the discursive terrain he occupies. He sees little ambiguity, simply "bad" ideology. To be sure, one can find the ideological commitments of one's adversary abhorrent, but one should at least attempt to understand those commitments in all their complexity when rendering judgment on their relative merits.

There is no doubt that Baraka's cultural nationalism was hotly contested by proponents of other forms of black nationalist politics. What gets lost in these sorts of caricatures of the moment is the prevalence of ideological contestation among "nationalists" throughout much of the black power era. Some with left-leaning commitments based on a form of black internationalism that emphasized an economic and racial analysis of the plight of black and brown peoples thought that Baraka's early nationalism was nothing but a "pork-chop" nationalist project. One might argue that standard accounts of the black power era too often take up the pork-chop characterization of cultural nationalism to the detriment of a fuller understanding of its political aims and ends. Scot Brown's wonderful book on Karenga's Us movement, *Fighting for Us: Maulana Karenga, the Us Organization and Black Cultural Nationalism,* demonstrates how political so-called culturally minded nationalists were. What gets lost in these crude reductions is how these ideological battles were waged and who won. Accounts like Watts's help hide the debate and contestation, leaving us with exaggerated figures and characterizations of winners that make it appear they were the only players in the game.

At a conference on Baraka at Amherst College I confronted Watts with this particular complaint. I suggested that he needed to complicate his conception of black nationalism during this period, because the aims of Baraka's NewArk project were different from, say, the political objectives of the Revolutionary Action Movement. His retort, in typical Watts fashion, was "Well, those negroes were crazy too!" His response generated a roar of laughter throughout the room. But here, clearly stated, is the problem of valuation: We can say they were crazy, but at least say they were crazy for interestingly different reasons.

Better Descriptions

Emotions tend to run high when discussing the black power era. Wounds still hurt. And some remain highly skeptical of anyone perceived to be trying to police the boundaries of blackness or to deny the significance of blackness in a country fundamentally shaped by white supremacy. What is striking is the extent to which that historical moment continues to exert pressure on contemporary African American politics. When young African Americans these days embrace radical politics they more than likely turn to Malcolm X and his ideological descendants than to Karl Marx. They express a profound pessimism, as Michael Dawson notes, about the legitimacy of American liberalism, and they do so in the name of political and social realities that accord race and racism primacy.[24] In short, one of the enduring legacies of the politics of black power (and this is by no means unique to this historical moment) is a racialized worldview and deep-seated skepticism about America. The skepticism often takes the form of a radical (and some would argue reasonable) distrust of white fellow citizens and a worldview that presumes their fate to be linked with that of other African Americans. The data show that these sentiments continue to inform black political opinion and animate the informal conversational networks—black everyday talk—within which African Americans deliberate about political matters.[25]

We could label much of this, as Dawson and Melissa Harris-Lacewell do, as examples of black nationalist ideology. But I question how productive the label actually is in accounting for political outcomes. Claims about self-determination, unique identity, and nationhood may translate into talk about an all-black political party, a separate nation-state, patronizing black businesses, or controlling black neighborhoods. But the data reveal considerable variation in how African Americans apply these ideas, which are often bound up with distrust of white fellow citizens. The relevant consideration here is arguably not whether we have confirmed the prevalence of black nationalist ideology in black public deliberation but whether we have isolated a key element in determining African American political orientations: trust.[26] We could then avoid the cumbersome task of describing all the different forms of black nationalism (since the term cannot otherwise be defined exactly) and turn our attention to the various ways the notion of trust impacts how African Americans think about protection, recognition, and association. In short, we could exchange the more troublesome term for less troublesome terms.

One way of interpreting the various claims of the Black Panther Party, for example, might involve the relation between ideas about citizenship and trust. The Panthers held the view, rightly or wrongly, that black skin historically marked persons as residing outside the protection of the nation-state and its attendant notions of citizenship. For them, the concept of citizenship in relation to African Americans revealed the profound levels of distrust between a subjugated population and the state: the state could not be trusted to ensure the safety of black communities precisely because its policies reproduced insecurities that defined the conditions of black living. In response, the Panthers powerfully resignified the idea of citizenship by challenging "the state's official performance of itself." Interpreted in this way, the spectacle of the Panthers political performances constitute what Nikhil Singh powerfully describes as "an insurgent form of visibility," which reveals a fundamental and reasonable distrust at the heart of their politics and, at the same time, "a literal-minded and deadly serious guerrilla theatre in which militant sloganeering, bodily display, and spectacular actions simultaneously signified their possession and real lack of power."[27] I am not suggesting here that the term *trust* constitutes *the* way of interpreting the efforts of the Black Panthers and of others who struggled during the black power era. I only want to demonstrate what might come of trading in one term for another.

The problem of valuation blocks the way to this sort of analysis. Too often such accounts presume a single real meaning of the term. Jerry Watts, for example, boldly asserts a definition of black nationalism and on that basis condemns its politics. But a closer examination of the interests attributed to black nationalism and the black power era might very well direct us to fundamental features of black political behavior, features that have been overlooked time and again because of the obfuscating work of categories like black nationalism and integrationism. If our interests and purposes as interpreters of African American life are to acquire a fuller grasp of African Americans' beliefs, choices, and actions, as they most assuredly are, then it is high time to discard the nettlesome approach aimed at delimiting the incredible complexity that define their actual lives.

Conclusion

My intention here has been to open up space for us to see more clearly how the politics of black power has shaped our current ways of talking about race and conceiving racial politics. I see no a priori reason to dismiss that politics as necessarily bad or uninteresting. Instead, I take seriously the fact that from early 1968 to as late as 1975 the various manifestations of black power provided the predominant political languages (and by implication, moral language) through which many young, poor and middle-class African Americans made sense of their lives. These languages involved ideas about identity, history, and agency that require critical examination because, as I have suggested, they inform how we talk about racial matters today. Failure to examine seriously the internal fissures of the period as well as its cultural metaphysics, I believe, constitutes a failure of nerve or, at least, a refusal to look the facts of black America's experiences squarely in the face.

What do we make, for example, of black preachers in our current moment allying themselves with a Republican administration in the name of black nationalism? How do we interpret the various ways nationalist desire has taken on a commodity form, in hip-hop culture and in Hollywood? How do we talk about the practical difference of these political formations in relation to contemporary problems like education, health, criminal justice, and the racial digital divide? All of these questions require, I believe, closer scrutiny of the ambiguities and ambivalences of a period that continues to captivate the political and cultural imaginations of many African Americans. Easy dismissals and caricatures only block the way to such analyses. Interpretation is obviously needed and, to my mind, the troublesome term *black nationalism* gets in the way of such efforts. I have suggested in light of my pragmatic approach that explication by elimination might help—that we ought to trade in the black nationalist label for the actual political behavior signified by the term.

My aim has been quite simple. I urge that we give up the task of stating, once and for all, what black nationalism is. We can indeed set aside the question of whether black nationalism has been correctly defined and ask instead whether the practices singled out by the phrase are worth debate and investigation. We can then set the term aside and proceed with the kind of thick description that will allow us to grasp the historical moment of black power in all of its complexity and, by extension, to describe more fully our own ambiguous inheritance as we face the challenges of the twenty-first century.

6

The Eclipse of a Black Public and the Challenge of a Post-Soul Politics

Have the past struggles succeeded! What has succeeded? yourself? your nation? Nature? Now understand me well—it is provided in the essence of things that from any fruition of success, no matter what, shall come forth something to make a greater struggle necessary.

WALT WHITMAN, *Leaves of Grass*

The old saying that the cure for the ills of democracy is more democracy is not apt if it means that the evils may be remedied by introducing more machinery of the same kind.... But the phrase may also indicate the need of returning to the idea itself, and of employing our sense of its meaning to criticize and remake its political manifestations.

JOHN DEWEY, *The Public and Its Problems*

Do we have to begin consciousness with a battle heroines and heroes like you have already fought and lost leaving us with nothing in our hands except what you have imagined is there?

TONI MORRISON, *Nobel Acceptance Speech*

Ours is a complicated historical moment, marked by enormous progress and by profound setbacks. We have witnessed over the last few decades a rapid expansion of the black middle class, the emergence of African American CEOs of Fortune 500 companies, and the inauguration of an African American woman as president of an Ivy League institution.[1] Moreover, with the appointments of Colin Powell and Condeleezza Rice as secretaries of state, we have even become the face of America to the world, representing our nation's foreign policies to the majority of black and brown peoples around the globe. By some measures, African Americans have finally found their place within mainstream American society. We no longer, some argue, need to retreat to racial enclaves for comfort and security. No longer, they might add, do we need to appeal to race in matters of politics. We have, for the most part, arrived.

But the tremendous progress evident in black America stands alongside the bleak reality that many African Americans have fallen beyond the pale. We have witnessed over the last few decades an expansion of the black "underclass." Large numbers of African American men and women find themselves caught within the intricate networks of the prison industrial complex: from 1954 to the present day the black prison population has grown by 900 percent.[2] Many African American children suffer from the chronic ills that attend growing up in poverty. Black babies, for example, are two and a half times more likely than white infants to die before their first birthday.[3] To be sure, a substantial number of African Americans are caught within a vicious cycle of poverty and violence that betrays any claim that all is well in black America.[4] These realities, some argue, demand continued struggle; we can ill afford to ignore the relevance of race in matters of politics, because America remains fundamentally shaped by white supremacy.

Hurricane Katrina seemingly affirmed the importance of race to American politics. The storm literally washed up and into our field of vision the black poor of New Orleans. Despite its yearly bacchanal, most knew New Orleans was a city deeply in trouble. The hundred thousand residents unable to evacuate the city lurked in the shadows—as the poor often do in such tourist locations—while visitors reveled in the unbridled freedom symbolized by the city. That ostensible freedom, however, obscured the fact that the poverty rate in New Orleans was 23 percent, that in some parishes the average adult income was less than eight thousand dollars a year, that most of these people lived in low-lying areas especially susceptible to flooding, and that the city struggled to breathe under the toxic effects of a not-so-underground drug economy.[5] In other words, we had in New Orleans before Katrina, as in many urban spaces throughout our country, a profound convergence of racial poverty and violence (hyperconcentrated in some areas), which the nation refused to address substantively beyond the standard calls for "getting tough on crime" and building more prisons. The response (or lack of response) to the disaster simply continued a policy of neglect—a willful ignorance about the conditions of living among poor people, especially black and brown poor people, in this country.

What was striking about this moment involved, among other things, the fact that many groped for a language to describe the horrible images they saw. And as they searched what was revealed with remarkable clarity was a startling inability on the part of many people, including black leaders, to avoid the easy trap of thinking about racism solely in terms of intentional prejudice. The structural dimensions of racism that revealed themselves in the very material conditions of poor black New Orleaneans could not be captured in a sound bite or in the traditional language of the civil rights establishment. Nevertheless, the easy formulation was ready at hand. Katrina was evidence of explicit, intentional racism. As Kanye West put it, "George W. Bush doesn't care about black people." Although this is probably true, it is a difficult claim to sustain, and it does not account for the tragedy as a whole.

Katrina revealed that the many challenges confronting black America require an imaginative and immediate shift in our political lexicon—that our traditional "vocabularies of struggle" require recalibration in light of the particular conditions of our current circumstances. This effort goes far beyond the narrow debate between those who would deny or accept the relevance of race to political matters. The question instead is how we address the actual problems African American communities confront, realizing that those communities fracture and fragment in varying ways and along different fault lines. What are our mobilizing tropes in light of this differentiation? How do they inspire us to respond passionately and intelligently to the problems at hand? Of course, these questions require a closer examination of what we mean by "our" and "us"; Katrina, after all, revealed the extraordinary class cleavages among African Americans.

I have tried to show, on pragmatic grounds, that there are ways to imagine "us" without falling into the trap of racial essentialism or succumbing to what Adolph Reed rightly decries as a misguided view of corporate racial interests. My aim has been to turn our attention to the actual "doings and sufferings" of black folk. There we find richly textured experiences that trouble any reductive account of the lives of African Americans. Time and again, appeals to racial identity and unity, or to notions of black history and agency, have masked, often to the detriment of the most vulnerable, the competing interests informing the political and moral choices of African Americans. Competing interests are ignored in favor of a form of racial politics that presumes, dangerously, that black individuals see themselves as *necessarily* in solidarity with other black individuals solely on the basis of race. This assumption, more often than not, results in a form of racial politics that relies heavily on a set of tropes that signal to those willing to listen that black interests, whatever they may be, are in jeopardy. We need only invoke the images of our past, or the many persons who gave their lives in the struggle for black freedom, to orient ourselves appropriately to any political matter. For some, these tropes stand in for democratic deliberation; they, in effect, do our thinking for us. But such invocations blind us to a crucial insight:

that democratic and participatory value must be the cornerstone of credibility for the notion of black politics; group consensus must be constructed through active participation. Even then, it is important to realize that often there will be no universal racial consensus on key issues; that some conflicts derive from irreconcilable material differences. Unity is always on specific terms and in pursuit of specific objectives.[6]

By my pragmatic lights, African American politics, if they are to be genuinely democratic, must, like the nation in general, embrace the full complexity of the racialized experiences of black folk (and not succumb to what I termed in chapter 3 the descriptive, theoretical, and existential problematic). That complexity will give the lie to any facile racial politics that fails to exemplify the black democratic energies necessary for a fundamental transformation in this nation.

In chapter 5, for example, I sought to unsettle a common characterization of the black power era and its attendant politics. For many, "black nationalism" signals a worrisome set of political commitments that requires condemnation, no matter the many ways in which that politics was articulated. This rejection habitually takes the form of a caricature of black nationalists and the era of black power. Such caricatures, however, block the way to a more nuanced understanding of the political choices of African Americans during this historical moment and, perhaps more importantly, conceal the ways that period and its various approaches to African American politics inform our current political choices. The phrase "black nationalism" and the emotions it carries in tow, I argued, get in the way of this sort of analysis.

My intention in this chapter involves an attempt, not so much to chart the various influences of black power on contemporary forms of African American politics, as to encourage a more imaginative and intelligent politics for the twenty-first century. I hold the view, and it is admittedly controversial, that the post-soul generation has lost its way politically, in part because our political imaginations have been captured by the symbolic significance of the black freedom struggle of the 1960s and 1970s. This state of affairs is all the more troubling given that the conditions that shaped and informed this historical period have been fundamentally transformed by the movement's successes.

In making this claim, I rely on John Dewey's account of publics in his book *The Public and Its Problems.* Dewey's view avoids some of the more troublesome aspects of the account of publics in the early work of the contemporary German philosopher Jürgen Habermas.[7] He does not assume, for example, that deliberation in the public sphere requires that we bracket the fact that some of us are wealthy and others are poor; that we are diverse in terms of gender, sexuality, ethnicity, and race; and that, in some cases, individuals are differentially treated because of these identities. These differences and the problems that may arise from them in a society like ours may even call into existence multiple publics that challenge restricted conceptions of the common good. For Dewey, this does not undermine democratic life but, instead, is a reflection of its vibrancy.

Dewey argued that publics come in and out of existence all the time. As we confront new social problems, as economic shifts and technological innovations transform our lives, the way we have traditionally gone about our business—including the way we have typically addressed problems—may no longer be effective and may even lapse into incoherence. Forces impact the form and content of our public deliberation and often lead to a disconnect between the way we talk about problems and the actual problems we face. Under these conditions, Dewey maintained, an eclipse of a public has taken place. Our task as social critics during such moments is to ask hard questions about the public under such conditions, to ascertain the various forces behind its eclipse, and to devise means and methods of organizing an emergent public into effective political action relevant to current social needs.

I suggest that Dewey's account of the eclipse of publics has special relevance to the contemporary challenges of post-soul politics. More specifically, I argue that the conditions that called the civil rights movement into existence have been fundamentally transformed by that very movement, and that continued uncritical reference to it as a framework for black political activity blocks the way to innovative thinking about African American politics. In pursuing this view, I begin with a brief account of the challenges confronting post-soul politics. I argue in particular that invocations of the trope of the black freedom movement functions in at least three ways: (1) as an indication of black piety, (2) as a characterization of the continuity between current and past racial realities, and (3) as a means to justify and authenticate the authority of a black political class. Each function is backward-looking in its orientation and, in some cases, inhibits the organization of an emergent public. I then turn to a more detailed discussion of John Dewey's account of publics. I give specific attention to Dewey's account of the emergence of the "great society" and the centrality of the "great community" to his view of democracy as a way of life. I suggest that conceptions of community that have informed African American politics in the past have given way to a fractured and fragmented public unable to identify itself. I argue for a conception of a great community colored a deep shade of blue, a view of community and democracy that takes seriously the complexity of racialized experiences in the United States and instantiates new forms of communication aimed at producing democratic dispositions capable of addressing the challenges of our current moment. I end by exhorting young African Americans to involve themselves actively in defining the contours of a post-soul politics without succumbing to the temptation of nostalgic longing for a past period of black political action. I urge them instead to take up the tools of their moment, to identify an emergent public, and to confront directly the social needs and opportunities it presents.

The Challenges of Post-Soul Politics

I should say a few words about what I mean by post-soul politics. On the one hand, the term simply refers to the period after the civil rights movement and black power era. It includes the political activity of persons born after the major legislative victories of the civil rights movement (the 1964 Civil Rights Act and the 1965 Voting Rights Act), the first of whom came of age during the Reagan years. On the other hand, "post-soul" references conditions and sensibilities. As Nelson George writes, the term "defines the twisting, troubling, turmoil-filled, and often terrific years since the mid-seventies when black America moved into a new phase of its history."[8] That new phase was marked both by many African Americans' experiencing unprecedented inclusion in American society, which altered the nature of their political commitments and actions, and by heightening levels of poverty and unimaginable violence, which circumscribed the life chances of large numbers of African American men, women, and children. The post-soul generation, as Mark Anthony Neal notes, experienced "the change from urban industrialism to deindustrialism, from segregation to desegregation, from essential notions of blackness to metanarratives on blackness, without any nostalgic allegiance to the past, but firmly in grasp of the existential concerns of this brave new world."[9] As this generation of African Americans addressed these changes—which gave their politics a different tone and timbre, their art a particular resonance—it also struggled to come to terms with the legacy of the civil rights movement and black power era. Indeed, this struggle with the past has in some ways overwhelmed the post-soul generation. It to this that I now turn.

BLACK PIETY

During and after Hurricane Katrina, Jesse Jackson and a host of other civil rights leaders likened the struggle over New Orleans to the mass movements of the 1960s. New Orleans demonstrated that African Americans remained second-class citizens in the United States and thus required continued struggle in relation to questions of citizenship. New Orleans, like the black freedom movement, constituted a struggle over black political empowerment, as elite whites attempted to seize the political reins of the city and remake New Orleans in an image quite different from its past. Indeed, New Orleans represented a threat to the tangible gains of "the movement"; it foreshadowed the looming battle over renewal of the Voting Rights Act. Jackson went so far as to claim that New Orleans is our era's Selma, Alabama, likening the struggle over the future of the city to the bloody crossing of the Edmund Pettis Bridge and the fight against segregation in the South.

Jackson's comparison was not that unusual. After the presidential elections of 2000 and 2004, we heard over and over again from a host of civil rights leaders how African Americans had died for the right to vote, and how the victories of the civil rights movement were being turned back. The tragic death of Martin Lee Anderson, a teen who died after a brutal beating at a boot camp in Florida, drew analogies to the civil rights movement as well. Students, legislators, and black leaders likened his death to that of Emmett Till, the fourteen-year-old whose brutal murder is often viewed as the spark of the civil rights movement. Students protesting Anderson's death even wore T-shirts comparing the two events. But how are we to understand such analogies? What kind of work do they perform in galvanizing black constituencies to address effectively their circumstances?

For many, invocations of the black freedom movement and its exemplars situate our efforts in a tradition of struggle and sacrifice. That tradition, to the extent that the trope of the black freedom movement carries with it a certain conception of character, also encourages us to act justly toward our fellows as we struggle for a more inclusive democracy. When civil rights leaders invoke "the movement" they refer, in effect, to a story—a political and ethical narrative—about black America's sojourn in the United States. That story ostensibly narrates the political and ethical lives of African Americans by establishing a tangible connection between the kinds of beliefs we currently hold and choices we now make and a history of black political action in the face of white supremacy in the United States.

This history often provides a set of interpretive tools for making sense of racialized experiences in America. Most young African American men, for example, have been told how to behave in the presence of police officers. We are told to speak respectfully, to appear nonthreatening, and to keep our hands in full view at all times. Most young African Americans have also been told of the importance of voting, usually by reference to the fact that people, African Americans in particular, have died for the right to vote and that participation in the electoral process honors their sacrifice. In both instances, knowledge acquired from past experiences orients the young and provides them with a kind of common sense aimed at securing desirable ends and avoiding certain consequences. Invocations of the story of the black freedom movement and its central characters also seek to orient us to continue the fight against racism in the United States.

From Martin Luther King Jr., Ella Baker, and Fannie Lou Hamer to Jesse

Jackson, these figures exemplify—as the story is told—the courage and moral fortitude necessary to confront racial apartheid in America and to secure the demands of a long-suffering people. References to the black freedom movement thus serve two simultaneous purposes: First, they often seek to call forth a particular political orientation; the listener is urged to take up a calling, to fight for, or at least to support, civil rights. That support shapes the person's choices and guides her actions. She, in effect, dedicates her life to fighting for justice or, minimally, supports those who do so. Second, they refer to loss and sacrifice. Many died for our current freedom, and recognition of this fact obligates us to act so as to honor their sacrifice. In calling upon us to show fidelity to the dead, invocations of the black freedom movement involve appeals to a conception of piety in which African American individuals are indebted to the black freedom struggle as an undeniable source of their being. This loyalty is expected to include not just expressions of gratitude to those sources but also displays of appropriate habits and character in confronting unjust practices.

I should distinguish this use of black piety from my earlier formulation in *Is it Nation Time?* There I argued that one of the distinguishing features of the black power era was a conception of black piety grounded in a particular understanding of blackness, which bound African Americans to one another, oriented them to a past in need of recovery, and provided a ballast for their lives by way of a reverent attachment to the sources of their individual identities. My use of black piety here, however, locates obligation not in the idea of blackness as such but, rather, in the notion of struggle on behalf of African Americans and principles of justice. The distinction matters. For some, the differences in the conception of black piety point to the substantive differences between the civil rights movement and the black power era. One version of the story holds that the latter represents a turn away from universal principles of justice that had previously informed African American struggle, toward a problematic black ontology that easily slips into a form of racial chauvinism.

Despite this difference, however, I want to describe both as instances of black piety, because both views can end up disciplining the political choices of African Americans (though they do not necessarily do so) by reference to the putative sources of African American existence. When Kenneth Blackwell, Shelby Steele, or John McWhorter put forward a view that runs counter to some notion of racial common sense, they are condemned for somehow betraying black people—or simply labeled Uncle Toms or race traitors. They are in effect being impious, turning their backs on the heroes and heroines who sacrificed and made possible their success. Whether the standard of judgment involves a tradition of black struggle or a more specific and troublesome conception of blackness, however, it threatens to constrain our ability to reimagine black political action, precisely because it presumes what that action ought to entail prior to experience. Our eyes remain fixed on the past and its exemplars who have already charted the path for us. Indeed, the likes of Martin Luther King Jr. and Malcolm X (and those who claim a direct connection to them) tower over our political imaginations, making us seem small and insignificant.

Members of the post-soul generation need not diminish the greatness of King, Malcolm, and all of those who sacrificed for our current freedoms to assert our own significance to the struggle for democracy. Their lives, with all of their power and limitations, model a standard of excellence that encourages excellence in our own lives. But we cannot be overwhelmed by the power of their presence to the point that we deny our own voice. Exemplars are a curious lot. They both inspire and potentially enslave. We must therefore be careful to strike the right balance between admiration and self-trust, not succumbing to the temptation of idolatry, which blinds us to our own unique excellences and potential greatness.[10] Instead, our orientation to the past and its exemplars must consist in a lively relation, one in which our thinking remains open-ended and imaginative recovery of the past does not obstruct efforts to invade successfully the future. All, as I argued in chapter 3, is not settled.

CONTINUITY WITHIN CHANGE

An appropriate conception of black piety presumes the importance of tradition to the formation of individual character, and that this tradition offers useful resources for the successful invasion of the future. But too often invocations of the black freedom movement proceed on the basis of a one-to-one correspondence between the political realities addressed by the freedom struggles of the 1960s and the current experiences of African Americans. When Jesse Jackson, for example, likened the struggles over the mayoral election in New Orleans to Selma, Alabama, he deployed the moral and symbolic weight of that historic moment to mobilize African Americans to turn out and vote in massive numbers. And they did. But what happens to the uniqueness of the situation in New Orleans in the analogy or translation? How do we account for the fact that the district judge who denied the petition to delay the 2006 mayoral election was an African American appointed by Bill Clinton? How are we to think about the 2000 presidential election and the debacle in Florida? Amid the justifiable outrage, one irony was lost on many: that the Supreme Court's reasoning was based on the very laws that helped secure many of the victories of the civil rights movement. In these instances, analogies with the 1960s obscure the nuances of the contemporary scene, thus affecting our descriptions and, by extension, our responses.

One might hold the view that racism—whether evidenced in de jure segregation or in schemes to "whiten" New Orleans—is always essentially the same and warrants a similar response. One might further argue that the most efficacious form of struggle against racism remains that of mass demonstrations. We know that when large numbers of African Americans "took to the streets" in the 1960s to challenge racial segregation, the nation, aided by television and print media, took notice and matters changed significantly. Descriptions of our contemporary problems as continuous with the black freedom struggle of the 1960s aim then, in most cases, to encourage us to act in a manner consistent, in both form and content, with that struggle. A wide range of black leaders constantly urges us—reasonably, given prior successes—to march and march again.

I should not be too glib. Mass mobilization of citizens publicly protesting government policies remains a crucial feature of American democratic life, and much has been achieved as a result. But too often African American communities find themselves encouraged to take to the streets not so much because of its efficacy, but because our descriptions of the problems demand that we do so. When we liken an event to Selma or invoke the death of Emmett Till, we in effect prescribe our response: we must act as black folk have always acted in the face of such terror. And the standard characterizations of responses all involve marching. But such a position tends to constrain the exercise of intelligent inquiry, precisely because we find ourselves habitually oriented to talk about and respond to the varied problems of African Americans in certain ways.

We forget that the power of marching in the civil rights era stemmed, in part, from the organization of public space. In the South, for example, Jim Crow ordered public space so as to reflect prevailing racial norms. Segregated restrooms and water fountains, back-door entrances to restaurants and stores, established customs regarding use of sidewalks—all of these prescribed how African Americans could navigate public space. To ignore these rules and restrictions was to risk one's life. In such a context, organized marching constituted a subversive act: it directly challenged the prevailing laws and norms of southern communities. In our current moment marching is not so powerful. The sight of black bodies marching in Washington, D.C., or in communities across the country, does not jolt the imagination as it once did. Were a large number of young black males in baggy jeans and long white T-shirts with platinum grills to march through communities' business districts demanding employment, they might unsettle some. But they would challenge black and white alike.

I am not suggesting that marching ought no longer to be a mode of political action. I simply insist that when we do march, we do so because it presents the most efficacious means of redressing a particular problem. We must not march simply because some black leader has declared the moment consonant with the struggles of the 1960s. To act in this way would be to shun one's responsibility to respond imaginatively to the specific conditions of one's living. Moreover, it reveals, as I argued in chapter 2, an inability to make the delicate distinctions requisite for both genuine political and moral progress.

A recent demonstration in Trenton, New Jersey, captures fully, I believe, this point. In June 2006 a thousand or so young African Americans, ranging from elementary school to high school age, gathered to protest a spate of gang-related violence terrorizing their neighborhoods. The children complained of pressures to join gangs and expressed deeply felt fears about playing outside with the constant threat of stray bullets. They simply desired peace. As these courageous young folk marched, they crossed a bridge at Mill Hill Park and were addressed by Trenton's mayor, Douglass H. Palmer. Palmer spoke of the civil rights activists in Alabama in 1965 who were attacked as they crossed the Edmund Pettis Bridge. "This is our Pettis Bridge," Palmer declared. "We're here together because we want peace in our city. We want people to put down the guns and put down the violence. It's not civil rights. We're talking about human rights."[11] Palmer's remarks, although heartfelt, revealed a profound inability to speak to the moment. The fact that many, if not most, in the audience knew more about the death of Biggie Smalls or Tupac Shakur than they did of the Edmund Pettis Bridge escaped him. Rather than finding the language to speak to the children and the issue in front of him, he relied on a confused array of clichés, invoking the civil rights movement, then awkwardly echoing the words of Malcolm X ("not an issue of civil rights, but of human rights"). Palmer's political imagination, like so many others, appeared exhausted. After he spoke, the children were clear about neither the nature of their problem nor what to do about it. As often happens, the need to locate and interpret a unique political reality and to articulate a way of dealing with it—the imperative of political and moral diagnosis and prognosis—was overshadowed by bad analogies and worn images. And the gangs still ride.

AUTHORITY OF A BLACK POLITICAL CLASS

Analogies based on current and past racial realities can serve to orient us more intelligently to the problems we face. When appropriate, they aid us in our efforts to make sense of racialized experiences by assimilating the unfamiliar to the familiar. An analogy may reveal something that would otherwise remain hidden, it may provide examples of courage or some other virtue, or it may clarify a dimension of a problem that enables us to resolve it more effectively. In any of these instances, the work of the analogy is forward-looking; it tells us something about our particular situation and about the kinds of action required to address it, orienting us such that we can address the problem without relying solely on luck. But too often analogies that purport to link the 1960s and our current moment obscure matters rather than clarify them. Perhaps Mayor Palmer simply wanted to urge the children of Trenton to be courageous, but his words offered little or no account of the context within which that courage would need to be exercised. Black leaders who frequently use these analogies may simply want to connect our current struggles with a tradition that offers resources that might aid us in our efforts, but too often the analogies are nonspecific and work only to justify the speakers' presence at the front of the march. The trope is thus used to authenticate a black political class:

many national black leaders base their claims to authority to represent African American communities either on appeals to their having participated in the struggles of the 1960s or on their connection to someone who did. Such appeals, of course, narrow the range of who can be considered a national black leader. Unless a member of the post-soul generation, for example, bears the imprimatur of someone who was a part of the black freedom movement (or is a child of an established member of the black political class), she will have to struggle mightily to acquire the gravitas needed to be taken seriously as a leader.

The problem, however, runs deeper. Invocations of the black freedom movement to justify the authority of a black political class reveal a much more troubling conception of African American politics: what Adolph Reed powerfully calls a politics of racial custodianship.[12] This politics presumes that there exists within black communities a viable distinction between the "masses" of African Americans, who need representation, and elites, whose role is to represent them. Reed rightly notes that "the term 'the masses' does not refer to any particular social position or constituency."[13] It does not help us understand the actual interests of those who are underemployed or those who describe themselves as hip-hop heads. And it does little to capture the commitments of those who struggle over high rents or those who are home owners. Indeed, as Reed writes, "the category assumes a generic, abstract—and thus mute—referent. It therefore reproduces the nonparticipatory politics enacted by the mainstream black political elite. The masses do not speak; someone speaks for them."[14]

This form of politics has not emerged simply because of the nominal elites' selfishness. The realities of Jim Crow shaped the form and content of black political activity in determinate ways. The denial of the vote and the real threat of violent reprisal for any public opposition to prevailing racist norms exerted enormous pressures on the form of public deliberation within African American communities:

compromise and silence became, for some, tools of the political trade. Moreover, the realities of white supremacy helped generate a conception of the group in which, without substantive deliberation, black elites defined the political agenda of black America and, without constraint or accountability, acted on it. The politics of racial custodianship, then, emerges out of a political context shaped by civic exclusion, the threat of racial violence, and the assumption of racial corporate interests represented by black elites who were not held accountable.[15]

Of course, de jure segregation is no more, and the threat of violent reprisal for publicly held positions is no longer sanctioned by the state. Yet the politics of racial custodianship remains, and its central trope is the black freedom movement. African American political leaders continue to invoke "the movement" to mobilize African American constituencies. In doing so, they often rely on a conception of black piety that obligates African Americans to act politically in certain ways and not in others; they sometimes presume a generic politics of racial advancement predicated on a correspondence between African American experiences then and now; and many continue to justify their place as representatives or brokers of black interests to the state. In each instance, the diversity of African American life is obscured, and the democratic values of accountability and open debate are denied. This makes it more difficult to imagine the formation of the dispositions so necessary for a vibrant democratic life—dispositions that appreciate, as Dewey argued, "the values of social life, to see in imagination the forces which favor our effective cooperation with one another, to understand the sorts of character that help and that hold back."[16] Instead, we find ourselves, time and again, urged to follow uncritically those who would have us believe that they represent *the* African American community.

Many, however, have come to see that such a politics simply fails to speak to our current moment and the complexity of African American conditions of living. What does such a moment signal? How are we to understand it in relation to the way we conceive of a post-soul politics? These questions, I believe, require an understanding of a national black public. What is this black public? And how are we to understand it under present conditions? Pragmatism, and specifically John Dewey, offer some resources to begin an answer.

John Dewey and the Eclipse of a Public

In 1927 John Dewey wrote that "optimism about democracy is today under a cloud."[17] He was responding, in part, to prevailing sentiments about participatory democracy. Walter Lippmann, in his important books *Public Opinion* (1922) and *The Phantom Public* (1925), had expressed the view that participatory democracy was not viable, because the opinions of everyday, ordinary citizens could be easily manipulated and consent manufactured by elites. To assume that ordinary Americans could engage in genuine deliberation about their conditions of living and the workings of government, given the quantity of information needed to do so effectively, was to fall into the worst kind of romantic thinking. Ordinary Americans simply did not have the time to become politically informed, which meant that deliberative democracy was a pipe dream. Lippmann suggested in its place a technocracy in which disinterested experts—persons who did not suffer from the irrationality so painfully evident among politicians—represented the best interests of American citizens too caught up in the daily demands of modern living.

Dewey acknowledged that the technological, economic, and bureaucratic developments of modern American life had fundamentally transformed the nature of social interaction among citizens. Americans were busy working, shopping, and pursuing the American dream. He conceded Lippmann's claim that the public in light of these developments seemed lost or bewildered. But Dewey rejected Lippmann's conclusions. The problem was not with the incapacities of everyday, ordinary people, nor was the problem inherent to the very notion of democracy. Matters were bad but not hopeless. What was required was a better understanding of the emergence of American democracy and a more intelligent pursuit of conditions that would enable it to flourish under continuously changing conditions. As Dewey put it, many "assume that democracy is the product of an idea, of a single and consistent intent."[18] The challenge involves recognizing the various ways ordinary Americans, in response to their environment, have forged the democratic way of life that we now associate, mistakenly, with liberal institutions. In other words, shifting attention from abstractions associated with democracy to the actual doings and sufferings of those who provide its content. Democracy, in Dewey's view, is not reducible to universal suffrage, free and frequent elections, or congressional and cabinet government. Instead, "political democracy has emerged as a kind of net consequence of a vast multitude of responsive adjustments to a vast number of situations, no two of which were alike, but which tended to converge to a common outcome. Much less is democracy the product *of* democracy, of some inherent nisus, or immanent idea."[19] When seen in this light we come to understand democracy as a historical phenomenon that is continuously reenvisioned, and it is here that Dewey's account of publics takes on added significance.

Dewey asserted that publics "consist of all those who are affected by the indirect consequences of transactions to such an extent that it is deemed necessary to have those consequences systematically cared for."[20] Say we find ourselves directly affected by a particular transaction. We work diligently, perhaps with the aid of friends, to secure consequences that favor us and to rid ourselves of others that do not. This mode of action is principally pre-political in the sense that it illustrates what we, as social creatures, do when faced with problematic situations. Such transactions are direct and their effects are primarily local. But when transactions affect people indirectly, Dewey argued, a more general public emerges and, in some cases, designated individuals ("officials") and agencies (the state) assume the task of conserving and protecting the interests of those affected. Both officials and the state emerge in response to human needs. As Dewey writes:

> Men have looked in the wrong place. They have sought for the key to the nature of the state in the field of agencies, in that doers of deeds, or in some will or purpose back of the deeds. They have sought to explain the state in terms of authorship. Ultimately all deliberate choices proceed from somebody in particular; acts are performed by somebody, and all arrangements and plans are made by somebody in the most concrete sense of somebody.[21]

In this view, the state is denied transcendental status. Instead, it is the consequence of efforts to protect the shared interests of those similarly situated. Officials are not disinterested elites or professional representatives. They are "indeed public agents, but agents in the sense of factors doing the business of others in securing and obviating consequences that concern them."[22]

Everyday people, however, are not mute; their representatives do not speak entirely for them. Everyday Americans speak insofar as they are committed to democracy as a way of life, which goes beyond liberal institutions to the very way in which individuals evidence certain values in their interactions with their fellows. Dewey insisted that we can only escape the reduction of democracy to a form of government, an *external way* of thinking as he called it, when "we realize in thought and act that democracy is a personal way of individual life; that it signifies the possession and continual use of certain attitudes, forming personal character and determining desire and purpose in all the relations of life."[23] Such an orientation entails embracing our responsibility to share in forming and aiding the activities of the various groups or associations within which we find ourselves; it demands "liberation of the potentialities of a group in harmony with the interests and goods which are in common."[24]

Obviously, Dewey rejected any view of American political life that would deny the centrality of everyday, ordinary people to the viability and vibrancy of American democracy. His was an unshakable faith in the possibilities and potentialities of ordinary people engaged in intelligent action.

> For what is the faith of democracy in the role of consultation, of conference, of persuasion, of discussion, in the formation of public opinion, which in the long run is self-corrective, except faith in the capacity of the intelligence of the common man to respond with common sense to the free play of facts and ideas which are secured by effective communication? I am willing to leave to upholders of totalitarian states of the right and the left the view that faith in the capacities of intelligence is utopian.[25]

Lippmann was right in stating that the fundamental transformations in the conditions of American life threatened

American democracy, but he failed to exhibit the requisite faith in the intelligence of common folk to respond effectively to those conditions.[26]

For Dewey, inventions in technology, industrialization, and urbanization and the ascendance of a new aristocracy made up of bankers and captains of industry radically transformed the quality and scope of indirect consequences. Yet the political forms of government that had developed under earlier and qualitatively different conditions persisted. As a result, Dewey argued, a new public remained inchoate and unorganized, and this public had "to break existing political forms" if it was to take shape.[27] These forms had developed in the context of communal living, as the habits of England and its legal institutions were adapted under pioneer conditions. In other words, American democratic life took shape in mutual comprehension experienced in face-to-face communities.

The machine age changed matters. It expanded and intensified the scope of indirect consequences, splintered and fragmented established forms of association, and formed "immense and consolidated unions in action, on an impersonal rather than a community basis."[28] Personal communal life gave way to the impersonal Great Society, which left us with abstract and highly mediated forms of social interaction. Americans *felt* indirect consequences but, under these conditions, failed to *perceive* them. As Dewey noted, "they are suffered, but they cannot be said to be known, for they are not, by those who experience them."[29] The challenge was to move from impersonal, shallow interactions to more meaningful forms of association: from the Great Society to what he called the Great Community.

New technologies did eclipse prior communal formations, but they could also, if intelligently utilized, aid in forging more meaningful forms of social interaction. Communication across various divides was necessary if genuine communal life, something so central to democracy, was to take shape. But again, this necessitated breaking through established political forms. It required the sort of undertaking that human beings engage in when confronted with problems. Dewey's view of the public foregrounds this sort of undertaking and keeps us mindful that our democracy is in constant need of attention and care.

Two features of Dewey's account of publics are particularly relevant to my discussion of the challenges of a post-soul politics. First, Dewey contextualizes the emergence of publics. He maintains that publics are historical phenomena that emerge in the context of specific attempts to address particular problems. As such, he avoids the tendency to reify political formations and to think of them as existing apart from the interests and habits that call them into being. Instead, Dewey urges us to situate historically political formations in the activity of groups as they seek to address indirect consequences. Contextualizing is particularly important in those moments when emergent publics cannot be identified because of the recalcitrance of extant political forms that block the way to more imaginative and intelligent political action. Second, Dewey's view conveys a profound faith in the capacities of everyday people. Although he agrees with much of Lippmann's position, he never gives up on the importance of participatory democracy. Instead, he argues for a more appropriate form of education that would aid in the formation of individuals with democratic character and that would equip them with the tools necessary for substantive and intelligent civic action. The answer to a bewildered public, then, is not to adopt a form of custodial politics but, rather, to expand democratic life and broaden the ground for individual self-development.[30] We must contextualize and historicize publics, and we must insist on the importance of the voices of everyday, ordinary Americans to democratic flourishing.

The Eclipse of a Black Public

Given the persistent legacies of white supremacy in the United States, the actions of many American whites in relation to African Americans have had far-reaching implications and have necessitated conjoint action on the part of African Americans to secure some consequences and avoid others. In short, a *national* black public has everything to do with responding to the persistence of racism in American society. From the national black convention movement of the early nineteenth century to recent responses to Hurricane Katrina, African Americans have sought forms of and created forums for political redress in light of the perceived effects of actions that extend beyond those immediately involved.

There have been, at least, three national black publics since the dawn of the twentieth century. The first involves what I call *mass migration and the problem of the color line,* in the period between 1903 and 1935 (from the publication of W.E.B. DuBois's *Souls of Black Folk,* the beginning of the Great Migration, to the invasion of Ethiopia by Italy). This period of black political activity was marked by the immediate effects of the consolidation of the white South and the subsequent mass migration of large numbers of

African Americans from rural areas to urban centers, from south to north. This public was eclipsed as international pressures and domestic retrenchment (the Great Depression and World War II) fundamentally impinged on the form and content of black political engagement. The second national black public, which I call *black internationalism and forgotten radical possibilities,* emerged between 1937 (with the Spanish Civil War) and was eclipsed by the onslaught of the cold war and a change in black politics corresponding with the *Brown v. Board of Education* decisions in 1954 and 1955. This period, one that involved the emergence of the United States as a global power and the beginnings of "third world" decolonization, was characterized by political languages reflective of broad global political patterns and economic crises, as well as pressures to limit the scope of black protest to the domestic domain. The third national black public, *civil rights, black power, and the age of Reagan,* emerged with the mass mobilization of African Americans to protest legal segregation in the aftermath of the *Brown* decision, the murder of Emmett Till, and the defiance of Rosa Parks in 1955, and was eclipsed in 1980 with the election of Ronald Reagan. This late period was characterized obviously by the successful challenge of Jim Crow, the rise and decline of the black power era, and a subsequent white backlash.[31] The boundaries of all three national publics were defined by the legality of white supremacist practices, which necessitated conjoint action and involved a wide range of discourses about collective racial advancement. In each instance, African American conjoint action changed, because of demographic shifts, international conflict, mass mobilization of black citizens, and the changing nature of race and racism in our country. Struggle remained a consistent feature of these publics, but that struggle looked different under different conditions.

During no other period in African American history was a national black public as active and vibrant as that of the 1960s and 1970s. This period resulted in the end of legal segregation, unprecedented growth in the black middle class, and the powerful expression of black cultural pride. It was also a moment marked by cities burning, violent encounters between the state and black citizens, and a palpable sense of white fatigue with regards to matters of race and civil rights. Indeed, the successes and failures of this moment stand alongside the tremendous transformations within African American communities and American society that have so complicated and intensified contemporary racial politics in the United States that a national black public cannot currently identify and distinguish itself. Some even ask whether there is such a thing as a black public under present conditions.

In his brilliant work *Black Visions*, Michael Dawson isolates a number of developments that impacted the form and content of the black public during this period. Intensified state repression and internal ideological fragmentation contributed to the ruin of many civil rights and black power organizations. COINTELPRO, among other federal programs, systematically targeted and harassed black leaders like Dr. Martin Luther King Jr. and organizations like the Black Panther Party. This program also sought to fuel internecine conflicts between black militant organizations, resulted in the arrest of many local and national leaders on trumped-up charges, and in some cases was involved in the assassination of targeted individuals. State repression often resulted in wholesale paranoia among many black activists. Black nationalist and leftist organizations increasingly experienced substantive internal rifts, which involved ideological consolidations and purgings that left many organizations weak; in some instances, it destroyed them outright. This contestation took place as much of what was left of the civil rights movement began to transform itself into what now can be called the civil rights establishment, an effective lobbying organization whose sole purpose was (and continues to be) to secure the gains of "the movement." A vast cadre of black elected officials (BEOs) also emerged as "a buffer class that helped delegitimate protest and circumscribe acceptable political discourse within the black community."[32]

Transformations in the political economy, Dawson maintains, also eroded the institutional basis of the black public. The shift in the U.S. economy from manufacturing to low-wage service industries adversely affected black laborers, as the shift to flexible accumulation weakened labor unions (just one in seven employed African Americans currently belongs to a union), transformed work forces, and increased the likelihood that African Americans would experience discrimination in labor markets.[33] Manufacturing losses in many northern cities were particularly devastating. William Julius Wilson notes that "between 1967 and 1987, Philadelphia lost 64 percent of it manufacturing jobs; Chicago lost 60 percent; New York City 58 percent; and Detroit, 51 percent."[34] Of course, global economic competition exacerbated matters in that the increasing demand for highly skilled labor left low-skilled African American workers on the margins of a new economy driven by technological innovation and the transition from hard to soft goods.

Dawson rightly notes that these transformations in political economy, in tandem with the successes of the civil rights movement, deepened class divisions within African American communities throughout the nation. The decline in manufacturing jobs—the primary vehicle for many African Americans to achieve middle-class status—destabilized the black working class. Indeed, "from the fourth quarter of 1974 through the fourth quarter of 1992, there were only five quarters in which black unemployment was below 10 percent."[35] Long-term unemployment among African Americans is now at its highest in twenty years, a phenomenon what William J. Wilson powerfully describes as the disappearance of work, and has left many African Americans living in concentrated poverty. The collapse of the civil rights coalition in the aftermath of the dismantling of legal segregation revealed white America's fatigue with regards to racial matters as well as the deep economic divisions within African American communities. To be sure, the internal fissures had always been present within African American communities, and now, without the unifying challenge of legal segregation, they began to evidence themselves in powerful and poignant ways. Class cleavages, strident criticisms of patriarchy and homophobia, and mainstream aspirations on the part of many black leaders all illustrated the difficulty of presuming a set of issues that define *the* black agenda. Moreover, the impact of that other important piece of 1965 legislation, the Hart-Cellar Immigration Act, which eliminated country-specific quotas on immigration, complicated the very idea of a "black" community. Between 1960 and 1984 some 604,104 immigrants from the Anglophone Caribbean and 141,109 from Haiti would come to the United States, greatly affecting the form and content of black cultural expression. Among the new arrivals was DJ Kool Herc, a Jamaican immigrant, who introduced us to the "break beat" and aided in the creation of the genre of music called rap. Dawson goes as far as to say that "taken together, the disintegration of the institutional bases of the black counterpublic since the early 1970s and increasing black skepticism regarding the existence of a bundle of issues and strategies that define a black agenda should lead us to question whether we can assert that a subaltern counterpublic exists—and if it does, how healthy is it?"[36]

This question, however, reveals more about the limitations of Dawson's approach than the actual problems faced. The concern is not whether a public exists but, rather, in what ways conjoint actions under present conditions might call a new public into existence and what blocks its emergence. Dawson is closer to the mark when he writes:

The dismantling of the formal structures of segregation ... combined with the increasing importance of identities based on other structures of stratification require that a black subaltern counterpublic would have to be reconstituted on a new understanding of the issues, including those of patriarchy and economic oppression.... Without such a broadening of what is understood to be the "black agenda," a unifying set of discourses and political agenda will not come to be.[37]

I am not so sure the aim should be a unifying set of discourses apart from particular problems that may necessitate broad-based political action. But I do agree, and here I would prefer to use Deweyan language, that we have witnessed the eclipse of a black public and need to devise means and methods of organizing an emergent public.

Economic realities (both local and global), technological developments (the computer age), identity formations (based on class, gender, sexuality, and ethnicity), and political transformations (the end of Jim Crow) have splintered and fragmented established forms of association among African Americans. We find ourselves instead awash in the Great Society, where the conception of "black community," which once informed notions of racial obligation and ideas about general racial advancement, persists primarily in nostalgic longings for a time past or in invocations of a politics formed in a context in which such notions of community actually made sense. But under present conditions this idea of black community and its attendant notions of group interests obscure the complex experiences that inform the varied political commitments and interests of African Americans, blocking the way to the formation of a black public more reflective of current conditions of living.

The challenge involves moving from a conception of black community that orients African Americans politically prior to experience—a view that often entails bad conceptions of black identity, history, and agency—to an understanding of black community consonant with an idea of Great Community. This view of community orients African Americans in such a way that democratic dispositions are forged, through new information and communication technologies, in intelligent and meaningful interaction with others. These interactions are, of course, colored a deep shade of blue.

They are genuinely informed by the stories of a blues people whose mere presence reveals the remarkable irony at the heart of our way of life, stories that shape our character as a nation and orient us to others in particular ways. In other words, the idea of great community has as a constitutive feature the tragedy of race, and the idea of black community reflects deep commitments to expanding democratic life and enlarging the possibilities for individual self-development.

This view of community will require breaking existing political forms. That is to say, it will require a reconceptualization of "black political activity as a dynamic set of social relations and interests that converge on some issues as consequential for broad sectors of the black population and that diverge from others, based on other identities and interest aggregations."[38] To achieve this will require a new orientation toward the black freedom movement, one that will free us to engage our contemporary problems imaginatively, intelligently, and in full view of the variety of African American political interests.

A Post-Soul Politics for the Twenty-first Century

The 1960s stand, negatively or positively, as a point of reference for all forms of political activity in our contemporary moment. Like the American Revolution, the Great Depression, and World War II—events that defined a generation—the black freedom struggle of the 1960s represents a defining moment for black America against which all other attempts at political insurgency are measured. In some ways, this is apt: the successes of the civil rights movement fundamentally changed the racial landscape in America. An emergent black middle class found greater access to America's wealth, and black America discovered a new sense of self-worth as its mass struggles produced tangible, though highly qualified, results. On one level, black America had never really experienced anything like the mass struggles of the sixties. The abolitionism of the antebellum period was relatively limited. The movement of Marcus Mosiah Garvey during the early twentieth century had a different ideological orientation: Garvey could care less about the soul of America. Yet, ironically, the historical anomaly of the struggles of the 1960s has become the standard model of political engagement for black America (and for a generation of white Americans who were also defined by that period).

The sixties occupy, and I mean this in its military sense, our political imaginations. This is the case not only because of the significance of the events, but also because of its *proximity* to our contemporary moment. African Americans who have battle scars from living in and fighting against racial apartheid in the United States are still alive. Mothers and fathers, uncles and aunts who remember Jim Crow are reminded of those experiences by living memories of humiliation. They have raised us and imparted to us their wounds and a reasonable skepticism about the moral capacity of some of their fellow white citizens. Leaders who came of age during that time of struggle also continue to lead black America and draw on the basic precepts and strategies that defined the period. They remain a vital force in American politics and, in some cases, a profound obstacle to innovative thinking. In the end, my point is simply this: those who struggled in the 1960s did not have the symbolic weight of "the 1960s" to contend with. We do. Old strategies and personalities continue to define how we engage in race-based politics. Yet, these old strategies and leaders stand alongside new problems and personalities that are not reducible to that moment of struggle. We live in a different time, a moment made possible by the extraordinary efforts of past generations. But our task is different because the conditions have changed. We must imagine a politics that revels in the diversity of African American life and esteems the democratic virtue of free and open debate, and insists on the capacities of everyday, ordinary folk to engage fully in what the rap artist Talib Kweli so brilliantly calls the beautiful struggle. What this politics will look like will depend on the particular problems faced and the specific forms of solidarity forged in efforts to secure some consequences and avoid others.

In accepting the 1993 Nobel Prize for literature, Toni Morrison spoke of the continuous task of the next generation of writers to possess language and to tell stories of the grandness of life. She told a story of an old, wise blind woman, a daughter of a slave, who was confronted by a few young people. One of them asked her, with the insolence of youth, "Old woman, I hold in my hand a bird. Tell me whether it is living or dead." After a period of silence and prodding, the blind woman responded, "I don't know whether the bird you are holding is dead or alive, but what I do know is that it is in your hands. It is in your hands."[39] I recall again what Ralph Waldo Emerson advocated in "The American Scholar," his 1837 Phi Beta Kappa address at Harvard. Among other things, he urged a new kind of thinking among Americans: "Our day of dependence, our long apprenticeship to the learning of other lands, draws to a close." I want a new kind of thinking regarding African American politics and democracy. And if this new thinking is to be emancipated it requires of the post-soul generation a declaration of independence. Then, to extend Emerson's remarks in a slightly different direction, the sluggard intellect of this generation will look from under its past successes and efforts and fill the postponed expectations of a people with something better than false promises and piecemeal victories. And the generations of old can truly say, with Morrison's wise woman, "Finally, I trust you now. I trust you with the bird that is not in your hands because you have truly caught it. Look. How lovely it is, this thing we have done—together."

Epilogue: The Covenant with Black America

Every generation has to accomplish democracy over again for itself; ... its very nature, its essence, is something that cannot be handed from one person or one generation to another, but has to be worked out in terms of needs, problems, and conditions of social life.

JOHN DEWEY, "Democracy and Education in the World of Today"

> I see a place where little boys and girls
> Are shells in the oceans not knowin' they a pearl
> No one to hold 'em while they growin'
> They livin' moment to moment without a care in the whole world

TALIB KWELI, "Where Do We Go"

We have come to the end of a language and are now about the

business of forging a new one. For we have survived, children, the very last white country the world will ever see.

BALDWIN, "Notes on the House of Bondage"

I have attempted to demonstrate over the course of this book how pragmatism helps sort out some of the more troublesome conceptual problems confronting African American politics. In doing so, I have emphasized the importance of experimentalism, asserted a profound faith in the capacities of everyday folk, and insisted that democracy be understood as a way of life. But my principle aim has been to clear the underbrush—to open the way for a more inspired form of African American politics animated by a profound commitment to democracy. I hold the view, and perhaps this reflects that I was born in 1968 and came of age during the Reagan years, that much of contemporary African American politics suffers from a woeful lack of imagination. We simply find ourselves, more often than not, imitating the methods of struggle forged in the 1960s and 1970s, and waiting, as if for Godot,[1] for the next great leader, the next Martin or Malcolm, to deliver us to yet another promised land. It reminds me of what Karl Marx wrote in *The Eighteenth Brumaire* about Hegel's claim that "all great historic-facts and personages appear, so to speak, twice. He forgot to add: the first time as tragedy, the second as farce."

Since February 2006, however, I have had the opportunity to be intimately involved in a moment that exemplifies what I mean by post-soul politics. Over the past eight years, Tavis Smiley, the powerful and prophetic African American media personality, has convened what he calls the State of the Black Union, a major discussion among various African American experts, thought leaders, policy makers, and activists about the conditions of African American living. The event airs on C-Span every February and draws regularly a viewership of over fifty-five million people worldwide. What is particularly striking about this gathering is that it has constituted a sort of yearly ritual. Folks gather around their televisions for an entire day literally glued to the discussion. The discussions take place live in front of large audiences who are invited to ask questions and to take the panelists to task. In short, the State of the Black Union constitutes a kind of public deliberative space, if only for a day, in which many African Americans (and others) throughout the nation sit and reflect with one another about their circumstances and, by extension, about the nation. It is a powerful illustration of democracy at work. But, again, the event is only one day.

In 2006, in conjunction with the State of the Black Union in Houston, Texas, Smiley released a book entitled *The Covenant with Black America,* a text that takes up ten important issues confronting African Americans in this country.[2] The book emerged out of discussions about defining the agenda of black America. Smiley had been challenged to deliver something more than an annual one-day series of panels. But the book turns out to be more than another top-down attempt to define the interests of African Americans; it is not a textual representation of custodial politics. Instead, Smiley (who perhaps is the first African American with a social conscience to have a substantial presence in television, radio, *and* print) went on *The Tom Joyner Morning Show,* a black radio show with an audience of ten million people, and asked African Americans to write in and list the most compelling problems they experienced. Issues ranging from health to education to criminal justice to the digital divide emerged, and Smiley convened a group of experts to write on these issues, collected a body of facts about them, listed best practices in response to the issues, and insisted that individuals hold themselves as well as politicians accountable in relation to them. The book materializes, then, out of a communicative space mediated by radio; its content reflects a broad-base consensus about *particular* problems faced and the need for conversation and debate about how *best* to respond to them.

On February 25, 2006, Smiley walked on stage, book in hand, to thunderous applause and proceeded to engage in this yearly rite of black democratic action. The difference, however, was that the deliberative space made possible by the State of the Black Union was now between the covers of a book and could move beyond a single day. In fact, Smiley organized what he called the Covenant Tour, in which town-hall meetings in local churches were held in twenty cities throughout the country to localize *The Covenant with Black America.* I had the privilege to participate in most of these meetings and witnessed firsthand the power of participatory democracy. Thousands of people gathered to discuss the content of the book and its relevance to their daily lives. In Baltimore and Washington, D.C., the issue of gentrification came to the fore. In Indianapolis, concerns over the state of African American children emerged as a central preoccupation. In Los Angeles, the issue of homelessness was important. In each city, some issue particular to the members of the community shaped the discussion of the Covenant, giving it special resonance and relevance to the participants.

Moreover, sustained criticisms of black leadership emerged. African Americans across the United States voiced a deep displeasure with the current black political class and demanded more accountability and responsibility. But the demands for accountability went beyond electoral processes; they involved a set of commitments, as evidenced in the Covenant meetings, to democracy as a way of living together. In each city, Smiley would say, quoting Kwame Ture (Stokely Carmichael), that "we are the leaders that we've been looking for." He would go on to paraphrase Ella Baker about not needing a strong, saviorlike leader. In each instance, the crowds erupted with applause. *The Covenant with Black America* affirmed that each individual indeed had the capacity to transform his or her circumstances. In fact, the orientation of the book and of those of us who support it is based on a profound trust that everyday black folk can in fact engage in intelligent action if proper conditions are furnished. It assumes, with John Dewey, that democracy is "the road which places the greatest burden of responsibility upon the greatest number of human beings."[3] As such, the book rejects outright the politics of racial custodianship and approximates the post-soul politics I commend in chapter 6.

While on tour we also acknowledged the generational divide—that many of us struggle with the burden of the symbolic weight of the 1960s. Smiley and I talked of our feelings of being born out of place and out of time: we did not march with Martin or organize with the students of SNCC; we did not stand post for Malcolm or serve breakfasts with the Black Panthers. Many young people nodded their heads in agreement and expressed their dismay with the challenge of asserting their own voice. But *The Covenant with Black America* offers an occasion to reimagine African American politics. A book stands at the center of this effort. That in itself is unusual. Moreover, the innovative ways information and communication technology have been deployed to forge solidarities around specific issues is unique in African American politics. But perhaps more important is the insistence on the centrality of the deliberative process. *The Covenant with Black America* exhibits "the faith that the process of experience is more important than special results attained, so that special results achieved are of ultimate value only as they are used to enrich and order the ongoing process."[4] This is what I mean by a post-soul politics: a form of political activity that exemplifies, in its very doing, a commitment to participatory democracy—that ensures, as far as possible, that everyday people, with varied interests, aims, and ends, engage one another in efforts to secure goods that are commonly shared.

The meetings also occasioned moments of dissent. In Harlem, a young woman, about twenty-five years of age, stepped to the microphone and declared in a powerful voice that people her age were not reading *The Covenant with Black America;* that the book was not a "how-to guide" for getting paid and thus was of little interest to many young people; and, perhaps most startling to the people in the room, that she would not vote in the upcoming election. The crowd moaned. What followed, however, was a remarkable exchange. The young woman explained herself. She did not care to vote, because she believed her vote would not count. The panel, which included Marc Morial of the Urban League and Bruce Gordon of the NAACP, offered counterarguments. I believed her conclusions represented an intelligible and reasonable judgment that our democracy was dysfunctional. Tavis Smiley then made an amazing gesture. He had announced earlier, as he did in every city, that the Republican and Democratic parties had agreed to host a conversation about the covenant with their presidential candidates. Now he not only offered her tickets for the events but proposed to fly her to them. The young woman ran back to the microphone and declared with amazing confidence, "I will do you one better. If you get me tickets to the events I will fly myself." She was not out to "hustle" her way into the forums or looking for some handout from Smiley; instead, like so many young African Americans, she simply wanted to participate meaningfully in a genuine process. This moment, for me, illustrated the power of the deliberative space afforded by the Covenant.

What I experienced throughout black America over the course of the tour was an extraordinary expression of civic energy, something very unusual in these dark political times. To be sure, we have witnessed over the past few decades a civic power outage in our country. Many of our fellow citizens are too busy trying to make ends meet or too preoccupied with their own selfish pursuits to engage in public matters. Moreover, moralists who are seemingly not committed to the democratic virtues of open and free exchange have sought to hijack American public life. They want to cultivate instead a pernicious provinciality that results not in the formation of democratic character but in blind dogmatism. I am reminded of the powerful words of William James: "A mind too narrow has room but for one kind of affection." This one kind of affection is often wrapped in the garments of piety. But as James says, "Piety is the mask, the inner force is tribal instinct."[5]

These realities should not lead us to retreat into separatist enclaves. Instead, those of us, few though we may be, must find the energy to draw on the resources of this powerful but fragile experiment in democracy, to save our country. The words of Ralph Waldo Emerson come to mind:

> The existing world is not a dream, and cannot with impunity be treated as a dream; neither is it a disease; but it is the ground on which you stand, it is the mother of whom you were born. Reform converses with possibilities, perchance with impossibilities; but here is sacred fact. This was also true, or it could not be: it had life in it, or it could not have existed; it has life in it, or it could not continue.[6]

We must believe, not in a naïve way, that our nation has life in it. *The Covenant with Black America* demonstrates that this is so and, in our current moment, constitutes a space where democratic hope can be found.

The Covenant with Black America stands within a particular tradition of struggle, a struggle of a blues people who found resources for democratic hope in the extraordinary capacities of ordinary people in spite of a wicked nation committed to wicked practices. The ideals of democracy inspired those who had been denied freedom and education to dream dreams, to imagine possibilities, and to hold on in the face of the withering storm—to will themselves into a new day. This tradition never believed the lie that this country was an example of democracy achieved but, rather, understood intimately its failures and shortcomings, its blindnesses and deformities. This tradition saw nevertheless not simply disease but possibility—understanding that the nation could have life if it would only learn to swing Duke Ellington style. It is a tradition that, at its best, cultivated democratic dispositions in the face of strange fruit dangling from poplar trees, insisted on effective freedom as African Americans imagined a day that their children and children's children would be able to actualize their capacities and potentialities, and struggled to ensure that every child would have access to the opportunity and skills to make good on the promise that is America. It is in these dark and trying times that we must turn to the power of Emerson's insight and the enduring purchase of traditions of struggle to muster the democratic hope and courage to challenge our nation and insist on a better future for our children—to educate them *and* ourselves into the habits of democracy so that this nation can be saved. I am convinced that the Covenant provides such an occasion—one not mired in the nostalgic longing of a glorious past but, rather, one that looks into a distant future to ensure a better life for those yet unborn.

In "Notes on the House of Bondage," James Baldwin reflected, among other things, on the challenges that young African American children face. He wrote, "What we see in the children is what they have seen in us—or, more accurately perhaps, what they *see* in us."[7] Baldwin understood fully the task before him: to raise his children in such a way as to make certain that "the American guile and cowardice [could not] destroy them."[8] His was a form of piety that was attuned to the lessons of tragedy in American life *and* forward-looking in its orientation, even until his last days. The epigraph to *The Covenant with Black America* reflects this orientation. The words of Terry Tempest Williams frame the ambition of the book: "The eyes of the future are looking back at us and they are praying for us to see beyond our own time." *The Covenant* instantiates a form of piety that begins with the dark side of American life; it confronts candidly the racialized experiences of this fragile experiment in democracy that cut short the lives of so many of our fellow citizens. The piety it commends is also forward-looking in its commitment to participatory democracy, in its insistence on speaking to the particulars of our current moment in a language informed by the past but shaped by the present, and in its steady resolve to secure a better world for our children and our children's children. This sentiment was given powerful expression in a town-hall meeting in Baltimore. The last question was from a young shy girl, about eight years of age. She asked timidly, "What can I do to help the Covenant?" Some answered to stand proud and never let anyone threaten her spirit. Others said make being smart cool. I simply said, in the democratic spirit of the Covenant, "Keep asking that question and tell us what you hear."

Notes

PREFACE

[1]   Albert Murray, *Stomping the Blues* (Cambridge: Da Capo Press, 2000), 250–51.

INTRODUCTION

[1]   Richard Rorty, *Philosophy and Social Hope* (New York: Penguin, 2000), 237.

[2]   Anna Julia Cooper, "The Gain from a Belief," in *A Voice from the South* (New York: Oxford University Press, 1990), 295.

[3]   Ibid., 303.

[4]   Ibid., 297, 304.

[5]   Charles Johnson, "Notes on a Personal Philosophy of Life," 1937. Quoted in George Hutchinson, *The Harlem Renaissance in Black And White* (Cambridge: Harvard University Press, 1995), 59.

[6]   Michael Magee, *Emancipating Pragmatism: Emerson, Jazz, and Experimental Writing* (Tuscaloosa:

University of Alabama Press, 2004), 12.

[7]   Cornel West, *The American Evasion of Philosophy: A Genealogy of Pragmatism* (Madison: University of Wisconsin Press, 1989), 5.

[8]   Ibid.

[9]   John Dewey, *The Quest for Certainty: A Study of the Relation of Knowledge and Action,* in Dewey, *The Later Works,* 1925–1953, ed. Jo Ann Boydston (Carbondale: Southern Illinois Press, 1981–90), 4:204.

[10]   My thinking has been greatly influence by conversations with Paul Taylor. His essay, "Pragmatism and Race," in *Pragmatism and the Problems of Race,* ed. Donald Koch and Bill Lawson (Bloomington: Indiana University Press, 2004), informs much of what follows.

[11]   John Dewey, *Art as Experience* (New York: Capricorn-Putnam, 1958), 290.

[12]   Hilary Putnam notes that this view involves at least four

important claims: (1) knowledge of facts (true singular statements) presuppose knowledge of theories (i.e., true statements about what is true in general, or in most cases); (2) knowledge of "theories" presupposes knowledge of facts; (3) knowledge of facts presupposes knowledge of values; (4) knowledge of values presuppose knowledge of facts. See Hilary Putnam, *Words and Life* (Cambridge: Harvard University Press, 1995).

[13]   Taylor, "Pragmatism and Race," 166.

[14]   Ibid.

[15]   William James, *Pragmatism* (Indianapolis: Hackett Publishing, 1981), 28.

[16]   John Dewey, "The Influence of Darwin on Philosophy" (1910), in *The Influence of Darwin on Philosophy, and Other Essays in Contemporary Thought* (Amherst, NY: Prometheus Books, 1997), 17.

[17]   C. I. Lewis, *Collected Papers* (Palo Alto, Calif: Stanford University Press, 1970), 108.

[18]   Stanley Cavell, *Emerson's Transcendental Etudes* (Stanford: Stanford University Press, 2003), 216. Cavell, in my view, simply reads Dewey too narrowly.

[19]   Saba Mahmood, *Politics of Piety: The Islamic Revival and the Feminist Subject* (Princeton: Princeton University Press, 2005).

[20]   Dewey makes this point in his essay "The Development of American Pragmatism," in *Philosophy and Civilization* (New York: Peter Smith, 1968).

[21]   Baldwin details the national myth that African Americans never believed: "that their [white Americans'] ancestors were all freedom-loving heroes, that they were in the greatest country the world has ever seen, or that Americans are invincible in battle and wise in peace, that Americans have

always dealt honorably with Mexicans and Indians and all other neighbors or inferiors, that American men are the world's most direct and virile, that American women are pure. Negroes know far more about white Americans than that.... The tendency has really been, insofar as this was possible, to dismiss white people as the slightly mad victims of their own brainwashing" (James Baldwin, *The Fire Next Time* [New York: Vintage, 1963], 101–2).

[22]   Cornel West, "Afterword: Philosophy and the Funk of Life," in *Cornel West: A Critical Reader,* ed. George Yancy (Malden, MA: Blackwell, 2001), 346–62.

[23]   Ibid., 91.

[24]   Ibid., 92; emphasis added.

[25]   Ibid., 104.

[26]   Henry Louis Gates Jr. makes such an argument in his essay "The Welcome Table," in *Lure and Loathing: Twenty Black*

Intellectuals Address W.E.B. DuBois's Dilemma of the Double-Consciousness of African Americans, ed. Gerald Early (New York: Penguin, 1994).

[27]   James Baldwin, *No Name in the Street,* in *The Price of the Ticket: Collected Nonfiction, 1949–1985* (New York: St. Martin's Press, 1985), 460.

[28]   Ibid., 552.

[29]   Ibid., 549.

[30]   Ibid.

[31]   Ibid., 550; emphasis added.

[32]   Ibid., 452.

[33]   Sheldon Wolin, "Political Theory: From Vocation to Invocation," in *Vocations of Political Theory,* ed. Jason A. Frank and John Tambornino (Minneapolis: University of Minnesota Press, 2000), 3.

[34]   James Baldwin, "White Man's Guilt," in *Price of the Ticket,* 410.

[35]   Ibid.

[36]   Wolin, "Political Theory," 7.

CHAPTER 1

[1] John Dewey, *Human Nature and Conduct: An Introduction to Social Psychology* (Amherst: Prometheus Books, 2002), 200.

[2] For readers who have not yet encountered the novel a brief summary: *Beloved* explores the devastating consequences of slavery in the lives of those who experienced the brutality of the Sweet Home plantation in Kentucky and carried those memories to freedom in Cincinnati. Central to the novel is an act of infanticide on the part of Sethe, a runaway slave who, after being brutally raped, escapes to Cincinnati, the home of her mother-in-law, Baby Suggs. When faced with the prospect of returning to slavery after experiencing twenty-eight days of freedom, Sethe slices the throat of her oldest girl, Beloved, and threatens to kill her two sons and youngest daughter, Denver. She is condemned to

death but eventually granted a reprieve. Upon her release, however, Sethe is ostracized by the African American community. She attempts to forge a life in relative solitude, but her home is haunted by the ghost of Beloved. Baby Suggs, the once proud and powerful preacher, dies of profound sadness and confusion. Sethe's boys, who survived her attempted murder, run away, leaving only her, Denver (who has an incessant need to hear stories of her place in Sethe's past), and the ghost of Beloved. Paul D, a former slave of Sweet Home, arrives in Cincinnati and reunites with Sethe. But their relationship is interrupted by the appearance of a young woman who calls herself Beloved. The past returns, literally embodied. Sethe comes to realize that Beloved is actually her daughter, and she becomes consumed with her. It is in the characters' efforts to come to terms with the haunting of the ghastly effects of slavery that the novel exudes its power. See Toni Morrison, *Beloved* (New York: Plume/New American Library, 1987); page citations in text refer to this edition.

[3]   Sidney Hook, *Pragmatism and the Tragic Sense of Life* (New York: Basic Books, 1974), 5.

[4]   I make this point in the epilogue to my book *Exodus! Religion, Race, and Nation in Early Nineteenth-Century Black America* (Chicago: University of Chicago Press, 2000), 166.

[5]   Hook, *Pragmatism and the Tragic Sense,* 13.

[6]   William James, "The Moral Philosopher and the Moral Life," in *The Will to Believe and Other Essays in Popular Philosophy* (New York: Dover, 1956), 202–3.

[7]   Ibid., 209.

[8]   Dewey, *Quest for Certainty,* 4:212.

[9]   Dewey, *Human Nature and Conduct,* 10–11.

[10]   Richard Bernstein makes a similar point in "Community in

the Pragmatic Tradition," in *The Revival of Pragmatism: New Essays on Social Thought, Law, and Culture*, ed. Morris Dickstein (Durham: Duke University Press, 1998), 149.

[11]   Dewey, *Quest for Certainty*, 4:3.

[12]   Ibid., 4:3.

[13]   Ibid., 4:6.

[14]   Ibid., 4:14.

[15]   John Kekes, *Facing Evil* (Princeton: Princeton University Press, 1990), 5.

[16]   Dewey, *Quest for Certainty*, 4:7.

[17]   For a more detailed account of Dewey's use of Darwin, see James Campbell, *Understanding John Dewey: Nature and Cooperative Intelligence* (Chicago: Open Court Press, 1995), chap. 2.

[18]   Dewey, "Influence of Darwin," 17. Elsewhere Dewey writes: "Men have never fully used the powers they possess to advance the good in life, because they have waited upon some power

external to themselves and to nature to do the work they are responsible for doing. Dependence upon an external power is the counterpart of surrender of human endeavor. Nor is emphasis on exercising our powers for good an egoistical or a sentimentally optimistic recourse. It is not the first, for it does not isolate man, either individually or collectively, from nature. It is not the second, because it makes no assumption beyond that of the need and responsibility of human endeavor, and beyond the conviction that, if human desire and endeavor were enlisted in behalf of natural ends, conditions would be bettered. It involves no expectation of a millennium of good" (John Dewey, *A Common Faith* [New Haven: Yale University Press, 1934], 46).

[19]   John Dewey, "The Need for a Recovery of Philosophy," in *The

Middle Works, 1899–1924, ed. Jo Ann Boydston (Carbondale: Southern Illinois University Press, 1980), 10:45.

[20]   Dewey, "Development of American Pragmatism," 24–25.

[21]   See Rorty, *Philosophy and Social Hope,* 51–52. Dewey invokes here the idea of natural piety. In *A Common Faith,* he writes, "Natural piety is not of necessity either a fatalistic acquiescence in natural happenings or a romantic idealization of the world. It may rest upon a just sense of nature as the whole of which we are parts, while it also recognizes that we are parts that are marked by intelligence and purpose, having the capacity to strive by their aid to bring conditions into greater consonance with what is humanly desirable." He expands on this theme at the end of the same volume: "We who now live are parts of a humanity that extends into the remote

past, a humanity that has interacted with nature. The things in civilization we most prize are not of ourselves. They exist by grace of the doings and sufferings of the continuous human community in which we are a link. Ours is the responsibility of conserving, transmitting, rectifying, and expanding the heritage of values we have received that those who come after us may receive it more solid and secure, more widely accessible and more generously shared than we have received it." (Dewey, *Common Faith*, 24, 86.)

[22]   Dewey, "Influence of Darwin," 15.

[23]   Dewey, *Quest for Certainty*, 4:205; emphasis added.

[24]   Dewey, *Reconstruction in Philosophy* (Boston: Beacon Press, 1948), 147.

[25]   See Gregory F. Pappas, "Dewey's Ethics: Morality as Experience," in *Reading Dewey:*

Interpretations for a Postmodern Generation (Bloomington: Indiana University Press, 1998). Pappas writes, "When a felt moral perplexity controls and pervades the development of the situation as a whole, we can designate the situation as a moral one" (118n10). Pappas's article is one of the best sketches of Dewey's ethics that I am aware of.

[26] John Dewey, *Ethics* (1932), in Dewey, *Later Works* 7:164.

[27] Ibid., 7:164–65.

[28] Ibid., 7:164.

[29] Dewey, "Three Independent Factors in Morals" (1930), in Dewey, *Later Works,* 5:280.

[30] Ibid.

[31] Ibid.

[32] Martha Nussbaum makes a similar point in her reading of Sophocles' *Antigone.* She writes: "One and the same action or person will frequently possess more than one of the attributes picked out by these

words—since in many cases they go together harmoniously. But they can be present separately from one another; and, even when co-present, they are distinct in their nature and in the responses they require. Many friends will turn out to be just and pious people; but what is it to be a friend is distinct from what it is to be just, or pious. The ordinary expectation would therefore be that in some imaginable circumstances the values named by these labels will make conflicting demands. Friendship or love may require an injustice; the just course of action may lead to impiety; the pursuit of honor may require an injury to friendship. Nor would each single value be assumed to be conflict-free: for the injustice of the city can conflict, as this Chorus will acknowledge, with the justice of the world below; and piety towards one god may entail offenses against another. In general, then, to see clearly the nature of each of these features would be to understand its distinctness from each other, its possibilities of combination with and opposition to each other, and, too, its oppositions within itself" (Nussbaum, *The Fragility of Goodness: Luck and Ethics in Greek Tragedy and Philosophy* [Cambridge: Cambridge University Press, 1986], 54).

[33] Dewey, "Three Independent Factors in Morals," 5:280.

[34] Hilary Putnam, *Renewing Philosophy* (Cambridge: Harvard University Press, 1992), 190.

[35] Ibid., 194.

[36] Dewey, "Three Independent Factors," 5:279–80; emphasis added.

[37] Dewey, *Human Nature and Conduct,* 150; emphasis added. Also see Melvin Rogers, "John Dewey and the Theory of Democracy Deliberation," (M.Phil. dissertation, Cambridge

University, 2000), chaps. 2 and 3.

[38] William James, "The Will to Believe" (1897), in *The Will to Believe,* 31. Also quoted in Putnam, *Renewing Philosophy,* 195.

[39] Arthur Schopenhauer, *The World as Will and Representations,* trans. E.F.J. Payne (New York: Dover, 1969), 2:573.

[40] Arthur Schopenhauer, "On the Suffering of the World," in *Essays and Aphorisms,* trans. R. J. Hollingdale (London: Penguin Books, 1970), 48.

[41] Charles Sanders Peirce, for example, wrote that there were three types of pessimists: "The first type is often found in exquisite and noble natures of great force of original intellect whose own lives are dreadful histories of torment due to some physical malady. Leopardi is a famous example. We cannot but believe, against their earnest protests, that if

such men had had ordinary health, life would have worn for them the same colour as for the rest of us. Meantime, one meets too few pessimists of this type to affect the question. The second is the misanthropical type, the type that makes itself heard. It suffices to call to mind the conduct of the famous pessimists of this kind, Diogenes the Cynic, Schopenhauer, Carlyle, and their kin with Shakespeare's Timon of Athens, to recognize them as diseased minds. The third is the philanthropical type, people whose lively sympathies, easily excited, become roused to anger at what they consider to be the stupid injustices of life. Being easily interested in everything, without being overloaded with exact thought of any kind, they are excellent raw material for litterateurs: witness Voltaire. No individual remotely approaching the calibre of a Leibnitz is to be found among them." Charles S. Peirce, *Collected Papers,* ed. Charles Hartshorne and Paul Weiss (Cambridge: Harvard University Press, 1935), 6:330–31.

[42] Dewey, "Need for a Recovery of Philosophy," 10:45.

[43] Dewey, *Reconstruction in Philosophy,* 178.

[44] Ibid., 179.

[45] James, *Pragmatism,* 128.

[46] John Dewey, *Experience and Nature* (1925), in Dewey, *Later Works,* 1:45, 42, 93.

[47] Dewey, *Experience and Nature,* 1:421.

[48] See James Campbell's insightful discussion of Dewey's meliorism in his text *Understanding John Dewey,* 260.

[49] John Dewey, *Ethics* (1908), in Dewey, *Middle Works,* 5:371. Also quoted in Campbell, *Understanding John Dewey,* 260.

[50]   Oliver Wendell Holmes, quoted in Dewey, *Experience and Nature,* 1:418–19.

[51]   Cornel West, "Pragmatism and the Sense of the Tragic," in *Keeping Faith: Philosophy and Race in America* (New York: Routledge, 1993), 108. West recognizes Hook's argument for a pragmatic sense of the tragic. However, he believes it "remains far from the depths of other tragic democratic thinkers like Herman Melville, F.O. Matthiessen, and Reinhold Niebuhr" (108).

[52]   Ibid., 110.

[53]   Ibid., 113.

[54]   Ibid., 116.

[55]   Ibid., 117.

[56]   Of course, Royce doesn't end here. He accepts "the sorrow of possessing ideals" and rejects Schopenhauer's conclusion that nonexistence ought to be preferred over a life of suffering. Royce maintained that although life is made up of endless battles it

is nevertheless not a complete failure. Self-sacrifice, giving oneself over to a great cause, helping and comforting those in need generate moments in which we can feel ourselves "in perfect union and harmony with the whole of conscious life." West rightly notes that Royce refused to give in to pessimism and argued that we must "dare to hope for an answer." For Royce, evil sounds a clarion call for us to struggle against it; the goal of conscious union of every conscious being with the whole of conscious life sustains the strenuous mood that makes that struggle worthwhile. In response to Schopenhauer's and, by extension, Lincoln's challenge, Royce wrote: "As for Schopenhauer's objection that the unrest predominates, we admit the fact. Schopenhauer's inference is that the will to live ought to be quenched. We reply that this is a matter not thus to be decided. As we first chose our goal by independent volition, so now we may choose how much hindrance of our endless efforts to reach the goal will be regarded as compensated by our occasional successes. Not the comparison of two sums is desired, but the verdict of volition upon the worth of two sets of experiences. Which will you choose? The last question is simply unanswerable, except by a direct act of will. Here are the facts: A goal, viz., self-forgetfulness in the contemplation and creation of the fullest and clearest universal conscious life; a struggle to reach this goal, a struggle with blind nature, with selfishness within, with hatred without; this struggle alternating with periods of triumph; the process of alternating struggle and occasional triumph an endless process. How like you this life? It is the best that you are apt to find. Do you accept it? Every man has to deal with these queries quite by himself, even as with his own eyes he must see colors. It is our province merely to suggest the ultimate questions" (Royce, "Pessimism and Modern Thought," in *The Basic Writings of Josiah Royce,* ed. John J. McDermott [Chicago: University of Chicago Press, 1969], 271–72).

[57]   West, "Pragmatism and the Sense of the Tragic," 114.

[58]   Dewey, *Quest for Certainty,* 4:240.

[59]   Ibid.

[60]   Dewey, *Reconstruction in Philosophy,* 178.

[61]   As Hilary Putnam writes in *Renewing Philosophy,* "For Dewey, the democracy that we have is not something to be spurned, but also not something to be satisfied with. The democracy that we have is an emblem of what could be. What could be is a society which develops the capacities

of all its men and women to think for themselves, to participate in the design and testing of social policies, and to judge results" (199).

[62] West, *American Evasion of Philosophy,* 228.

[63] Cornel West, "Subversive Joy and Revolutionary Patience in Black Christianity," in *The Cornel West Reader* (New York: Basic Books/Civitas, 1999), 438.

[64] Rorty, *Philosophy and Social Hope,* xxix.

[65] Ibid.

[66] Dewey, *Quest for Certainty,* 300.

[67] Dewey writes in "The Influence of Darwin on Philosophy" that "old ideas give way slowly; for they are more than abstract logical forms and categories. They are habits, predispositions, deeply engrained attitudes of aversion and preference. Moreover, the conviction persists ... that all the questions that the human mind has asked are questions that

can be answered in terms of the alternatives that the questions themselves present. But in fact intellectual progress usually occurs through sheer abandonment of questions together with both of the alternatives they assume—an abandonment that results from their decreasing vitality and a change of urgent interests. We do not solve them: we get over them" (19).

[68] Dewey, *Common Faith*, 82. Dewey still must confront the challenge of George Santayana—his interest in human solitude and his insistence on the importance of the comic. See Henry Levinson's brilliant *Santayana, Pragmatism, and the Spiritual Life* (Chapel Hill: University of North Carolina Press, 1992).

[69] Schopenhauer, *World as Will and Representation*, 1:252–53. Also quoted in Nussbaum, *Fragility of Goodness*, 79.

[70]   Friedrich Nietzsche, *On the Advantage and Disadvantage of History for Life,* trans. Peter Preuss (Indianapolis: Hackett Publishing, 1980), 10.

[71]   Terry Otten, "Transfiguring the Narrative: *Beloved* —from Melodrama to Tragedy," in *Critical Essays on Toni Morrison's "Beloved,"* ed, Barbara H. Solomon (New York: G. K. Hall, 1998), 287.

[72]   Ibid., 291.

[73]   Amanda Smith, "Toni Morrison" (interview), *Publisher's Weekly,* August 21, 1987, 51. Also quoted in Otten, "Transfiguring the Narrative," 288.

[74]   Otten, "Transfiguring the Narrative," 288.

[75]   Carol Schmudde, "Knowing When to Stop: A Reading of Toni Morrison's *Beloved,*" *CLA Journal* 37, no. 2 (December 1993): 121.

[76]   Baldwin, *Fire Next Time,* 98.

[77]   Nussbaum, *Fragility of Goodness,* 80–81.

[78]   See George Hutchinson, "Pragmatism and Americanization," chapter 1 in *Harlem Renaissance in Black and White.*

CHAPTER 2

[1]   Ralph Waldo Emerson, "The American Scholar. An Oration before the Phi Beta Kappa Society, at Cambridge, August 31, 1837," in *Emerson: Essays and Lectures* (New York: Library of America, 1983), 53.

[2]   Dewey, "Three Independent Factors in Morals" 5:280.

[3]   Much of this paragraph reflects my engagement with Robert Brandom. See his important essay "Freedom and Constraint by Norms," in *Hermeneutics and Praxis,* ed. Robert Hollinger (Notre Dame: University of Notre Dame Press, 1985), 175–78, as well as his article "Truth and Assertibility," *Journal of Philosophy* 73 (1976): 137–89.

[4]   Rorty, *Philosophy and Social Hope,* xxiv.

[5]   I use the term *archeology* here only to call up the image of excavation, not in the sense in which Michel Foucault uses it.

[6]   Glaude, *Exodus!*

[7]   Stuart Hall, "Cultural Identity and Diaspora," in *Colonial Discourse and Post-Colonial Theory: A Reader,* ed. Patrick Williams and Laura Chrisman (New York: Columbia University Press, 1994), 393.

[8]   Amy Gutmann, *Identity in Democracy* (Princeton: Princeton University Press, 2004), 40.

[9]   Tommie Shelby and Lionel K. McPherson distinguish what they call five modes of blackness: (1) the racial dimension, (2) the ethnic dimension, (3) the national dimension, (4) the cultural dimension, and (5) the political dimension. What follows from the multidimensionality of black identity, for Shelby and McPherson, is that (1) an individual may exemplify only a

subset of the five dimensions, (2) each mode may be exemplified but to different extents, and (3) because each is rather vague and certainly contested, disagreement among African Americans about the label "African American" often arises. See Shelby and McPherson, "Blackness and Blood: Interpreting African American Identity," *Philosophy and Public Affairs* 32, no. 2(2004): 171–92.

[10]   Gutmann, *Identity in Democracy,* 38. Also see Joseph Raz and Avishai Margalit, "National Self-Determination," in *Ethics in the Public Domain: Essays in the Morality of Law and Politics* (New York: Oxford University Press, 1994).

[11]   This view of black identity is not limited to Molefe Asante, Minister Louis Farrakhan, and other self-described black nationalists. Established civil rights leaders such as Jesse Jackson and Al Sharpton repeatedly appeal to such ideas

about black identity and the obligations that follow from them. I discuss this issue more directly in chapter 6.

[12] Frantz Fanon, *The Wretched of the Earth* (New York: Grove Press, 1963), 210.

[13] See John McWhorter, *Losing the Race: Self-Sabotage in Black American* (New York: Free Press, 2000) and *Authentically Black: Essays for the Black Silent Majority* (New York: Gotham Books, 2003).

[14] For an elegant treatment of these issues, see Paul Taylor, *Race: A Philosophical Introduction* (Cambridge: Polity Press, 2004).

[15] Alan Ryan, "Pragmatism, Social Identity, Patriotism, and Self-Criticism," *Social Research* 63, no. 4 (1996): 1041–64.

[16] Pappas, "Dewey's Ethics," 110–11.

[17] Dewey, *Human Nature and Conduct,* 38.

[18] John Dewey, *Ethics,* 7:306.

[19]   Tommie Shelby, *We Who Are Dark: The Philosophical Foundations of Black Solidarity* (Cambridge: Harvard University Press, 2005), 10.

[20]   Ibid., 223.

[21]   Paul Taylor makes this useful distinction in *Race: A Philosophical Introduction.*

[22]   Watkins offered this analogy: "On my passage to Philadelphia, two men, the one white and the other colored, fall overboard—five passengers, all white men, and myself, behold the heart-rending scene—the drowning men cry for help—the five white men having contracted a deep-rooted hatred against a sable hue, & actuated by a sympathy of color, and a supposed identity of interest with the drowning man, run en masse, to succor him; I, finding the colored man neglected from an unworthy principle, spring to his rescue, and stretch out, not one hand to the white man (who has already abundant

help) and the other to the colored man, but I reach out both hands to him who has none to help him." (*The Colored American,* September 15, 1838, 118.)

[23]   James, *Pragmatism,* 30.

[24]   John Dewey, *Ethics,* 7:306.

[25]   Ibid.

[26]   Here I allude to a broad transracial antiracist politics that isn't reducible to the experiences of racism, but finds its common basis in a commitment to justice. But I also recognize that bonds of solidarity forged in the context of similar treatment are viable and can be the basis of a powerful politics, if rightly articulated.

[27]   Robert Gooding-Williams, "Politics, Racial Solidarity, Exodus!," *Journal of Speculative Philosophy* 18, no. 2 (2004): 124.

[28]   Glaude, *Exodus!,* 11–12; emphasis added.

[29]   I am using the term *works* to signal my use of James, who wrote, "Any idea upon which we can ride, so to speak; any idea that can carry us from one part of our experience to any other part, linking things satisfactorily, working securely, simplifying, saving labor; is true for just so much, true in so far forth, true *instrumentally.*" This is a "view that truth in our ideas means their power to work" (James, *Pragmatism,* 30).

[30]   For a brief pragmatic account of community see Richard Berstein, "Community in the Pragmatic Tradition," in Dickstein, *Revival of Pragmatism,* 141–56. My thinking about narrative relies on Jeffrey Stout's explication of historicism in his brilliant book *The Flight from Authority: Religion, Morality, and the Quest for Autonomy* (Notre Dame: University of Notre Dame Press, 1981). Stout writes:

Human character, and therefore the capacity to act freely, is shaped not only by its actual past but also by the unending activity of bringing that past to consciousness in narrative. Narrative is thus essential to both the primary formation of character in the education of the young and the continuous re-formation of character in moral discourse and reflection. *It matters greatly that we tell stories, that we tell the right stories, and that we tell them well. Bad stories produce bad people—people who cannot act, or who cannot act well, because they lack the virtues of a well-formed character.... In neglecting the imperative to narrate well, we impoverish ourselves.* (259; emphasis added)

With Berstein and Stout's view in mind, I am reluctant to accept the conclusions of Anthony Appiah, "Race, Culture, Identity: Misunderstood Connections," in Appiah and Amy Gutmann, *Color Conscious: The Political Morality of Race* (Princeton: Princeton University

Press, 1996). After defending an analytical notion of racial identity, Appiah cautions against "too hearty an endorsement of racial identification." He ends up encouraging what he calls a banal postmodernism where "we live with fractured identities; we engage in identity play; find solidarity, yes, but recognize contingency, and, above all, practice irony." The importance of communities and the narratives so critical to them seemingly gets squeezed between postmodern play and Rorty's private ironist.

[31]   Charles Taylor, *The Ethics of Authenticity* (Cambridge: Harvard University Press, 1991), 39.

[32]   See P. Taylor, *Race.*

[33]   John Dewey, "Postulate of Immediate Empiricism," in Dewey, *Influence of Darwin,* 230 To make the point a bit clearer, we might apply Dewey's view to the example of phlogiston: only by taking the presence of phlogiston as

real and as fully real, he would argue, are we able to claim any basis of experienced knowledge of phlogiston. As Dewey writes, "It is in the concrete thing as experienced that all the grounds and clues to its own intellectual or logical rectification are contained." He goes on to say, "It is because this thing, afterwards adjudged false, is a concrete that, that it develops into a corrected experience ... whose full content is not a whit more real, but which is true or truer."

[34]   James, *Will To Believe*, 2–3.

CHAPTER 3

[1]   Robin D. G. Kelley, *Freedom Dreams: The Black Radical Imagination* (Boston: Beacon Press, 2002).

[2]   *David Walker's Appeal ... to the Coloured Citizens of the World, but in Particular, and Very Expressly, to Those of the United States of America*, ed. Charles

M. Wiltse (New York: Hill and Wang, 1965), 3.

[3]   Cornel West, *Prophesy Deliverance!* (Philadelphia: Westminster John Knox Press, 1982), 109.

[4]   James H. Cone, *God of the Oppressed* (New York: Orbis Books, 1997), 28.

[5]   I should note the irony here. Cornel West claims just the opposite in his essay on the historicist turn in philosophy of religion. See West, *Keeping Faith,* 127.

[6]   James H. Cone, *Black Theology and Black Power* (New York: Seabury, 1969; Maryknoll, N.Y.: Orbis, 2001) and *A Black Theology of Liberation* (Philadelphia: Lippincott, 1970; Maryknoll, N.Y.: Orbis, 1986).

[7]   James Cone's work touched off a storm of debate. The critical works of Major Jones, Cecil Cone, Charles Long, Gayraud Wilmore, Deotis Roberts and William Jones pushed the basic assumptions of Cone's theological

project. See Cornel West and Eddie S. Glaude Jr., eds., introduction to *African American Religious Thought: An Anthology* (Louisville: Westminster John Knox, 2003).

[8]   See Victor Anderson, *Beyond Ontological Blackness: An Essay on African American Religious and Cultural Criticism* (New York: Continuum, 1995), 93.

[9]   West, *Prophesy Deliverance!*, 109.

[10]   See Dwight N. Hopkins, *Introducing Black Liberation Theology* (Maryknoll, N.Y.: Orbis, 1999), 4.

[11]   Cone, *Black Theology and Black Power,* 28; emphasis added.

[12]   Stephen Bush, a graduate student in Princeton's religion department, made this powerful point in a paper for my course "Black Power and Its Theology of Liberation."

[13]   Dwight Hopkins notes four basic building blocks in the construction of black liberation theology: the historical context

of slavery; the unique reading and interpretation of the Bible; considerations about method (that is, how our thinking about Jesus Christ is *systematically* connected to the project of liberation); and the significance of the black freedom struggle, particularly black power. See Hopkins, *Introducing Black Liberation Theology*, 34–41.

[14]   This is somewhat different than Emile Durkheim's analysis of members of society worshipping themselves through religious symbols. As Ernest Gellner suggests, "Society [and proponents of black cultural nationalism] no longer worships itself through religious symbols; a modern streamlined, on-wheels high culture celebrates itself in song and dance, which borrows (stylizing in the process) from a folk [or ancient] culture which it fondly believes itself to be perpetuating, defending, or reaffirming" (Gellner, *Nation*

and Nationalism [Ithaca: Cornell University Press, 1983], 57).

[15] See Vincent Harding's powerful essay "The Religion of Black Power," in West and Glaude, *African American Religious Thought.*

[16] Quoted in Gayraud Wilmore, *Black Religion and Black Radicalism: An Interpretation of the Religious History of African Americans,* 3rd ed. (Maryknoll, N.Y.: Orbis Books, 1998).

[17] Cone, *Black Theology and Black Power.*

[18] James H. Cone, "Black Spirituals: A Theological Interpretation, 1972," excerpt from *Spirituals and the Blues,* in *Risks of Faith: The Emergence of A Black Theology of Liberation* (Boston: Beacon Press, 1999), 18.

[19] Ibid., 24–25.

[20] Cone, *Black Theology of Liberation,* 25.

[21] See the introduction to Eddie S. Glaude Jr., ed., *Is It Nation*

Time? Contemporary Essays on Black Power and Black Nationalism (Chicago: University of Chicago Press, 2002).

[22]   The romantic pedigree of this sentiment should be readily recognizable: self- or communal definition, not subject to external influences and insulated from outside interference in order to express the self's or community's inner personality, is part of what Isaiah Berlin terms the critical "turning point" of the Romantic revolution. See Berlin, "The Romantic Revolution: A Crisis in the History of Modern Thought," in *The Sense of Reality: Studies in Ideas and their History,* ed. Henry Hardy (New York: Farrar, Straus and Giroux, 1996).

[23]   Cone, "Black Spirituals," 17.

[24]   This raises a range of broader questions about the role of religion in black public deliberation.

[25]   Stout, *Flight from Authority*, 258.

[26]   Nietzsche, *On the Advantage and Disadvantage of History for Life*, 52.

[27]   "It depends on one's being able to forget at the right time as well as to remember at the right time; on discerning with strong instinctual feelings when there is need to experience historically and when unhistorically" (ibid., 10).

[28]   Ibid., 10; emphasis in original.

[29]   Ibid., 19.

[30]   Ibid., 21–22.

[31]   Ibid., 19.

[32]   Ibid., 62.

[33]   Hayden White, *Tropics of Discourse: Essays in Cultural Criticism* (Baltimore: Johns Hopkins University Press, 1978), 32.

[34]   Nietzsche, *On the Advantage and Disadvantage of History for Life*, 38.

[35]   See Stout, *Flight from Authority*, chap. 12.

[36]   In the case of black theologians, history simply shades into theology. As Cone writes: "Whites may suppress black history and define Africans as savages, but the words of slavemasters do not have to be taken seriously when the oppressed know that they have a somebodiness that is guaranteed by the heavenly Father who alone is the ultimate sovereign of the universe" ("Black Spirituals," 26).

[37]   Baldwin, *Fire Next Time*, 81; emphasis in original.

[38]   Dewey, "Need for a Recovery of Philosophy."

[39]   John Dewey, *Democracy and Education* (New York: Free Press, 1916), 214.

[40]   Dewey, "Need for a Recovery of Philosophy," 10:6.

[41]   Dewey, *Experience and Nature*, 1:18.

[42]   West, *American Evasion of Philosophy*, 89.

[43] John Dewey, *Experience and Nature,* 1:33.

[44] Dewey, *Democracy and Education,* 214.

[45] Dewey, "Need for a Recovery of Philosophy," 10:45.

[46] Ibid., 8–9.

[47] Stout, *Flight from Authority,* 261.

[48] John Dewey, "Experience and Objective Idealism," in *Influence of Darwin,* 220–21.

[49] Morrison, *Beloved,* 274.

[50] The point, then, is not whether pragmatism has a tragic vision, but rather, presupposing such a vision, how it orients one to the world and to others.

[51] David Paul Mandell, "The History of Political Thought as a 'Vocation': A Pragmatist Defense," in Frank and Tambornino, *Vocations of Political Theory,* 135.

[52] Dewey, "Need for a Recovery of Philosophy," 10:10; emphasis added.

[53] Dewey, *Experience and Nature,* 1:309.

CHAPTER 4

[1]   Ira Berlin, *Generations of Captivity: A History of African American Slaves* (Cambridge: Belknap Press, 2003), 4.

[2]   The ideas for this essay emerged in some extraordinary conversations with Professor Raboteau and in our jointly taught course on African American religious history.

[3]   I have framed the issue in language associated with a "modern" conception of the self and freedom (e.g., Kant's distinction between autonomy and heteronomy). This view presupposes what has been called a "prejudice against prejudice"—that is, an acknowledgement that we moderns have emerged from the provincialism of Christian superstition. But in the case of African Americans, I suggest, this very language puts in place the possibility of imagining oneself in modern terms.

[4]   Richard Rorty, *Consequences of Pragmatism: Essays,* 1972–1980 (Minneapolis: University of Minnesota Press, 1982), 87; emphasis added.

[5]   Many have taken Rorty to task for his reading of pragmatism and of John Dewey. See, for example, Robert Westbrook, *John Dewey and American Democracy* (Ithaca: Cornell University Press, 1991); James Kloppenberg, "Pragmatism: An Old Name for Some New Ways of Thinking," in Dickstein, *Revival of Pragmatism;* Richard Shusterman, "Dewey on Experience: Foundation or Reconstruction," *Philosophical Forum* 26, no. 2 (winter 1994); Hilary Putnam, *Renewing Philosophy* and *Pragmatism: An Open Question* (Cambridge: Harvard University Press, 1995); and Martin Jay, *The Songs of Experience: Modern American and European Variations on a Universal Theme* (Berkeley: University of California Press, 2005).

[6]   John Dewey, "Appendix 2: Experience and Philosophic Method," in Dewey, *Later Works,* 1:372.

[7]   Joan Scott, "The Evidence of Experience," *Critical Inquiry* 17, no. 4 (summer 1991): 777.

[8]   Ibid., 777.

[9]   See also Lois McNay, "Agency and Experience: Gender as a Lived Relation," *Sociological Review* 52, no. 2 (2004):173–90.

[10] Judith Butler, "For a Careful Reading," in *Feminist Contentions: A Philosophical Exchange* (New York: Routledge, 1995), 137.

[11] Dewey, *Quest for Certainty,* 4:232.

[12] John Dewey, "Intelligence and Morals," in *Influence of Darwin,* 74.

[13] Walter Johnson, "On Agency," *Journal of Social History* 37, no. 1 (fall 2003): 113–24.

[14] Saidiya V. Hartman, *Scenes of Subjection: Terror, Slavery, and Self-Making in Nineteenth-Century America*

(New York: Oxford University Press, 1997).

[15]   Hartman writes: "I argue that the barbarism of slavery did not express itself singularly in the constitution of the slave as object but also in the forms of subjectivity and circumscribed humanity imputed to the enslaved; by the same token, the failures of Reconstruction cannot be recounted solely as a series of legal reversals or troop withdrawals; they also need to be located in the very language of persons, rights, and liberties. For these reasons the book examines the forms of violence and domination enabled by the recognition of humanity, licensed by the invocation of rights, and justified on the grounds of liberty" (ibid., 6).

[16]   My use of *antihumanism* refers to a position associated with Michel Foucault. It should be noted that his is a very specific way of understanding

humanism, which presupposes a notion of "reason" as fundamental to human nature or a form of foundationalism in which knowledge has indubitable foundations that are characteristic of how human beings think. Hence Foucault's rejection of any claim that presumes a subject that stands outside of power. Deweyan pragmatists reject any conception of the human agent apart from experience and presume antifoundationalism as a core tenet of their position.

[17] The paradigmatic figure I have in mind is Gayraud Wilmore and his important work, *Black Religion and Black Radicalism.*

[18] One certainly does not have to assume an emancipatory teleology when assessing the actions of black agents, religious or otherwise. We can still ask of the religious actor: Is this particular act ethical and/or politically acceptable? My intention here is not to

deny such efforts. I only want to call attention to how a narrow view of black agency truncates historical descriptions of African American religious life, which in turn contributes to truncated descriptions of African American life generally.

[19] Mahmood, *Politics of Piety,* 14–15.

[20] Ibid., chaps. 1 and 4.

[21] Dewey insists that individuals and the choices they make play a crucial role in the transaction. But these choices are not viewed as the consequences of a "will" that stands apart from experience and the various ways of talking that shape them.

[22] Berlin, *Generations of Captivity,* 162.

[23] Ibid., 168.

[24] Ibid., 173.

[25] Ibid., 193.

[26] See Peter Kalm, *Travels into North America,* 2nd ed., reprinted in vol. 13 of *A General Collection of the Best*

and Most Interesting Voyages and Travels, ed. John Pinkerton (London, 1812), 503. See Albert Raboteau, *Slave Religion: The "Invisible Institution" in the Antebellum South* (Oxford: Oxford University Press, 1978), 102.

[27] Quoted in Raboteau, *Slave Religion,* 123.

[28] Nathan Hatch, *The Democratization of American Christianity* (New Haven: Yale University Press, 1989), 9. See also Gordon S. Wood, "Ideology and the Origins of Liberal America," *William and Mary Quarterly,* 3rd ser., 44 (1987): 637.

[29] David Wills, *Christianity in the United States: A Historical Survey and Interpretation* (Notre Dame: University of Notre Dame Press, 2005).

[30] Nathan Hatch writes: "Charles Colcock Jones, the Presbyterian most vitally concerned about [the Christianization of the slaves], reported a total of less

than three hundred black Presbyterians in 1848, when black Methodists and Baptists numbered almost 125,000. Earlier he had noted the explosive growth of Methodism among blacks in the Revolutionary era, from less than two thousand in 1787 to over forty thousand in 1815. He also estimated an equal number of black Baptist by the second decade of the century" (*Democratization of American Christianity*, 102). See Charles Colcock Jones, *The Religious Instruction of the Negroes in the United States* (Savannah, 1842), 55–62, and *Thirteenth Annual Report of the Missionary to the Negroes in Liberty County (Ga.)* (Charleston, 1848), 45–55.

[31] See Albert Raboteau, *Canaan Land: A Religious History of African Americans* (Oxford: Oxford University, 2001), 19.

[32] As David Wills puts it, "The largest and most influential

Protestant churches fractured well before a confederacy of southern states made an armed effort to divide the country in 1861. The Presbyterian division of 1837 into New School and Old School bodies involved a number of doctrinal and ecclesiastic issues, but the legitimacy of slavery was the undercurrent.... The succession of the Methodist Episcopal Church, South from the Methodist Episcopal Church and the creation of the Southern Baptist Convention were explicitly about northern efforts to enforce restrictions on slave-holders respectively, as bishops and foreign missionaries.... Northern and Southern Methodists were not reunited until 1939, nor Presbyterians until the 1970s, while Baptists have never reunited" (*Christianity in the United States*, 28–29).

[33]   *In Permanence and Change,* Burke uses this phrase to

describe how established ways of living often blind us to various dimensions of our living and "train" us to respond in bad ways: "In the complexities of social experience, where the recurrence of 'like' situations is always accompanied by the introduction of new factors, one's total orientation may greatly influence one's judgments of likeness. A good Catholic may feel that priests and guides are alike; a good Marxian may feel that priests and deceivers are alike. And since much of our means-selecting is done on the basis of comparisons (as when the man chose to sit on the chair with the tack because it looked like a chair without a tack), we see how orientation, meansselecting and 'trained incapacity' become intermingled" (*Permanence and Change,* 3rd ed. [Berkeley: University of California Press, 1984], 14).

[34]   See West and Glaude, introduction to *African American Religious Thought,* xviii–xxii.

[35]   Orlando Patterson, *Slavery and Social Death: A Comparative Study* (Cambridge: Harvard University Press, 1982), 74.

[36]   Berlin, *Generations of Captivity,* 4–5.

[37]   Otherwise, Patterson's use of the concept of social death would appear incoherent.

[38]   Amy Hollywood, "Agency, Gender, and the Divine in Religious Historiography," *Journal of Religion* 84 (2004): 514–28.

[39]   Ibid., 527–28.

[40]   Raboteau, *Slave Religion,* 126.

[41]   I want to resist the temptation to read this as a sufficient condition for the exercise of slave agency. That is, the indeterminacy of signification takes us only so far; it is a necessary but not sufficient condition, for the material realities of the slave's condition still loom large.

[42]   Raboteau, *Slave Religion,* 177.

[43]   Ibid., 306.

[44]   Black liberation theologians like James Cone sought to translate the prophetic black church tradition into an idiom of black power. Or, said differently, they sought to maintain the relevance of African American Christianity in the face of secularizing forces by positing it as a source of revolutionary praxis. See Cone, *Black Theology and Black Power,* or Wilmore, *Black Religion and Black Radicalism.* Both Cone and Wilmore frame "black Christian agency" in principally political terms. What is surprising (and somewhat fascinating) is that these theologians were not in extended conversation with historians, like Raboteau, who were, at the same time, forging the field of African American religious history.

[45]   Raboteau, *Slave Religion,* 317.

CHAPTER 5

[1]   Robin D. G. Kelley has played a crucial role in the revisionist historiography about the black power era. His numerous books, articles, and students attest to the scope of his influence. Also see Nikhil Singh, *Black Is a Country: Race and the Unfinished Struggle for Democracy* (Cambridge: Harvard University Press, 2004); Timothy Tyson, *Radio Free Dixie: Robert F. Williams and the Roots of Black Power* (Chapel Hill: University of North Carolina Press, 2001); Penny Von Eschen, *Race against Empire: Black Americans and Anti-colonialism,* 1937–1957 (Ithaca: Cornell University Press, 1997); Lance Hill, *The Deacons for Defense: Armed Resistance and the Civil Rights Movement* (Chapel Hill: University of North Carolina Press, 2004); and Mary Dudziak, *Cold War Civil Rights: Race and the Image of American*

Democracy (Princeton: Princeton University Press, 2000).

[2] I make this claim in the introduction to my edited volume, *Is it Nation Time?*

[3] See Clifford Geertz, "Thick Description: Toward an Interpretive Theory of Culture," in *The Interpretation of Cultures* (New York: Basic Books, 1973).

[4] I am thinking, for example, of Brent Edwards, *The Practice of Diaspora: Literature, Translation and the Rise of Black Internationalism* (Cambridge: Harvard University, 2003); Michelle M. Wright, *Becoming Black: Creating Identity in the African Diaspora* (Durham: Duke University Press, 2004); Peniel Joseph, *Waiting 'Til the Midnight Hour: A Narrative History of Black Power* (New York: Henry Holt and Co., 2006) and the edited volume *The Black Power Movement: Rethinking the Civil Rights-Black Power Era* (London: Routledge, 2006); and Fred Moten, *In the Break: The*

Aesthetics of the Black Radical Tradition (Minneapolis: University of Minnesota Press, 2003).

[5]   Jeffrey Stout, "Theses on Black Nationalism," in Glaude, *Is It Nation Time?*, 242.

[6]   Ibid., 242–43.

[7]   Wilson Moses, *Classical Black Nationalism: From the American Revolution to Marcus Garvey* (New York: New York University Press, 1996), 2.

[8]   Ibid., 2.

[9]   Ibid., 4.

[10]   The participants in the Gary Convention were quite diverse in their ideological commitments. Left-leaning nationalists stood alongside cultural nationalists and union organizers as well as mainstream civil rights organizers. For a detailed account of the convention see Komozi Woodard, *A Nation within a Nation: Amiri Baraka (LeRoi Jones) and Black Power Politics* (Chapel Hill: University of North Carolina Press, 1999).

[11]   William Van DeBurg, ed., *Modern Black Nationalism: From Marcus Garvey to Louis Farrakhan* (New York: New York University Press, 1997), 4.

[12]   Brittani L. Kirkpatrick, "Contemporary Notions of Black Nationalism and Their Implications for Twenty-first-century Black Political Thought," senior thesis, Princeton University, 2005, 105.

[13]   Ibid., 118.

[14]   Stout, "Theses on Black Nationalism," 242.

[15]   James, *Pragmatism,* 25.

[16]   See W. V. Quine, *Word and Object* (Cambridge: MIT Press, 1960), 258–59. Also quoted in Jeffrey Stout, "What Is the Meaning of a Text?" *New Literary History* 14 (1982): 2. Much of my thinking about this matter has been shaped by Stout and this essay.

[17]   Stout, "What Is the Meaning of a Text?," 2.

[18]   Cornel West, *Prophetic Reflections: Notes on Race and*

Power in America (New York: Common Courage Press, 1993)

[19]   Stout, "What Is the Meaning of a Text?," 5.

[20]   Jerry Gafio Watts, *Amiri Baraka: The Politics and Art of a Black Intellectual* (New York: New York University Press, 2001), 20.

[21]   Ibid., 467.

[22]   Ibid., 5.

[23]   Ibid., 7.

[24]   Michael Dawson, *Black Visions: The Roots of Contemporary African American Political Ideologies* (Chicago: University of Chicago Press, 2001), 85–86.

[25]   Melissa Harris-Lacewell, *Barbershops, Bibles, and BET: Everyday Talk and Black Political Thought* (Princeton: Princeton University Press, 2004), chap. 3.

[26]   See Danielle S. Allen, *Talking to Strangers: Anxieties of Citizenship since Brown v. Board of Education* (Chicago: University of Chicago Press, 2004).

[27]   Nikhil Singh, "The Black Panthers and the 'Undeveloped Country' of the Left," in *The Black Panther Party Reconsidered,* ed. Charles E. Jones (Baltimore: Black Classic Press, 1998), 83.

CHAPTER 6

[1]   The CEOs are Richard Parsons of Time Warner, E. Stanley O'Neal of Merrill Lynch, and Kenneth Chenault of American Express. Dr. Ruth Simmons is the first African American president of an Ivy League institution (Brown University).

[2]   Of the 2.1 million inmates in American prisons, 910,000 are African American. One out of every three black males born today will spend time in prison, as will one out of eighteen black females (six times the rate for white women). See Tavis Smiley, ed., *The Covenant with Black America* (Chicago: Third World Press, 2006), 53–54.

[3]   W. Parker, "Black-White Infant Mortality Disparity in the United States: A Society Litmus test," *Public Health Reports* 118 (July–August 2003): 336. Also quoted in Smiley, *Covenant with Black America,* 8.

[4]   In the United States, 12.7 percent of the population lives below the poverty line—about thirty-seven million people. As of 2004, 9.4 million African Americans live in poverty. See David Wessel, "Changing Attack in Poverty Tactics, An Old Debate: Who Is at Fault," *Wall Street Journal,* June 15, 2006.

[5]   Michael Eric Dyson, *Come Hell or High Water: Hurricane Katrina and the Color of Disaster* (New York: Basic Books/Civitas, 2006), 5.

[6]   Adolph Reed Jr., *Stirrings in the Jug: Black Politics in the Post-Segregation Era* (Minnesota: University of Minnesota Press, 1999), 49.

[7]   I am aware that Habermas revisits his conception of the

public in his book, *Between Facts and Norms: Contributions to a Discourse Theory of Law and Democracy,* and corrects many of the mistakes evident in his earlier formulation. In fact, he comes to a position much like that of John Dewey's. But African American theorists, in the main, continue to refer to *The Structural Transformation of the Public Sphere* and offer criticisms of the view put forward there. Nancy Fraser's important criticisms of Habermas loom large in this regard. See her insightful essay, "Rethinking the Public Sphere: A Contribution to the Critique of Actually Existing Democracy," in *Justice Interruptus: Critical Reflections on the Postsocialist Condition* (London: Routledge, 1997).

[8] Nelson George, *Post-Soul Nation: The Explosive, Contradictory, Triumphant, and Tragic 1980 s as Experienced by African Americans (Previously Known as*

Blacks and before That Negroes)
(New York: Viking, 2004), ix.

[9]   Mark Anthony Neal, *Soul Babies:
Black Popular Culture and the
Post-Soul Aesthetic* (London:
Routledge, 2002), 3.

[10]   This point was greatly
influenced by my colleague
Jeffrey Stout's work. See his
Democracy and Tradition
(Princeton: Princeton University
Press, 2005), 173.

[11]   *Princeton Metro Times,* June 15,
2006.

[12]   The main argument of this
section is indebted to the work
of Adolph Reed Jr. See his
Stirrings in the Jug, p. 18 and
chaps. 2–3.

[13]   Ibid., 16.

[14]   Ibid., 16.

[15]   Ibid., 18–20.

[16]   John Dewey, "The Moral
Significance of the Common
Schools Studies," in Dewey,
Middle Works, 4:208.

[17]   John Dewey, *The Public and Its
Problems* (Chicago: Swallow
Press, 1954), 110.

[18]   Ibid., 110.

[19]   Ibid., 84.

[20]   Ibid., 15–16.

[21]   Ibid., 17–18.

[22]   Ibid., 19.

[23]   John Dewey, "Creative Democracy—The Task before Us" (1939), in Dewey, *Later Works*, 14:226.

[24]   Dewey, *Public and Its Problems*, 147.

[25]   Dewey, "Creative Democracy," 14:227.

[26]   I do not want to give short shrift to Lippmann's criticisms. His pessimism about the capacities of ordinary people extends beyond a simple judgment about their intelligence and amounts to a realistic assessment of the structural obstacles to its application. How do we, for example, acquire the requisite information to act intelligently when Rupert Murdoch and a small number of others own the major media outlets? What are we to make of genuine political

participation when corporate money has so sullied the political process? Systemic problems do block the way to intelligent action on the part of everyday people. I am not so sure, however, that Lippmann's appeal to technocrats remedies the problems. Dewey insists, and I agree, that any remedy to the structural maladies in our democracy must include the genuine participation of everyday folk. Our challenge is to figure out how to ensure this under present conditions.

[27]   Dewey, *Public and Its Problems,* 31.

[28]   Ibid., 126.

[29]   Ibid., 131.

[30]   Dewey's understanding of the importance of education to democracy underscores the fact that his "faith" in the capacities of ordinary folks isn't naïvely utopian. We are able to act intelligently because we have been (or should be) equipped to do so. This is why Dewey

believed *Democracy and Education* was the best account of his overall moral and political philosophy.

[31] A wonderful book charting the confluence of African American political activism and white backlash is Robert O. Self, *American Babylon: Race and the Struggle for Postwar Oakland* (Princeton: Princeton University Press, 2003).

[32] Dawson, *Black Visions,* 40.

[33] Ibid., 38.

[34] William Julius Wilson, *The Bridge over the Racial Divide: Rising Inequality and Coalition Politics* (Berkeley: University of California Press, 1999), 31.

[35] Dawson, *Black Visions,* 38.

[36] Ibid., 41.

[37] Ibid., 42.

[38] Reed, *Stirrings in the Jug,* 50.

[39] Toni Morrison, *The Nobel Acceptance Speech* (New York: Knopf, 1993).

EPILOGUE

[1]   I am indebted to my dear friend and intellectual confidante, Melvin Rogers, for the Samuel Beckett reference.

[2]   Houston was a particularly meaningful site for the annual symposium and the launching of the book. Hurricane Katrina had left many African Americans angry as the nation sat back and allowed its own citizens, dark though they may be, to be cast as refugees. Many displaced New Orleaneans had made their way to Houston, trying to put together the pieces the storm left in its wake. The symposium and the book then were framed by a palpable sense, once again, of national betrayal.

[3]   John Dewey, "Democracy and Education in the World Today" (1938), in Dewey, *Later Works,* 13:154.

[4]   Dewey, "Creative Democracy," 14:228–29.

[5]   William James, *Varieties of Religious Experience* (New York: Random House, 1994), 370.

[6]   Ralph Waldo Emerson, "The Conservative," in *Ralph Waldo Emerson: Essays and Lectures* (New York: Library of America, 1983), 177.

[7]   James Baldwin, "Notes on the House of Bondage," in *Price of the Ticket,* 667.

[8]   Ibid., 668.

Front Cover Flap

In this timely book, Eddie S. Glaude Jr. makes an impassioned plea for black America to address its social problems by recourse to experience, and with an eye to the future rather than the fixed ideas and categories of the past. Central to Glaude's mission is a rehabilitation of philosopher John Dewey, whose ideas he applies to a renewal of African American politics.

According to Glaude, Dewey's pragmatism, when attentive to the darker dimensions of life—what we often speak of as the blues—can address many of the problems that plague contemporary African American discourse. How blacks think about themselves, imagine their own history, and conceive of their own actions can be rendered in ways that escape bad ways of thinking that assume a tendentious political unity among African Americans simply because they are black, or that short-circuit imaginative responses to problems confronting actual black people. Drawing deeply on black religious thought and literature, *In a Shade of Blue* seeks to dislodge such crude and simplistic thinking and replace it with a deeper understanding of black life in all its variety and intricacy. Only when black political leaders acknowledge such complexity, Glaude argues, can the real-life sufferings of many African Americans be remedied.

Heady, inspirational, and brimming with practical wisdom, *In a Shade of Blue* is a work of political commentary on a scale rarely seen today. To follow its trajectory is to learn how African Americans arrived at this critical moment in their history and to envision where they might head in the twenty-first century.

Back Cover Flap

EDDIE S. GLAUDE JR. teaches religion and African American Studies at Princeton University. He is the author of *Exodus! Religion, Race, and Nation in Early Nineteenth-Century Black America* and editor of *Is It Nation Time? Contemporary Essays on Black Power and Black Nationalism*, both published by the University of Chicago Press.

Back Cover Material

"Eddie Glaude is poised to become the leading intellectual voice of our generation, raising questions that make us reexamine the assumptions we hold by expanding our inventory of ideas."
TAVIS SMILEY

"Glaude is a leading young African American scholar who has a fine historical sense but is not shackled by the past. He is critical of the blind spots of the classical pragmatists for their failure to deal with the problem of racism. But here he presents an exciting interpretation of pragmatism, revealing the way Dewey combines a profound sense of tragic choices with a passionate commitment to how ordinary folk can further genuine democratic practices. With deft eloquence he shows how this pragmatic orientation clarifies key issues for understanding the past and contemporary politics of black America."
RICHARD J. BERNSTEIN

"Eddie Glaude is the towering public intellectual of his generation. He also is a superb scholar and academic pioneer in his profound synthesis of American pragmatism, African American thought, and religious studies. There is simply no one else like him emerging on the intellectual scene!"

CORNEL WEST

THE UNIVERSITY OF CHICAGO PRESS
www.press.uchicago.edu

issues hindered
by invocation of,
postsoul politics
blocked by
prestige of,
proximity to
contem porary
moment,
See also black
nationalism,
black history
Baldwin on,
black theology
and,
competing
interests ignored
in appeals to,
race language as
essential in
accounts of,
racial solidarity
based on,
seen as
predetermining
orientation to
problems,
black identity,
archaeological
approach to,

in black politics of
1960s and 1970s,
black theology's
conception of,
competing
interests ignored
in appeals to,
as conscription,
as constantly
remade,
as cultural
identity,
as emerging
within complexly
organized
interactions,
expressivist
conception of
racial self,
and group
narrative,
how we think
about as
mattering,
as live
hypothesis,
and other
identities,

www.ingramcontent.com/pod-product-compliance
Lightning Source LLC
Chambersburg PA
CBHW010139270326
41926CB00023B/4505